Table of Contents

PREFACE

The project of compiling some written material in order to preserve, at least in outline, a record of the Diocese of San Joaquin has been long in the making. With the intent of recording the memories and recollections of what the Episcopal Church in this diocese was like in its early years and development, as well as the decades of the seventies and the eighties the collecting of materials began some years ago.

The Rev. George Woodgates offered to begin the process about fifteen years ago. For several years Fr. Woodgates gathered information which he passed on to one of our diocesan historiographers, Fr. Paul Levine, Rector of Turlock. Fr. Paul carried on the work and collected photographs for several years.

More recently, Fr. Chris Kelley, our other historiographer was asked to carry on the project. He gathered much material from the churches and was able to get photographs of many of the churches and their incumbent clergy. This is the kind of work that can go on and on, but, with the passage of time material gathered years before becomes obsolete or requires extensive editing.

When Archdeacon Williamson retired, I challenged him to help us with the project. He responded in the affirmative and went to work on his word processor. There is a danger in saying "thank you" to one person because for sure you may well forget others. Nevertheless, I must take this chance and say "thank you" to Archdeacon Williamson, the historiographers of San Joaquin, Fr. Woodgates, the staff of the Diocesan office, and my wife, Barbara, for their help in making this book possible. Finally, but very importantly, "thank you" to the Order of San Joaquin, which has helped to subsidize this project.

+ Victor M. Rivera,
Bishop of San Joaquin
Epiphany 1988

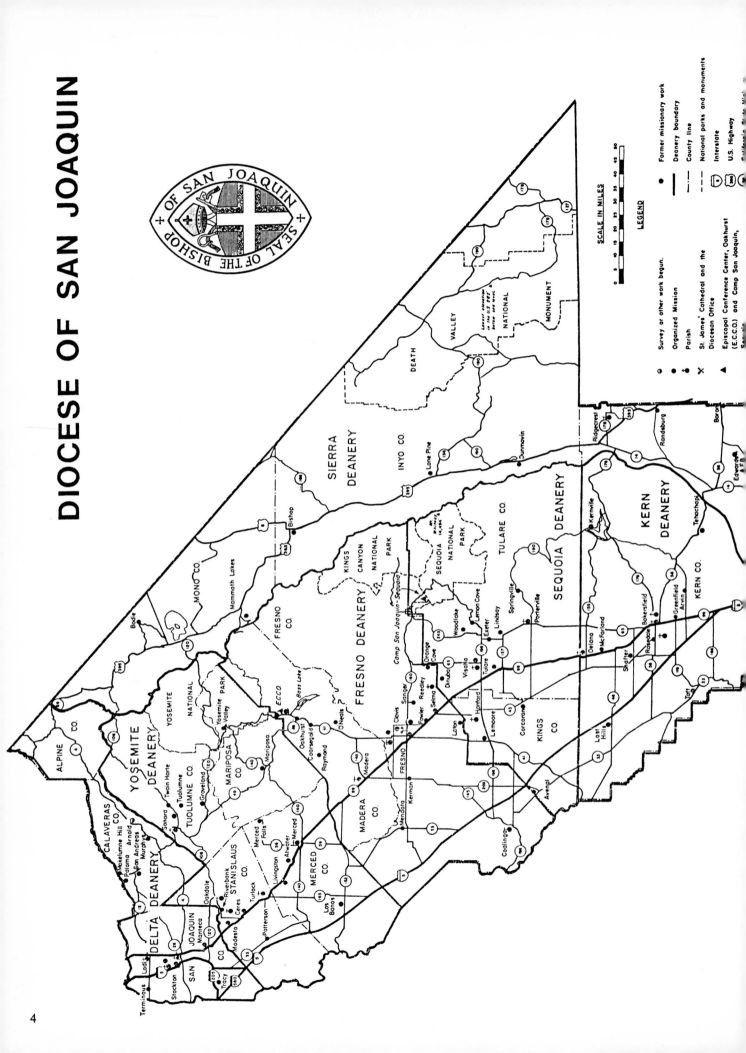

DIOCESE OF SAN JOAQUIN

SEAL OF THE BISHOP OF SAN JOAQUIN

FOREWORD

A review of the episcopate of any bishop is more than the record of an individual; it is that, of course, but it is really the record of all those many individuals who have had a part in helping to shape the ministry of that particular bishop. There is a sense in which every member of the diocese will have had some part to play in that history, but the particular contribution of only a few can be given both because of space limitations and also because the specific contributions of only a few out of the thousands of members can be known.

In Bishop Rivera's episcopate there is the need to acknowledge the leadership of the fledgling diocese during the tenure of his two predecessors, Louis C. Sanford (1911-1944) and Sumner F. D. Walters (1944-1968). It was from the results of their labors that Bishop Rivera was enabled to continue the development of the diocese during his tenure (1968-1988). He served this diocese under Bishop Walters as Rector of St. Paul's, Visalia, almost from the beginning of Bishop Walter's consecration, assuming the position in 1945, and continuing until his own consecration in 1968.

It is for the people of St. Paul's, Visalia, that Bishop Rivera and his family have their strongest feeling of attachment and identification. To most of them he is still familiarly known as "Father Vic." In a record such as this it is impossible to give recognition to everyone deserving of mention for the simple reason that even with the best of intentions one would be likely to overlook some and thereby to possibly give unwitting offense. It is hoped, therefore, that all who have shared in his ministry will understand the reason for not attempting to list names for credit. Some individuals will be mentioned in the course of this account for the role they played in particular events. It is hoped that those not named will know that they are nonetheless deeply appreciated for their contribution to this diocese.

The years of Bishop Rivera's ministry as priest and then as bishop covers a span of 44 years. These years embrace the now seemingly halcyon period of the mid-forties to the mid-fifties. Then came the turbulent years of the late fifties to the seventies. A time that profoundly affected our western societies and raised issues that have divided society at large in seeking their resolution. Inevitably the churches have been affected by these same issues, and similarly polarized in their attempts to respond.

Immediately following World War II and continuing into the fifties there was an upsurge in church attendance and church membership for virtually all denominations. The acquisition of land and facilities for the new congregations springing up preoccupied the attention of church leaders and it seemed there would be no end to the growth. It was a period when the annual report of Episcopal Church statistics noted with pride that our membership was increasing at a faster rate than the birthrate, and confidence was expressed that the trend would continue. Baptisms were up, Confirmation classes were often quite large, Church Sunday School attendance was at an all-time high. This church fielded over 400 foreign missionaries into the mid-fifties and all indicators were that this trend too would continue.

But it was not to last. The assassination of President John F. Kennedy might be taken as a turning point in our somewhat euphoric national mood. It would oversimplify things to say that the war in Viet Nam caused the national tumult that ensued, but it did provide a focal point for all sorts of real and imagined grievances. The church reflected this in its own responses and an unprededented polarization of the national church ensued. That the liberal element in the church came to dominate was not necessarily a reflection of the majority membership attitude. Nevertheless, programs were enacted by General Convention through sometimes questionable and manipulative tactics that left good people on both sides of the issue in question. In short, religion in the mainline denominations in this country became politicized as it had not been since the Civil War era.

The result of these highly complex and interwoven issues was a slowing of church growth and a gradual decline in attendance and membership, beginning in the mid-sixties and continuing to this day. In 1968 this church claimed 3,588,435 baptized members and 2,280,077 communicants. In 1985 (the latest year for which national figures are available) we report 2,972,607 baptized members and 1,881,250 communicants. Needless to say, the same general trends are to be noted in the Diocese of San Joaquin. Now, in the eighties, nearly all mainline Christian denominations are trying to cope with similar trends and all are anxiously scanning the religious horizon for that cloud that may presage the spiritual rains that will once again make the fertile the fields for evangelism and conversion. A significant indicator of what has happened in this church with regard to the once deeply held belief that "There is no other name under heaven whereby men might be saved" than that of Jesus is that the number of missionaries in the foreign field fell from a high of nearly 500 in the fifties to fewer than 100 in the eighties. In fact, there was an explicit rejection of the missionary thrust of this church as being a form of "imperialism."

A similar attitude prevailed here at home, and, instead, the dominant notion was that what was needed was not to change men's hearts and minds so much as to reform the structures of society. A kind of Rousseaun idea held sway that all men are born in innocence and it is only the wicked structures of society that subvert that original innocence. Evangelism and conversion of individual men and women were scornfully rejected, and social engineering was substituted. To be sure there were those who did not agree with this assessment of Man's real needs, and sought to stem the tide by orthodox teaching and praxis.

Bishop Rivera and his wife Barbara have both long recognized the signs of diminishing church growth and attendance and their causes and have striven earnestly to carry the message to this diocese. Indeed, Bishop Rivera stated from the beginning of his episcopate that his three principles emphases were: 1) evangelism and church growth, 2) Christian Education, and 3) Stewardship. This account of his episcopate will attempt to assess the record in each of these three areas. It should be noted, however, that success or failure in any of these is due to the kind of support elicited from all in this diocese, clergy and laity. Bishop Rivera has often sounded the clear call for implementation of programs to accomplish these ends, but in the final analysis the results depend upon the measure of support given from the diocese taken as a whole.

The first portion of this account is a chronicle of this diocese from its earliest days. The policy I have followed as editor of these pages is to begin with the brief history of each congregation in their chronological order of admission. Following that record comes as assessment of Bishop Victor M. Rivera's episcopate.

It should be explained that this is not history in the sense of scholarly research, instead, it is for the most part, an account by people who are members of the congregations. They have graciously responded to a request for a summary history of their congregation.

A scholarly history of this diocese would be a subject worthy of a scholar's attention, and it is to be hoped that some one will, in the not too distant future, undertake just such a history. This preliminary work would be no more than the core for such a study, but the account herein contained is the only attempt to date and contains much that would be of interest to a research scholar. In the meantime, it is hoped that every congregation will find some person or persons who would undertake to carefully chronicle their own history, with as much detail as possible. In so doing some future historian may indeed call you blessed!

I would be remiss in not acknowledging the research and writing done by the Rev. Christopher Kelley in the preparation of this record. Virtually, the entire record of the individual congregations is the result of his labors, and my only contribution has been that of some slight editing in some instances. For Fr. Kelley it was a "labor of love" since so much of the history of this diocese bears the indelible imprint of the missionary zeal of his great-grandfather, the Rev. Douglas O. Kelley.

Advent, 1987
The Ven. Wayne B. Williamson

CHAPTER ONE

The Early Years

The year 1910 marks the beginning of what was then called the Missionary District of San Joaquin, embracing fourteen counties that collectively make up the central third of the State of California. The first bishop was Louis C. Sanford (1911-1942). His successor was Sumner F. D. Walters (1944-1968). The third bishop, Victor M. Rivera, was consecrated September 19, 1968, and at the time of this writing is still the incumbent. He has, however, announced his intention to retire upon reaching the mandatory canonical age for retirement in 1988.

In his book PROVINCE OF THE PACIFIC, Bishop Sanford states that Bishop Nichols of California, foreseeing the creation of a fourth unit of the Church out of the State of California took the initial step of forming the unofficial "Church Association of the San Joaquin." Formal action was taken on September 10, 1894, when the San Joaquin Convocation was organized in Fresno. Even then he is said to have envisioned its establishment as a Missionary District, which did, in fact, take place in 1911. At the same time Louis Childs Sanford was elected first Bishop of the newly formed Missionary District of San Joaquin.

When it was officially designated a Missionary District, San Joaquin listed 5 parishes, 10 missions, and 14 clergy. There is no record of the number of baptized members, but communicants were listed as being 1,687. Fifty years later at a Special Convocation held at the Church of Our Saviour, Hanford, a petition was officially approved and addressed to the Sixtieth General Convention of the Protestant Episcopal Church asking for the "ratification of the formation of a new diocese out of the whole Missionary District of San Joaquin . . ." The petition was received favorably by the 1961 General Convention meeting in Detroit, Michigan, thereby establishing the Diocese of San Joaquin.

When San Joaquin was made a diocese the record shows that there were 19 parishes, 23 missions, and 56 clergy. Also listed were 15,872 baptized members and 9,461 communicants.

Any attempt to relate the history of the Episcopal Church in the San Joaquin valley would be remiss if the labors of the Rev. D. O. Kelley were not noted. Douglas Ottinger Kelley, Apostle of San Joaquin, was born on Kelley's Island in Lake Erie, Ohio, 1844. He died in 1918. While in his freshman year at Hobart College, Geneva, New York, he enlisted in the U. S. Army and served in the Civil War until his capture and imprisonment in Richmond, Virginia. After the war and his release he read law and was admitted to the Bar. In 1868 he accompanied the famed missionary-educator James Lloyd Breck to California and established himself as a lawyer in San Francisco.

He organized the Church Union of San Francisco, and was instrumental in the establishment of the Episcopal Old Ladies' Home (a designation that would surely provoke adverse comment today!) and St. Luke's Hospital. He served as editor of the Pacific Churchman for many years.

In 1872 he was ordained Deacon at St. Peter's, San Francisco, and subsequently was priested by Bishop Kip. His marriage to Amelia Fletcher occurred in 1874, and there were eight sons and one daughter born to the couple. Two of his sons also entered the priesthood of this Church. His many years of service in San Joaquin began in 1879. As the subsequent fruit of his labors the following parishes and missions owe their existence:

St. Paul's Bakersfield
St. James', Fresno
St. John's, Lodi
Trinity, Madera
St. Luke's, Merced
St. Paul's, Modesto
Good Shepherd, Reedley
St. John's, Tulare

Church of Our Saviour, Hanford (he was responsible for the first services, or first regular services, in Coalinga, Fowler, Laton, Lemoore, Sanger, Selma, and Visalia)

CHAPTER TWO

The Foundations Are Laid

ST. JOHN'S PARISH, STOCKTON

At the time of its being made a Missionary District the oldest church congregation was St. John the Evangelist, Stockton. It is also the third oldest Episcopal Church on the West Coast. The Rev. Orlando Harriman, Jr., conducted the first services on Sunday, August 25, 1850, and the parish was organized that same evening and named by the Rev. Mr. Harriman. He remained at St. John's for a month and "failing to obtain support, and on account of ill health" he left.

Services were resumed under lay leadership by Mr. J. M. Bissell, the Junior Warden on April 27, 1851, in a building owned by Captain Weber, founder of Stockton. Occasional services were taken by Dr. Orange Clarke and the Rev. John Morgan. With the impending move of Mr. Bissell from Stockton, a meeting was held to determine the parish's future. Although a Rev. John Reynolds was resident in Stockton at the time, Mr. Bissell recorded that the Vestry wished to maintain its "independence" and "its inalienable right" of "choosing for themselves . . . their own minister." Reynolds (from San Diego) was "permitted to occupy St. John's Chapel . . . but he was not recognized by any authority in the parish . . . as the minister of this Church." For all its Episcopal polity the Episcopal Church has had a strong strain of "congregationalism" from Colonial Days, and there is no evidence that that spirit is abating.

Bishop Kip visited Stockton on February 18, 1854, shortly after his arrival in California. The Vestry promised a budget of $200 per month for Church and clergyman. Bishop Kip nominated the Rev. Joseph S. Large of Indiana to be Rector. The Vestry acquiesced and the Rev. Mr. Large arrived on November 17, 1854.

Captain C. M. Weber generously donated two lots and a third was purchased. As the holder of a Mexican Land Grant, Captain Weber was in a position to donate land for all of Stockton's original churches and old public squares and schools. Large resigned in April 1856 and the Vestry called the Rev. Elijah W. Hager of Marysville as their second Rector. Under his leadership the first brick church was erected in 1857-58. Bishop Kip consecrated the church building on Sunday, June 20, 1858. St. John's has thus occupied the same site since Gold Rush days. The oldest stained glass window in the San Joaquin valley was installed at the time over the altar. It is now above the entrance from El Dorado Street.

Hager was succeeded by the Rev. David F. McDonald, from May, 1859 to March, 1862. He was followed by the Rev. J. G. Gassman of Sonora who left in April 1866. Next the Rev. Elias Birdsall served from June 1866 to June 1868. He wrote articles on his trips to the San Joaquin valley which alerted the Rev. D. O. Kelley to the need for mission work there. Following Birdsall was Dr. James Lloyd Breck (see LESSER FEASTS AND FASTS, April 2) who supplied services from Benicia until March 1869. He was succeeded by the Rev. William P. Tucker who left in little more than a year to become Headmaster of St. Augustine's College, Benicia. The Rev. Mr. Birdsall was called back and he remained until July 1872.

A Mission Sunday School was established during this time which flourished under his successor, H. L. Foote, of San Francisco. It lasted for some 20 years, when it became idle, and was sold to meet debt on the new church building. Following Foote's resignation the Vestry called Birdsall back for his third time as Rector — a record of sorts, surely. Birdsall again resigned in November 1880. The Vestry then called the "tenth" Rector, the Rev. E. H. Ward, who served from January 1881 until June 1885. In August of 1885, E. C. Mills became Rector and served until September 1888. At the recommendation of Birdsall the Vestry called W. J. Lemon of Detroit. Under his leadership the new church and guild hall were built. The hall was built first from funds gathered by the Women's Guild and the Sunday School, a total of $9,200. The parish supplied an additional $3,100 for the purpose.

In November 1891 the old brick building was razed and the bricks sold to help meet the cost of the new building. The cornerstone was laid on April 4, 1892, and the building was completed and the first service held on December 18, 1892. Lemon then resigned because of his wife's ill health. He was succeeded by D. L. V. Moffett in December 1893. During this time the mission at Lodi was assisted and pews from old St. John's were given them. Moffett resigned in September 1895, and, in the same month, Daniel G. MacKinnon was called to the parish. He arrived in November. In October 1896, the Convention of the Diocese of California met for a week in Stockton, with Bishop Nichols.

In the preceding year, the General Convention had created the Diocese of Los Angeles. Bishop Nichols called for the creation of a Convocation of San Joaquin; Stockton, however, was part of the Convocation of San Francisco at the time. By early 1898, the clearing of the debt on St. John's was within reach, and an effort was made to enable the consecration to take place on Easter Sunday, April 10. With $1,500 yet to raise and Easter only a few days away, Mrs. Wm. H. Crocker, formerly Ethel Sperry of Stockton, who had given the carpet for the building, was sent a wire in Europe where she was at the time, asking for assistance. She generously promised to cover the remaining sum. Bishop Nichols then consecrated the church building as planned. In February, 1899, St. John's was transferred to the Convocation of San Joaquin.

MacKinnon resigned in January 1900, and was followed in August of that year by the Rev. John T. Bryan, who stayed one year. In December 1901, Bishop Nichols presided at the Vestry meeting and nominated Alfred S. Clark, who was duly elected and assumed his duties at once. Ill health forced him to resign in January 1905. He was succeeded by R. H. Starr of New York who served until May 1908.

A number of supply clergy followed Dr. Starr, but one young man, William T. Renison, "won the hearts of all the people in the parish," and was called to be Rector in October 1908. He remained for 14 years — the longest rectorship to date. Renison resigned in January 1922 to accept a call to Church social work as chaplain of the Syracuse Seaman's Institute. He retired in 1947, and returned to Stockton to serve as a voluntary assistant until his death in 1957.

Hugh E. Montgomery became Rector on July 15, 1922. His was an innovative ministry that succeeded in greatly enlivening the parish. He was elected Dean of the Northern Deanery in 1924, and held many other elective positions in the District of San Joaquin. In 1925, the Rev. Mr. Montgomery was called to All Souls' Parish, Berkeley, California.

C. P. Leachman was called in late 1927 but served a scant six months. He was followed by the Rev. Seth C. Hawley. In spite of its being the beginnings of the Great Depression period members of the Church living in the Terminous area of Northwest Stockton opened a small chapel, consecrated by Bishop Nichols as "Emmanuel Chapel." The Rev. Mr. Hawley resigned in 1939.

He was followed by the Rev. George F. Pratt of Hoquiam, Washington. Stockton prospered during the years of World War II. During the late '40s the church was extensively renovated, and the crypt was made into classrooms. On July 3, 1950, St. Anne's, Stockton, was opened in Lincoln Village to serve north Stockton. The Rev. Mr. Pratt left St. John's in the fall of 1950.

Late 1950 saw the Rev. Paul E. Langpaap called from his first cure at St. Timothy's, Bishop, to be Rector of St. John's. A concern over the move of parishioners out of downtown assumed major proportion during his tenure. With one exception, other pioneer Stockton churches had moved from the city center to the suburbs. St. Stephen's was organized as a parochial mission of St. John's on September 27, 1954, and property purchased with the idea that it might be the site for St. John's to relocate; but a reversionary clause in the deed was settled by Charles Weber, III, in a quit-claim in 1955. In 1957, adjacent property to St. John's was purchased from Chase Chevrolet, providing the church with desperately needed office space and room for the "Budget Shop," which opened in 1964.

In January 1958, the Rev. Peter Barker succeeded Paul Langpaap who had accepted a call to Seattle, Washington. During Peter Barker's tenure a Master Plan Committee was set up to examine the location question in detail. The study proved inconclusive. However, by the 1970's, renovation and renewal of the downtown area was progressing, and in 1972, the Stockton Cultural Heritage Board declared St. John's Guild Hall an historic city landmark, in recognition of its unique Nordic style. In 1975, complete restoration of the second floor of this building was made.

The Rev. Charles Smith became Rector in January 1971 and remained until the Spring of 1974. In August, on the eve of St. John's 125th Anniversary, The Rev. James T. Booth left his position as a Canon of St. James' Cathedral, Fresno, to be the new Rector of St. John's.

In the last several years St. John's had generously and graciously provided accommodation for the newly formed Filipino Mission, Holy Cross, under the leadership of The Rev. Justo Andres. It has also provided a much needed social service in the downtown Stockton area under the leadership of Fr. Booth. They have a regular meal service for the needy and provide various other social services as outreach to those in need.

By the end of 1987, St. John's church building was undergoing extensive restoration. Under the leadership of Fr. Booth, not only is the church structure being overhauled, but a new interest is developing in mission responsibility to the community and to the thousand of Filipinos, Hmongs, Vietnamese, and Mexican-American communities that are settling in this valley.

ST. JAMES' PARISH, SONORA

Historic St. James' is located in the "mother lode" area of the gold rush days of early California. It was founded in December of 1859. Sonora, like other mining communities in the "mother lode," experienced a rough and rugged period in the early mining days. In 1859, a group of loyal churchmen, who had remained in Tuolumne County after the boom days of the gold rush had ended, discussed the possibility of having a church of their own. Three men — Cabel Dorsey, Abner Pitts, and Frederick Salter — comprised the committee that started the move towards building a church in Sonora.

They began by drafting a letter to Bishop Kip in San Francisco outlining their plan. In a short time Bishop Kip was able to assign a man who was capable of filling the position, the Rev. John G. Gassman, a native of Norway, who arrived in Sonora on December 17, 1859. He was enthusiastic about the challenge and had considerable skill as a builder, and his ideas for the plan and architecture of the church were useful in the construction.

The church was built over the abandoned workings of the Bonanza Mine, one of the richest pocket mines in California. The first service was held in the new church building on October 4, 1860, and it was consecrated in November 1870 by Bishop Kip.

In 1868 the west side of the building was damaged by fire when the United States Hotel across the street burned. This necessitated extensive repairs to the church. In 1949 the building was again carefully renovated and modernized. Further renovation was done in 1970 and 1973.

Since 1860, St. James' Episcopal Church has occupied its position on Washington Street, overlooking Sonora's business district. It is a testimony to the faith and consecration of those who planned and built it; and to the loyalty of those who have maintained it. But above all it is a symbol of the changelessness of Almighty God and of the fact that men do feel that they must worship Him; the same yesterday, today and forever.
(Taken in part from an article by Mr. John Germain, The Tuolumne County Historical Society Quarterly)

St. James' has had twenty-eight Rectors, Deacons and an Assisting Priest from its beginning. At the time of Bishop Rivera's accession to the episcopate the Rev. Galen Onstad was the Rector. He retired in 1971 and was succeeded by the Rev. Ronald Swanson who, at the time of his call, was a Canon on the staff of St. James' Cathedral, Fresno. During Swanson's tenure mission congregations were begun in Sonora, St. Michael's, established in February 1983, and Groveland, Grace Church Mission, in February 1985. The Rev. Ronald Swanson resigned in 1987 and at the time of this writing the congregation is being served by the Rev. Dr. William E. Craig, former Director of St. Francis' Home For Boys.

ST. PAUL'S PARISH, BAKERSFIELD

Bakersfield was said to have been founded "in the middle of nowhere" by Col. Thomas Baker, beside the Kern River. When the "city fathers" refused to give the railroad the concessions desired, surveyors routed the line to the east and created a new "town" Sumner, and for years refused to acknowledge the existence of Bakersfield only a little more than a mile to the west.

Its strategic position in Kern County was accentuated by the discovery of oil in May 1899, and its importance could no longer be denied. When Bishop Kip first visited the site in October 1855 there was nothing but a dusty plain beside the dry Kern River bed. The only unarmed member of an Army patrol, Bishop Kip conducted the first Anglican Eucharist in Kern County at Fort Tejon, where all the officers were found to be confirmed Churchmen. One, a licensed lay reader, had been conducting services.

In 1855, word spread that there was gold to be found in the Kern River valley, and Havilah became the County Seat. Lay readers conducted services there occasionally. Access to the lower Kern Valley was difficult at best, and the gold had to be extracted with heavy equipment rather than hand tools, as was the case in the Mother Lode country. In 1866, the County Seat was moved to Bakersfield. Rails finally reached Kern County in 1874.

The Rev. D. O. Kelley first visited Bakersfield and held services on Sunday, June 29, 1879. After conducting regular services in the Fall, St. Paul's was the first of his foundations to be officially organized on December 1, 1879. There were about a dozen communicants, "including several men." First services were held in a large new Railroad Avenue School House, located where the Beale Library now stands. Mrs. Walter Chittenden and her husband brought their small organ on a wagon from their home for each service. Only the Roman Catholic and Methodist Churches had preceded the Episcopal Church in Bakersfield.

Bishop Kip made his first return to the area April 18, 1890, and confirmed eight persons. The service was held in the small Methodist house of worship. A remark of Bishop Kip's concerning the inadequacy of the place for worship resulted in the women organizing as St. Paul's Guild and they assisted materially in support of the mission. In January 1882, Deacon Thomas A. Griffiths came as resident missionary. He remained for a little over a year when ill health forced his retirement; he succumbed the following July at home in New Jersey. There is a memorial window in the Children's Chapel honoring him.

He was followed by Mr. H. Horace Clapham, who was studying for the ministry in Fresno under D. O. Kelley. Mr. Clapham conducted services twice monthly until his ordination when he became resident missionary in July 1885.

Property was purchased at 17th and Eye Streets, and funds raised. A wooden church with steeple was erected in the fall of 1886, and a delighted Bishop Kip dedicated it on Sunday, November 21, 1886. Only $470 remained unpaid of the $3,000 total cost. The building was free of debt by January 1888 and the consecration was done by Bishop Nichols on January 18, 1891.

St. Paul's was granted parish status by the Diocese of California on March 4, 1891. In May, the Claphams left for Los Gatos, but not before he had begun services on Easter Day in Rosedale for the English colony there. Frank D. Miller began serving on October 14, 1892, and was instituted as Rector in February 1893. David Holmes, an Oxford graduate from England, came by way of Montana and served briefly in 1897. In December of that same year he was succeeded by Hobart Chetwood.

Another Englishman, Edward Morgan, began his rectorship on September 1, 1898. It was his first parish after graduation from Church Divinity School of the Pacific, then located in San Mateo. He introduced the first processional Cross, eucharistic lights, and vestments to the parish. In January 1900, St. Barnabas' Guild for women was organized. In 1901 the 12-year old wooden building was moved to the corner of Kern and Lake Streets, "Kern City", to be used for the parochial mission of St. Barnabas. The Rev. Hugh Ramsey came to assist with this mission. This made room for a brick church which was built for a cost of $16,000 and opened by Bishop Nichols on January 1, 1902.

At the same service, the white memorial altar was consecrated as a memorial to Romualdo Pacheco, 12th Governor of the State of California. He was the father of Mrs. William Tevis. The Tevis's also gave six brass candlesticks, the altar cross and vases, the altar rail (now in the chapel), and the Tiffany window. Mrs. Tevis had seen the entire group in the Italian exhibit at the Pan-American exhibition in Buffalo, N. Y., in 1901, and was so impressed that she purchased it entire for the church then being planned. It is said that President William McKinley had knelt before the altar only a few hours before his assassination. The marble font was given by a friend of Mrs. Tevis, and the rose window was given by the four Tevis sons.

At the same time, a red frame St. John's Chapel was built in Rosedale, and consecrated on February 14, 1904. A lot for the guild hall was donated in 1904. Edward Morgan often returned the Church his monthly salary of $50. When it was rumored a saloon might be built beside the church on Chester Avenue, he used his own money to buy the lot and had a two-story office building put up. The oil boom brought a great influx, and Fr. Morgan established missions at Rio Bravo (1902), and at Greenfield (1903). A slump in oil prices brought a recession and the missions were closed when Morgan resigned in 1905 to take a position in New York City. He was succeeded by Walter B. Clark who left in 1907.

David M. Crabtree, a Southerner, was called from Washington, D. C. as the next rector. A fine preacher he soon had the church filled again. He married in Bakersfield, but found that he and his wife could not live on their small salary; he left in the Spring of 1912.

St. Barnabas' Chapel was put up for sale. When the building was sold to Calvary Baptist Church in 1912, the bell went with it with the consent of the donor Mrs. Cooper. St. John's, Rosedale, was later used as a residence and storehouse; when threatened with demolition in 1950, it was purchased by St. Paul's parishioners and given to Pioneer Village Museum. In 1965, it was restored and opened as the village church, and so dedicated by Bishop Walters.

For a three month period St. Paul's was served by Bishop Anson Rogers Graves, retired Bishop of the Platte. He and his wife lived in the study and cooked their meals in the guild hall. In October 1912, Charles Hitchcock, another Englishman, became Rector. Hitchcock resigned early in 1914, moving to Australia. He was followed by Benjamin E. Diggs, a Southerner with "high church" tendencies. In June 1915, during the District Convocation, the church, now free of debt, was consecrated. Plans for a large guild hall were started, but abandoned in the face of considerable dissension. Diggs became the center of controversy over his alleged abrupt and tactless manner with those who disagreed with him. In Spring 1919, he resigned, but was prevailed upon to remain by his supporters. Attendance and income fell and Bishop Sanford was forced to intervene after the 1920 parish meeting. After $1,500 was borrowed to pay his salary arrears, Diggs resigned and became assistant to the Bishop of Colorado.

In October 1920 the Rev. George E. Renison, an expert in Indian work, was called from Minnesota. He succeeded in reuniting the parish family. The young people were organized and Sunday School flourished. The church had no rectory at the time so the six Renisons were housed with various church families until the women were able to purchase a small house on 20th Street. In January 1921, however, he was recalled to his Indian work. March 1921 saw the Rev. William Cash arrive from San Francisco. He conducted services and helped organize the first mission in Taft in 1922. A rectory was purchased on H Street, but in 1924, Cash accepted a call to Merced.

The short tenure of the clergy hint at problems, and it was nearly a year before William E. Patrick, a Harvard graduate, came from Santa Paula as Rector. He stayed for sixteen years, the longest tenure in the parish. He served as a Chaplain in the military during World War I and was decorated. Eventually, he served as national Chaplain of the American Legion.

The family of five children were too many for the rectory, so it was rented out to a parish family, and the Patricks bought a home. The Sunday Church School was built up to an enrollment of 200. A festive celebration of St. Paul's 50th anniversary was held in 1929 despite ominous signs from Wall Street. Bakersfield was one of the last to feel the effects of the Great Depression, but church income dropped and Patrick volunteered to take a $600 annual reduction in salary. Refugees from the Dust Bowl greatly changed the demographics of Bakersfield. Later, with the U. S. facing entry into World War II, Patrick was granted "leave of absence" in February 1941 to serve as chaplain at Fort Lewis, Washington. Later he resigned the parish to serve overseas and was awarded the Bronze Star medal for meritorious service.

Ralph Cox, a Chicagoan trained at C.D.S.P., came from Porterville as next Rector. He remained for nearly thirteen years. His marriage while serving St. Paul's was one of the last official acts of Bishop Sanford and one of the first for Bishop Walters. The parish received many memorials of men who died in service during World War II. In 1947, the Women's Auxiliary was organized; members were then divided into guilds. They organized the first annual parish Barbeque for a fund-raiser, an event that continues to the present day. In 1951, a new parish hall was built in a brick design that matched the church. The old wooden hall was sold to a Baptist congregation and moved to Lakeview Avenue.

The disastrous earthquake of 1952 changed the face of downtown Bakersfield and severely damaged St. Paul's. A second quake a month later doomed the structure. In all, seven downtown churches had to be demolished. Valuable glass and the marble altar were salvaged for the new building. Services were held in the parish hall until September. The property was sold for $145,000 and a new site was purchased on 17th Street, between B and C for $40,000 from the Hay family, parishioners. Most of the balance went to pay off debts on the new hall. Services were conducted in the Elks Hall while the new church was being built. The new church was built of concrete for $194,000. As the building itself neared completion, long-smoldering discontent flared against the Rector's allegedly "dictatorial and abrupt manners." Mr. Cox resigned and went to Connecticut. In December, the former Rector, William Patrick, conducted services for their 75th anniversary.

In November 1954, the Vestry called Clarence W. Franz from Trinity Cathedral, Phoenix. He arrived to begin 1955 as Rector. An attractive person and excellent preacher he attracted many and it became necessary to add a 9:30 A.M. family service, and church school enrollment reached 300 baby-boomers. By Spring, he presented 61 for Confirmation, and in the Fall, 33 more. Franz introduced professional fund-raising to pay off the debts and build a parish hall and classrooms. In

January he tendered his resignation. When he did so he was presented with a scroll of 350 names in appreciation and a large gift of money. On February 27, 1956, an early morning fire destroyed the guild hall. $9,000 from insurance was used toward the planned new building.

The Rev. Dr. Frederick A. Schilling, a professor at C.D.S.P. came weekly to hold services. He so impressed the Vestry that he was called to be Rector as soon as the 1956 seminary Spring term ended. A new rectory on Sunset Avenue was purchased. Old wounds were healed and the parish prospered. In two years he presented 132 candidates for Confirmation. For the first time, St. Paul's hired an assistant, the Rev. Ralph Jeffs, formerly in another denomination as chaplain at the Tehachapi prison. While serving as assistant he studied under Dr. Schilling and was ordained at St. Paul's. In the fall of 1958, he was appointed Vicar of St. John's Mission, Tulare. Dr. Schilling resigned in May 1958 to become Rector of St. Jude's, Burbank.

Victor R. Hatfield from Marysville came next. He took office in September. To him fell the responsibility for leading the congregation in the financing and building of the new units. John Atkinson, retired from Taft, and Frederick Stillwell, retired from Ridgecrest, assisted. In June 1960, the loan on the first buildings were paid in full, four years ahead of schedule.

"Father Harry" Leigh-Pink, an English born, Canadian trained priest, became Associate Rector when Atkinson moved to Porterville. He served as chaplain to Canterbury Club at Bakersfield College. Being a former newspaper man, Bishop Walters asked him to assume the editorship of the diocesan newspaper in a new format. The request, being made on Epiphany, Father Harry chose THE STAR as the new name. Later he was appointed Vicar of St. Stephen's, Stockton, which he served for about four years before returning as Associate at St. Paul's in 1968. He retired in 1971 in Bakersfield where he died in 1973.

July 1960, saw ground broken for the new buildings, to cost a total of $250,000. The Building Fund then held $61,799. At the same time, San Joaquin was becoming a Diocese, and the Diocesan Advance Fund was opened. St. Paul's pledged $52,000 to this even as building was going on. On April 9, 1961, Bishop Walters dedicated the new facilities. There were 1,002 members on the records in "Good Standing," and 346 church school pupils. The Rector was honored by being named an Honorary Canon of the Cathedral. For several years he served as Secretary of the VIIIth Province. He was among the nominees for Bishop in 1968.

St. Paul's assisted materially in the founding of the All Saints' Mission in southwest Bakersfield in 1966. Many of St. Paul's parishioners were transferred to the new mission. This required a change in the loan repayment rate from $2,000 to $500 per month. Canon Hatfield retired to Cambria in 1968. Dr. John W. Ellison was called to take Canon Hatfield's place. A Colorado native, schooled at Harvard and Virginia Seminary, he was at St. Clement's Pro-Cathedral, El Paso, when called to Bakersfield. His published works included the first computerized concordance of the RSV Bible. His Bible study classes drew not only parishioners but clergy from other traditions. He also got the church involved in Meals-On-Wheels, taking 60 hot meals each noonday to shut-ins. Other churches took part under St. Paul's leadership. Three men went to seminary from St. Paul's during Dr. Ellison's tenure: Charles Threewit, an Union Oil executive, Bill Chase, and Mark Lawrence. In 1976, Dr. Ellison organized a Bi-centennial celebration for Bakersfield, attended by several thousand. After the February Convention in 1979, Dr. Ellison left for a parish in Sacramento.

The Rev. Harry Leigh-Pink resigned in November 1971, and Peter Van Hook came the following summer, directly from C.D.S.P. In 1974 he accepted appointment to St. Raphael's Mission, Oakhurst. The Rev. Thomas B. Hubbard was called from Sherrill, N. Y., to be Associate Rector. When he left in January 1978, a lay Intern for Christ, Joe Parker, was engaged to work with the parish youth. In August, he left for Portland. Much work refurbishing St. Paul's buildings, organ, and grounds was done in anticipation of the Centennial in 1979.

The Rev. John D. Spear, former Dean of St. James' Cathedral, Fresno, is the latest in the succession of clergy at St. Paul's. During his tenure the Rev. Thomas Barnett followed by the Rev. Roger Grist have served as assistants. Fr. Spear has served the diocese in Shafter, St. Luke's, Bakersfield, and interim at Delano. As of this writing he is still the Rector of St. Paul's, Bakersfield, Chairman of the Stewardship Committee for the Diocese, member of the Standing Committee, and Dean of the Kern Deanery.

ST. JAMES' CATHEDRAL, FRESNO

Fresno County's first white settlement was at Fort Miller, a site now covered by Millerton Lake. In October 1855, Bishop Kip visited Fort Miller and conducted services there. He appointed the Fort's doctor as a lay reader. The desolate, dusty, parched plains did not then offer any prospect of future prosperity until A. Y. Easterby conducted his first experiments with irrigation in the Fresno area. In 1872, the railroad reached a point near Easterby's field and changed the prospect greatly. Following a vote in 1874, the county seat, buildings and all, was loaded on wagons, hauled from Millerton to the new site of "Fresno City," and reconstructed. By 1875, Fresno had a population of 600, including some 200 Chinese. Before 1879, Episcopal priests W. C. Powell and Elias Birdsall stopped in Fresno City on exploratory trips through the San Joaquin valley and held a service or two.

In June 1879, on his own initiative, the Rev. D. O. Kelley toured the Central Valley by rail, staying for two Sundays in Fresno. He visited one of the first irrigated vineyards in the valley, and sensed the importance of this for the future of the town. In September, he was sent back to Fresno by the Board of Missions and took up residence, doing his missionary work up and down the valley from this center. In formal organization, St. Paul's, Bakersfield, predates St. James' by two weeks; St. James' was organized December 15, 1879. Two Tupper brothers, former Confederate soldiers, worked with Fr. Kelley, a former Union Officer, as Warden and vestrymen, all but six or eight communicants were women at the start. Services were held in W.D. Tupper's law office, then in a shanty-like hall, later in a vacant school room.

In 1881-82, two lots were given to the Church by the Railroad, at Fresno and N Streets, opposite the present-day City Hall and Memorial Auditorium. Kelley bought and paid for four adjacent lots, and a brick church facing Fresno Street, and a frame parsonage, were built with generous assistance from the East. As a Deputy to General Convention in 1880, Kelley made it a special point to help form the American Church Building Fund, and had scoured the East for help in Fresno. As a result the church was consecrated December 7, 1884. In Eastertide, 1888, St. James' Church became a parish, and D. O. Kelley was elected its first Rector. At the time it was a thing of note to record that all seven men on the Vestry were also communicants. Ten years later 275 communicants were listed, of whom 140 were in "good standing." The first postulant for Holy Orders had also come from the parish and went to Nashotah House. Bishop Nichols called Fr. Kelley to his staff in San Francisco, and he left the parish on July 8, 1891.

William Lucas was the second Rector, from March 6, 1892 to 1900. He also served as first Dean of the San Joaquin Convocation. Harvey S. Hanson was third Rector, September 1900 to August 31, 1911. During his tenure the original brick church was demolished and a new cornerstone laid by Bishop Nichols on September 8, 1901. The new church, facing N Street, was built during 1902, with a debt of some $7,000, which was rapidly reduced in the next few years. A handsome rectory was also built.

Upon the creation of the Missionary District of San Joaquin in 1910 Fresno became the See city. By agreement between Bishop Louis C. Sanford and the Vestry of St. James', it became the Pro-Cathedral, thus realizing the dream of its founder over forty years earlier. On nomination by the Bishop, and confirmation of the Vestry, the Rev. G. R. E. MacDonald of Hanford became the first Dean. R. W. Rhames was appointed Canon, and J. H. Waterman was made an honorary Canon. The Pro-Cathedral was consecrated on October 27, 1911. In 1925, St. James' Church was officially made the Cathedral Church of the Bishop of San Joaquin.

Following Dean MacDonald's retirement in 1929, the Very Rev. Arthur W. Farlander served as Dean through the Depression years, 1929 to 1936. The unique high altar in St. James' was carved by Canon Frederick D. Graves, in memory of his father, former Bishop of Kearney (Western Kansas), and for 14 years Rector of St. James', Sonora, and of his mother; it was finished in 1938. At the same dedication, the carved Good Shepherd pulpit was also installed. It was made in England for St. Stephen's Church, San Francisco, around 1896. When the church was closed, the pulpit was put into storage and later donated to St. James' Cathedral, via Dean Malloch, by Canon George H. B. Wright of San Francisco, former Rector of St. Stephen's.

Dean Farlander was followed by James M. Malloch, from 1936 to 1955. Dean Malloch was different, to say the least! He would often arrive late for services, using this as an excuse not to wear vestments. He stands out in the set of clergy photographs by virtue of the fact that he always wore his tie. Together with a Roman Catholic priest and a Jewish rabbi, Dean Malloch was featured on a popular radio program and had a high profile in Fresno. A sculpture group in downtown Fresno commemorates this "Forum". People remember that Dean Malloch's "sermons" were often entertaining book reviews.

During his episcopate Bishop Sanford lived in Fresno on Peralta Street. His successor, Bishop Sumner Walters, because of a long-standing rift (unresolved during his tenure) between him and the Deans of his time, made St. John's, Stockton, "his church," while St. James' continued to have the title of Cathedral Church.

In 1951, Sanford Hall was built as a parish hall for the Cathedral. The great Central Valley earthquake of 1956 severely damaged the church, making it unsafe. City inspectors condemned the old church, and from April 1, 1957, the parish hall was used for services until a new site on East Dakota at Cedar was prepared. The Chapter first bought property in the area that later proved to be directly under the flight path from the new Fresno Air Terminal. The situation was somewhat improved when a local dairyman was kind enough to trade that for the present site.

Harry B. Lee, succeeded Dean Malloch in 1955, after a year as Associate Dean, and served from 1955 to 1970. In 1960, under Dean Lee, the present facilities were erected for a cost of

$270,000. The new Sanford Hall now serves as worship space; offices for the Cathedral Parish and the Diocese, and a day school are also located there. In 1961, the Cathedral Parish moved. Parts of the old Sanford Hall downtown now serve as office of the Fresno Chamber of Commerce. During the final years of Bishop Walter's episcopate, Diocesan House was constructed, and under Bishop Rivera, the center of diocesan administration returned to Fresno. Future development of the property and facilities is in abeyance.

Dean Lee was followed by the Very Rev. John D. Spear, Dean from 1970 to 1978. It was a time of great change and social unrest, together with the introduction of a new Prayer Book. In 1971, the present St. James' Parish Day School was established. It continues to provide a lively educational program for children from pre-school through sixth grade.

The sixth, and present Dean, is the Very Rev. George C. Ruof, who has served since February 1979. The Episcopal School Center has been expanded to include children in grades 3 through 6, and a larger enrollment is found in day care for younger children. Programs in Bible Study and Christian Education, and care for needy in the community through the Dean's Food Cupboard, together with a ministry to California State University students in Fresno, formerly supported by the diocese, are now integral parts of the Cathedral's outreach. Plans for construction to include a multi-purpose building adjunct to the Cathedral worship center are foremost in the list of projects at St. James'.

CHURCH OF THE SAVIOUR, HANFORD

Following the Civil War, Hanford became a kind of "English Colony." A number of Englishmen settled there to raise wheat, but their agricultural methods were unsuitable, resulting in the surface soil being heavily impregnated with salts, forcing a change in use.

People in Lemoore, a few miles to the south of Hanford, invited the Rev. D. O. Kelley to come for a service. He gladly obliged on Wednesday evening, February 18, 1880. Attending that service were two sets of English brothers, who asked him to come to Hanford the next morning and celebrate the Holy Communion for them. They offered their home to him as a place to stay on his visits. "St. John's Mission, Tulare County" was then promptly organized, to include Tulare City, Hanford, Lemoore, and Visalia, with Hanford as its center.

The English connexion proved helpful. By 1882, a small chapel had been built, primarily with English funds. It was decorated in High Victorian fashion of the Gothic Revival. In December 1886, the name was changed to "The Church of the Saviour", which may reflect Oxford Movement sympathies, for this was the name of a grand church built in the industrial slums of Leeds entirely at the expense of Dr. Edward B. Pusey, a leading figure in the Oxford Movement in England.

The Hanford Mission was "somewhat peculiar" from the beginning because nearly all of the 20 or so communicants were M-E-N, and Englishmen at that, so that the locals thought of it as "the English Church". The men, however, were far from exclusive, and actively encouraged Fr. Kelley to draw Americans into the Church; his two confirmation classes totaled 12, of whom 11 were American women. American males on the frontier were apparently not notable for their "church going" habits. In 1885, the Robinson family donated land for a cemetery plot, and Bishop Kip, who by then was nearly blind and having to be led carefully around the cornerstakes, came for the consecration.

In 1887, C. S. Linsley was appointed Vicar of Hanford, with charge of the Tulare County Mission. By April 9, 1891, Hanford was able to become a parish, and Linsley was elected its first Rector. He remained until 1898. Following him was C. G. Adams who came October 1, 1898, but served for less than a year. F. J. Mynard arrived October 1, 1899 and remained until 1904. D. M. Brookman served as Rector for only a few months in 1905.

The Rev. G. R. E. McDonald was Rector from 1905 until 1911, when Bishop Sanford appointed him Dean of St. James' Pro-Cathedral. During his tenure, however, the brick church was built on a new and better site. The land was acquired and the cornerstone laid in 1910. The cost of the new building was "not to exceed $16,000."

At the time there was considerable controversy over moving the church site "across the tracks" to the central site in the growing city of Hanford. Although the controversy eventually died down, a number of items were lost or disposed of in the move, including a pedal organ, the lytch gate and portico. The lectern was sent to Bishop Graves in Coalinga, but was later "found" and returned. After the completion of the "new" church building, the small chapel was placed on logs and rolled up the dirt road to its present location, pulled by horses. It was then used as a parish hall, children's church, and even as a makeshift gymnasium, until its restoration in 1966.

The 1882 church building is fine example of Victorian architecture, with original works of art imported from England and Italy. The walls of the sanctuary and chancel are covered with passion flowers and Tudor roses, hand-painted by an early member of the congregation. Other seco-wall-painting includes life-size (sic) angels and saints, scripture texts painted on scrolls, etc. Another member of the church did much of the original wood carving. Since its restoration, the chapel has been used for mid-week and Holy Day services, small weddings, etc. It is an important part of downtown Hanford, sponsored by the Hanford Chamber of Commerce.

From earliest days, members of the Church of the Saviour have been active in the community. Members have served on the City Council and as Mayor. For several years, the parish sponsored a tutoring program for children in the community. The Churchwomen have, at various times, rolled bandages, provided food and clothing for needy persons, etc. Members are currently involved in such community organizations as Homecoming, Heritage League, Scouts, hospital volunteers, etc. One member has, for eight years, operated the King's Transcribers Library, providing taped books for the blind. Prior to that, she recorded textbooks for the state schools. Other members have been or are involved in the Navy League, Alcohol Board, and many other civic organizations. Through all the years the Church of the Saviour has also taken an active part in the life of the diocese.

As 1987 comes to an end the Church of the Saviour is without a Rector. The Rev. Alexander Patience resigned as of December 1 and accepted the call to be the Rector of the Church of the Holy Communion in Dallas, Texas.

ST. LUKE'S, MERCED

As early as 1872, Merced Episcopalians gathered in private homes for occasional services conducted by the Rev. William H. Dyer of Sonora, and the Rev. W. H. Hill. Several children were baptized, according to a hand-written record dated 1892. Merced, "Gateway to Yosemite," began as one of many "railroad towns" in the Central Valley. The Rev. D. O. Kelley arrived by rail and conducted services on Trinity Sunday, June 8, 1879. He also conducted a burial and a baptism that day, and visited potential parishioners. Sporadic services and visits were made, and on April 8, 1880, Bishop Kip visited. Evening Prayer, a baptism, and one confirmation was conducted. In November 1880, the Rev. William L. Mott, brother-in-law of D. O. Kelley, was appointed Missionary to serve both Modesto and Merced. He took residence in Modesto and began holding services in both places. St. Luke's Mission was organized on August 20, 1881.

During the summer of 1883, chiefly through the efforts of the Rev. William Mott, lots were secured from the Central Pacific R. R. Company, fronting on the Court House, and considerable funds were raised for a chapel or guild hall. Then on September 9, 1883, Mott died suddenly in Modesto "to the great grief of the little band of church people in Merced." The chapel was then only partially completed, but was ready for services on December 30, 1883, when the congregation numbered 34, with two communicants. St. Luke's remained on this site at 20th and M Streets until 1975, when a new facility was built at 350 West Yosemite Avenue, across from Merced College.

D. O. Kelley resigned charge of St. Luke's on October 1, 1884, and the Rev. Scott Jeffreys was appointed to Fr. Mott's place. He did not remain long, and after some time the Rev. W. H. Dyer came in the summer of 1886, ministering occasionally for about a year. "Owing to unfortunate conditions the mission fell into a sad state of discouragement, and the chapel itself was for a time abandoned to the ravages of weather and roaming beasts." A parishioner described it as "fearfully befouled," and home to pigs and chickens.

The Gurr family from England had settled in the McSwain area, known as "the British Colony." During part of 1889 and 1890, the Rev. Harry J. Gurr, temporarily in residence, received Bishop Nichol's permission to re-open the chapel for services. He managed to rally a few to his assistance, cleaning the chapel and "making it fit again for services." In the fall and summer of 1891, however, it again became "unoccupied and dismantled and the few people greatly disheartened." Bishop Nichols had just appointed D. O. Kelley as General Missionary for what is now three dioceses, and gave him Merced for priority attention, to promise the people that Merced would not be abandoned again, once services were revived. After he had succeeded in once again encouraging the support of the people he moved his family to Merced in December. Additions were made to the chapel and new seats were put in. A Sunday School was organized and hopes were revived. Mr. Alfred R. Gurr, lay reader was of great aid in the conduct of the services.

The Rev. Octavius Parker took charge of Merced on September 1, 1892, and served until 1903. He is described as "a short, stout Englishman, who always wore a tall silk hat, and was kindness in itself. He was truly the 'shepherd of his flock'." Clergy listed for Merced also include W. M. Bours, the Rev. George H. Jenks, MD., a Rev. Mr. Lane; in 1904 the Rev. Edwin Johnson for about six months, the Rev. Nelson Saunders, 1905-07, the Rev. Jonathan Nicholas, 1907-08,

W. H. Hawken, 1909-11, and W. L. Greenwood, 1911-13, who was ordained in Merced. At that time, in spite of the rapid changes of clergy, it looked as if self-support and parish status were in sight.

Fr. Hawken, later Bishop Sanford's Archdeacon, returned to Merced from 1913 to 1921. He was a skilled carpenter and built a larger church and vicarage. The old chapel was moved to connect the new buildings in a U-shape. They remained this way until 1960, when the residence was made into offices. This new church was opened for services on Easter Day, April 4, 1915, with orchestra and full choir. By 1919, the debt on the rectory was paid, a remarkable feat, considering the small congregation and the difficult times. Many memorials were given to the new church. These were removed and placed in the present building. A beautiful carved altar with reredos, given in 1917, was used as one piece until it was moved to the new building in 1975, when the altar was separated from the reredos so the priest might go behind the altar and face the congregation, according to the latest fashion. A font of granite from Raymond, given in 1920, now stands at the rear of the nave in the new building.

On November 1, 1921, Hawken resigned to become General Missionary and Archdeacon of the District; on the same date, the Rev. W. H. Pond, a deacon, became Vicar. A Rev. Mr. Woods traveled from Fresno by bus on occasion to celebrate the Eucharist. From 1924 to 1937, Mr. Cash was Vicar. He established a Brotherhood of St. Andrew at St. Luke's, which became a major stablizing factor. The Rev. George Purchase was Vicar from 1942 to 1944. A young Canadian priest, the Rev. Mr. Scott, became Vicar in 1944. He spearheaded the drive to become a parish, and this was achieved in 1947.

In 1949, the Rev. John Christensen brought more expansion and refurbishing changes. Many of St. Luke's present parishioners studied under the leadership of this fine theologian and great preacher from 1949 to 1954. He helped organize St. Alban's, Los Baños. He held the first service of Evening Prayer there on September 24, 1950, in the Women's Club. The mission was formally organized April 22, 1951, with Bishop Walters officiating. Christensen also travelled monthly to conduct the Eucharist at Yosemite Chapel. Additionally, he held the first services in Mariposa at the Ivers-Tiscornia Mortuary in 1949. He organized St. Luke's lay readers for services in Yosemite Valley, Mariposa, Ballico, Livingstone, Winton, Atwater, and Castle Air Force Base. He resigned for reasons of ill health in early 1954.

On Ash Wednesday, March 3, 1954, the Rev. Robert Carwyle Gould became third Rector. The Cornell property beside St. Luke's to the east was purchased. By 1960, the parish had grown from 34 members in 1879 to 214 families. This was a time when mainline churches were growing everywhere. In 1954, St. Luke's CHIMES began publication. It became a parish institution under Ed McDonald, growing from a brief newsletter to a widely read monthly magazine of some 40 pages. Fr. Bob resigned from St. Luke's on April 19, 1960. Chaplain Lang from Castle AFB took services for a time.

Fr. Jack Livingstone was called as fourth Rector. A new rectory was bought on West 26th, facing Applegate Park, the old rectory was made into offices. Steel tie-rods were inserted into the nave "to hold the building together." Six apartments belonging to the parish (to the rear of the offices) were rented out. In Atwater on November 13, 1960, St. George's Chapel was started, with Sunday School and Morning Prayer staffed by St. Luke's parishioners. On November 16, the

Vestry received a petition from five people in Mariposa that a mission be established there as well. They had met with Fr. Christensen for a number of years and had now found a regular place for meeting. On December 4, Fr. Livingstone celebrated the Eucharist for them in Mariposa. Tragically, on Christmas Eve, Fr. Jack and his brother Fr. Joseph Livingstone, were involved in a train/auto collision. Fr. Joseph was killed and Fr. Jack was comatose for six weeks. St. Luke's was served by a series of visiting priests; and Merced's Lutheran Pastor conducted Morning Prayer on one occasion. By March 1961, Fr. Jack was in his office part of each day, and took part in the Sunday services.

By June 1961, discussion was well along on selling the church site and moving to East Merced. But a "drastic financial situation" required a real estate loan. To make matters worse, the offerings for October 15 were stolen. St. George's Chapel was closed for the summer and unable to reopen as planned that Fall due to problems finding quarters and the financial state at St. Luke's. St. Andrew's, Mariposa, however, had funds enough to buy land and make the down payment on a Wurlitzer organ. The portable altar from Atwater was taken to Mariposa. One spring Sunday each year was set aside when the Rector of Merced, with Cherub, Junior, and Senior Choirs went to Mariposa for divine service with the parochial mission. Afterward everyone went to the Mariposa Fairgrounds for a picnic; this practice continued until the late 1960s, building a lasting relationship between the Merced and Mariposa congregations. One year after St. Andrew's Mission was started, the land was completely paid for, and the deed handed to Bishop Walters. Twelve from Mariposa and 20 from Merced were confirmed in November 1961. Fr. Livingston, though back "full time" since June 1962, resigned in February 1963.

In June 1963, the Rev. Edward E. Murphy was called from San Andreas to be fifth Rector. He took up his new position in August. Interestingly, he had gone to C.D.S.P. from Colorado without a sponsoring church. Bishop Walters accepted him as from San Joaquin, and St. Luke's sponsored him, 1955 to 1958, without knowing him! He had worked as special Assistant to Bishop Walters for a time before coming to Merced. Fr. Ed continued the Migrant Ministry in union with other churches in the summer. He kept a monthly appointment in Mariposa for the Eucharist, and started weekly Bible Study classes there Mondays in the basement of the Veterans' Building. He was also very active in laymen's conferences in California and Arizona, participating in "Faith At Work," Billy Graham's Crusades, and other projects. He is also credited for bringing notable spiritual leaders to Merced, such as the late Gertrude Behanna, Rosalind Rinker, Bruce Larson, and others.

In September 1964, the Rev. Walter Clarke, rector of St. Alban's, Los Baños, met with St. Luke's Vestry to propose a "team ministry" between Los Baños, Merced, and Mariposa. This came into being in 1965 when Clarke moved to Merced and became Associate Rector, in charge of "yokefellow" groups (Elton Trueblood's "small group" ministry concept). This lasted until 1968. On Trinity XIX, 1964, Fr. Murphy announced his engagement to Lorraine Costa Stribling, a native of Merced and parishioner since 1960. Bishop Walters conducted their wedding at St. John's, Stockton, on Sunday, December 6, 1964, upon the conclusion of a Northern Deanery EYC weekend at St. Paul's, Modesto, at which 145 young people serenaded them about 3 A.M. by strumming "Here Comes the Bride" on guitars.

A piece of land out in the country was held for St. Luke's for $1.00 while plans were developed for building. The city was rapidly spreading northward, and Merced College was soon to be located across the street. Later Merced Mall and housing was built up around it and the site was no longer isolated. In December 1974, ground was broken and construction begun. The new building was ready in June 1975. The downtown property was sold to Security Pacific Bank, and the old building was burned by the Fire Department "for practice" after valuables were removed.

In the meanwhile, in September 1967, two parishioners, JoAnn Wright and Janeeme Clarke, with the Bishop, Rector, and Vestry's support, began a Day School with 20 pre-school children. Year by year, another grade was added until it reached the 8th grade and an enrollment of 182 pupils, and a graduating 8th grade class in 1984 and 1985. Difficulties with running a Junior High led the Board of Trustees to curtail the program at the 6th grade. There were other difficulties in more recent years when the School Board was no longer comprised of Episcopalians and the control of the school was no longer under the control of the rector and the diocese. This led to unfortunate misunderstandings and no little acrimony because of the failure to understand the relationship of the school with the diocese and the Bishop as Corporation Sole. With the aid of the Canon Chancellor, the late James Barnam of Fresno, the matter was eventually settled with the school being clearly brought under control of the church and the diocese. The staff today includes eight full-time teachers, two part-time, three aides, a librarian, a secretary, and an Extended Day Care Director. This care is offered for students of the school from 7:30 A.M. until 5:30 P.M. weekdays. An annual auction in support of the school has raised as much as $79,000. The Constitution of the school now makes clear the relation between the Church and the Board.

In 1978, the mission work at Atwater was revived. Three vestry members and about 20 families transferred to the new St. Nicholas' church. This resulted in about $25,000 a year reduction in St. Luke's budget, but the "investment in mission" was soon repaid to St. Luke's spiritual benefit, and recovery of the budget as well. St. Luke's has sent at least four men to seminary, and seen several ordinations as well.

St. Luke's has been prominent in inter-church work in Merced. A "Concern Group" in the tumultuous late '60s met weekly for a Brown Bag luncheon in the Parish Hall. Fr. Murphy and the Rev. Tom Wynne from Antioch Baptist Church took the initiative in contacting the other clergy and concerned laity. The group continued to meet for several years, and it was felt that this open communication between leaders of the black and white communities of the city did much to avert serious trouble. Later, the group studied the new books on "sex education" being introduced in the public schools. This led to the formation of an official Merced Human Relations Commission. Several other inter-church projects and proposals involved St. Luke's, such as, exploration of ideas of shared facilities (when St. Luke's was considering its move), and an "ecumenical high school," involving Lutherans, Anglicans, and Roman Catholics. From 1981 to 1983, this received serious consideration, but Fr. Murphy's serious illness in 1983 slowed the momentum and the group eventually dissolved.

The Women's Guild has been a vital part of St. Luke's since 1883, raising money through bazaars, teas, etc., "until they tired of doing the same work each year, so they rested for a time." Guilds have been formed from time-to-time to meet the schedule requirements of different groups of women. For a time the Episcopal Church Women kept meeting, although no one was willing to be President. The title "Convenor" was accepted by some, however. In early 1987, it was voted that "Presidents" would again take the place of "Convenors" in order to comply with

Deanery and Diocesan guidelines. The Daughters of the King have also been an important and active part of parish life and renewal.

In December of 1987 the Rev. Edward Murphy has announced his intention to retire in 1988 after a long ministry at St. Luke's and in this diocese.

ST. PAUL'S, MODESTO

At the time the Central Pacific Railroad was being built through the San Joaquin Valley, it was proposed that the town site where the line bridged the Tuolumne River be named for one of the company officers. He declined out of modesty, however, in 1870 it was named "Modesto," in his honor. By 1871, the treeless streets had 75 buildings. By 1874, the grammar school boasted 286 pupils, and by 1878, ten doctors were practicing medicine in the city. At the same time, other, less desirable influences were prevalent, so a secret citizens' group, the "San Joaquin Valley Regulators," put a large group of prostitutes, gamblers, and sundry other undesirable characters on an outbound train (wouldn't the A.C.L.U. love that today!). With the passage of time agriculture built a strong economic base with a great diversity of irrigated crops, and livestock.

In 1878, traveling Episcopal priests found "many people ready to encourage the establishment of a mission in this region." April 29, 1871, Bishop William I. Kip visited Modesto, "read the service, preached, and baptized an infant." The Methodist "house of worship" was used on that occasion. On Pentecost Sunday, June 1, at his own suggestion, the Rev. Douglas O. Kelley made Modesto his first stop, held morning and evening services in the United Protestant Church, where fourteen received Communion. During the week he met with local churchmen. A nucleus of Episcopalians clearly wanted the regular services of the Church.

After settling in Fresno that Fall, Fr. Kelley conducted services at Modesto from time to time. In 1880, his brother-in-law the Rev. William Lucas Mott took up residence in Modesto as Vicar, and St. Paul's was formally organized on November 3, 1880.

By 1882, the congregation included 30 families, 60 adults and 36 children, and the mission held property at Fourteenth and H Streets. The Railroad donated two lots, as was its policy; two more lots were purchased for a total of $970. Another property was bought for $5.00. A small but attractive wooden church, and a parsonage were built. Mott obtained subscriptions of $1,500 from family and friends in Central New York, San Francisco, and Oakland. Bishop Kip wrote, "Mr. Kelley and Mr. Mott in Modesto have together made the most efficient mission in the diocese." Tragically, Mott died suddenly on September 9, 1883.

It was not until July of 1884 that Henry Scott Jeffreys, Curate of Trinity Church, San Francisco, was sent as Missionary. He stayed but a year and then took a position at St. Paul's, Los Angeles. W. H. Dyer came in September 1885. In November, the church was officially incorporated as "St. Paul's Mission" in an effort to clear title to the land; incorporation was to last for 50 years. The vote is recorded "carried unanimously by a majority of the members voting." For the next year there was difficulty meeting the mortgage payments until, with the permission of the court, a Dr. Hart made a new mortgage at lower rates. Mr. Dyer left in 1887. For a time, D. O. Kelley again "filled in" until R. M. Edwards was appointed Vicar in 1890. He had charge of missions in Stanislaus and Tuolumne Counties, but stayed little more than a year. During this time Modesto had services on first and fifth Sundays. Edwards was called to assist at Trinity, San Francisco, but his wife remained behind to take charge of the entertainment to raise funds to paint the church and "rectory."

The Rev. Octavius Parker took charge of Modesto, Oakdale, and Sonora on June 5, 1891, but on September 1, 1892, he relinquished Sonora, taking on Merced and Madera instead. The Modesto property was now in "very delapidated condition" and he spent over $1,000 on repairs and improvements. He was an outstanding missionary, later appointed the first Missionary of the Episcopal Church to Alaska, but is said to have "failed in the spiritual work at Modesto." He left Modesto in October 1894, and the church buildings were closed for several years thereafter. For a few months in 1898, William Higgs lived in the rectory and held services.

In 1899, Tracy R. Kelley, D. O. Kelley's eldest son, came to Modesto as a high school teacher. With Bishop Nichols' hearty permission, he reopened the church and parsonage as lay reader, organist, and janitor. His father made monthly visits from San Francisco for the Holy Communion. With the school year, four adults and several children were baptized and the Sunday School was reopened. Nine adults were presented for Confirmation. When Tracy Kelley was hired at a San Francisco High School, he continued to return each weekend by train to Modesto to hold services. Under this arrangement he presented two more Confirmation classes to the Bishop. Tracy Kelley may properly be credited for saving St. Paul's from extinction. On February 11, 1900, the handsome wood-gothic church was consecrated, but stability was yet in the future. In 1902, D. O. Kelley was appointed Priest-in-charge once again, until William Edgar Couper came as missionary in 1904. He left in June 1907.

A parishioner, Lay Reader A. L. Walters, who was later ordained, held things together for a time; then Archdeacon Scriven from British Columbia took services until March 1908. For most of the remainder of 1908, C. L. Linsley was Priest-in-charge. For a few months in early 1909, the resident priest was C. E. Maimann; he also had charge of Oakdale. In December 1909, D. O. Kelley presided at the annual meeting. At the end of 1909, W. H. Hawken was assigned to Modesto and while in charge secured important improvements to the church, including the building of the chancel. On June 20, 1910, St. Paul's was regularily organized and incorporated as a Parish. By early 1911, however, the rectory was declared "old and inadequate." Hawken became the first Rector but left after March 1911 to serve other missions; he later became Archdeacon.

In April 1911, W. H. Wheeler was called as second Rector. Talk of building a guild hall was prominent in the parish at the time. In December, the Vestry granted the Rector permission to hold services in Turlock as might be convenient, but he left in April 1912 for a church in Oakland. J. R. Atwill was appointed *locum tenens* for six months, and the parish house was erected in that year for the sum of $2,300. The Ladies' Guild was chiefly responsible for this accomplishment. From April 1913 to May 1915, William P. Williams was Rector. He came from Iowa, then left for Connecticut. He continued to hold services in Turlock during his tenure. In July 1915, the Rev. Charles Hitchock came as Rector, having served Grass Valley, Ferndale, and Bakersfield. He set about a complete canvass of the parish "for the Lord's Treasury", and reported about $40 more a month for the parish. He ordered fifty new prayer books, hoping the Guild would pay the bill as he had received only $2.50 to pay for them. He left in May 1916. It was not until the following spring that Oliver Kingman became Rector, but after serving one month, ill health forced his resignation.

A. L. Walter, now in priest's orders, came from Hemet as *locum tenens* in June-July 1917, and was called as Rector in August. A "Grand Opening" was set for the first Sunday of October at which all members were invited to bring suggestions for improving attendance and activities. A Harvest Festival, boys' choir, and visitation of parishioners and others were subsequently planned. It was suggested that a list of those "having insufficient reason for not coming be handed to the Rector in order that these people can be induced to attend." The Women's Auxilliary was appealed to, to assume the debt on the parish hall. Money continued to be in short supply to the treasury. The Vestry threatened to resign for lack of support if sufficient pledges were not received by May 15, 1918. There are no Minutes from that May until April 23, 1919, but Walters continued as Rector throughout. $7.20 in taxes were paid and "the remainder in the treasury (to) be paid to the Rev. (Mr.) Walters as part of the amount owing him." A successful pledge campaign took place in early 1920, and only $500 remained on the Guild Hall debt. Walters' resignation was accepted at that time "with deepfelt regret."

In July 1920, the parish called the Rev. Harold S. Brewster as Rector. He was described as "a brilliant, deeply spiritual scholar", and remained for seven years — the longest pastorate at St. Paul's to that date. Lively social events — dances, minstrel shows, musical comedy, and such are recorded. The Women's Guild reported a membership of 156, and its budget for 1921 was $5,785. Suggestions were made that the men also organize. In 1923, St. Paul's hosted the District's annual Convocation. Brewster almost resigned in 1924, apparently over salary arrears, but the parishioners scrambled into action and secured enough to go on. By 1926 the Treasurer despaired, and, in September 1927, Fr. Brewster was made Dean of the Cathedral in Fargo, North Dakota. Archdeacon Hawken and Lay Reader Paul Shimmon covered services for about three years. Persian-born, Shimmon had completed seminary nearly 30 years before, and was now priested to serve Modesto. The Vestry called for cooperation among all parishioners. At the same time tax delinquencies were reduced.

In January 1931, the parish called the Rev. Thomas C. Maxwell as Rector (though Archdeacon and Bishop had recommended return to mission status). At the same time, he was appointed Vicar of Turlock and Oakdale. The rectory was "uninhabitable", and a firm of wreckers gave $25 for the lumber. The Maxwell family lived in Berkeley until a house was rented for them in Modesto in 1933. The widely-experienced priest was granted leave to live with his family Monday through Wednesday each week, and so was effectively "half-time Rector." Meeting even such modest salary was a strain. On March 29, 1933, a special arrangement was made and St. Paul's reverted to Mission status, Maxwell's salary and travel expenses to be met in part by the District for the work at Oakdale and Turlock. By 1934, the Committee felt able to promise him a home telephone, to be maintained by the church.

On February 9, 1938, a severe storm downed electric lines on the church and it burned; little was salvaged. Modesto people presented Fr. Maxwell with a purse, especially to replace his water-damaged personal books. Sunday services were held at the Jewish Community Center. Groups went into action to raise funds for a new church building; "not at the present site" Fr. Maxwell insisted. Episcopalians and non-Episcopalians responded to appeals for funds. A new site was purchased at 17th and I Streets for $7,500, but plans to build a rectory first were scrapped. Despite all this, St. Paul's hosted the Convocation of January, 1939, using the Guild Hall, the Jewish Center, and the Presbyterian Church. By September 1939, plans were drawn for a gothic style building in concrete, with a wood-beam ceiling. A door to door solicitation was discouraged, but several businesses made donations. Groundbreaking was held on Sunday, March 17, 1940, and Dedication on September 18. St. Cecilia's Guild (newly formed for the purpose) bought rows of seats from the Tivoli Theatre in San Francisco for $120.76, including sales tax. On August 18, 1942, Fr. Maxwell died suddenly, having been Vicar through a difficult eleven years.

Bishop Sanford then recommended the Rev. Edward Birch, Irish-born world-traveler, for one year, under the supervision of the Rural Dean of Stockton. The Vestry soon decided to call him as Rector, and set itself the goal of regaining self-support. The eloquent Mr. Birch resigned in January 1944 to accept a commission in the Canadian Army. Bishop Walters first visited in February, dedicated the War Shrine, and addressed the question of local leadership. Alvin Hilgeman was called to St. Paul's, but served only two months.

In September 1944, the Rev. Harry B. Lee was called. The Vestry took on more indebtedness and finally bought a rectory after years of thwarted efforts. St. Paul's was incorporated as a Parish on February 15, 1945. By the end of the year, movement was afoot to build a new hall. In 1946, the Vestry was looking for a suitable lot on which to build a rectory, and in 1947, Mr. Lee stressed the need of space for church school, a project estimated at $40,000. Plans were accepted in October. A letter of 1948 to the parish expressed his expectation that the parish membership would double in five years; church seating for 500 would be needed. Groundbreaking for the Hall was on January 23, 1949. The $84,685 building was completed later that year.

Many hours were spent trying to dispose of the old property (which had been leased). It was finally sold for $21,000 in early 1952, a smaller amount than a previous bid. Many physical improvements, and stained glass windows were added. By this time parish finances had become stronger and more dependable. In September 1950, the Vestry granted, then withdrew permission for a year's leave of absence for Mr. Lee. They feared "disruption of the prosperous condition" of the church. Harry Lee then resigned and served for a time in Napa before going to St. James' Cathedral, Fresno, in 1955.

The Rev. H. Ward Riley was called as next Rector from Sonora in November 1950. The Vestry proceeded to employ a professional fund-raiser to help retire the debt of $30,000. In Wiley's first year, all records in giving and Sunday School attendance were broken as Baby-boomers began flooding in. This influx did not continue, however. In November 1952, Wiley submitted his resignation, effective February 1, 1953, and left for Auburn. The Rev. Wilbur Caswell (retired) then became Priest-in-charge. Caswell was severely injured in an automobile accident in March 1953, but wrote out sermons for laymen to read. From his hospital room he wrote to appeal for a large Easter offering and reminded parishioners, "Whether you make a pledge or not, you cannot consider yourself in 'good standing' unless you are taking some share in support of your church. And the best way to do this is to apply for weekly envelopes, and indicate what you believe is possible to contribute weekly, monthly, or annually."

The Rev. Robert Chidwick accepted a call to be the next Rector as from June 1, 1953. The English-born artist and priest had been a choir boy at Westminster Abbey; he trained at Wycliffe

College, Toronto. A live radio broadcast from the church was undertaken in September, and the Vestry noted that "no liquor be allowed on church property" even for weddings. The Presiding Bishop launched a "Builders for Christ Fund" but the Vestry voted to refuse it, even after a special appeal from Bishop Walters. On October 3, 1954, the Treasurer reported the church "solvent". Mr. Chidwick followed up on the newly confirmed and expressed appreciation of their attendance at Holy Communion; he urged the Bishop consider confirmation at an earlier age "when indelible impressions are made and lifelong habits formed." He made special approaches to families "detached from fellowship" who "appear to be somewhat confused in their thinking on spiritual matters."

Finances continued to be a problem, and the Women's Guild was unable to help the Vestry to the extent asked. St. Paul's sent a contribution of $500 to the "Builders for Christ" campaign, although the Bishop had requested they meet a quota of $2,000. Fr. Chidwick made an "irrevocable decision" to resign in December 1958. The parish called Fr. Caswell back as interim priest. He served again through February 1959.

In March 1959, Fr. Charles Williams assumed the rectorship. A new rectory was purchased as the old one was too small and needed extensive repairs. A Council of Advice was formed by June to give voice to all parish groups. A Memorial Fund was also set up. The District asked St. Paul's for $28,800 to make progress toward Diocesan status "at a very inopportune time" for the parish, but the Vestry agreed to it on a schedule of payments to be determined later. Fr. Williams had a keen interest in everything happening; activity bubbled up and it was clear he needed clergy assistance. St. Paul's had grown from 191 communicants in 1945 to 534 in 1960. Fr. Edward A. Groves, Jr., a man of wide experience, became Associate Rector on February 14, 1960. Hopes were expressed even then of a parochial mission in Ceres. The parish had to take out a loan to retire the previous debt and meet the year's expenses. In April 1961, the parish invited British Evangelist, Canon Bryan Green, co-sponsored by the Modesto Council of Churches, for a 9-day Crusade. This was enthusiastically supported, even by Episcopalians. The title "Associate Rector" created much confusion, and in May, Fr. Groves presented his resignation as such, though he was kept on at the same salary and allowances for some time. In October, Fr. Arthur Beckwith, recently retired from Oakdale, agreed to assist as a "supply priest," not on the "regular parish staff."

Bishop Walters was urging the creation of another congregation in Modesto at the time, but in January 1962, the Vestry told the Bishop that "the mood and atmosphere" were not right for the involvement of St. Paul's staff in such a venture, and urged that any other mission be under the Diocese. At Thanksgiving, the entire offering was given for the new Mission of St. Dunstan. St. Paul's was feeling cramped on its property and investigated the acquisition of the adjacent city park; the impossibility later forced St. Paul's to relocate. Bookkeeping became an issue in the Fall of 1964, and in May 1965, Fr. Williams submitted his resignation, overwhelmed by personal problems. It was accepted with regret. Fr. Beckwith supplied, together with the Rev. Norman Van Walterop, a worker priest. An accounting firm made several suggestions to clarify finances.

Dean Malcolm E. McClenaghan was called from Trinity Cathedral, Sacramento, as Rector in September 1965. He had begun his ministry in the Evangelical and United Brethren, then served several mid-Western Episcopal churches and the Cathedral in Kansas City. In Sacramento he helped set up a $3-million housing project for the elderly. It was said that he blew into St. Paul's like a fresh wind, "sometimes of hurricane proportions." Following trends of the day, he discouraged the existence of guilds because some tended to be cliques; fund-raising activities were discouraged, and parishioners were exhorted to give of their own income rather than spend efforts raising money from other sources. He supported faith, study, and prayer groups, and education and service guilds, and the "PEP" (Presbyterian-Episcopal-Program). "He did not always carry all parishioners with him in the directions he intended to go, but he fearlessly pursued his goals." Hindsight sees some wisdom in various of his aims. The Vestry told him to deal with dissidents by "closing his ears to this group and go(ing) ahead with your own plans." The rectory was sold and the Rector was given a loan toward a down-payment, relieving the Vestry of that responsibility. Financial accounts were put on the national standardized basis. The EYC worked off its indebtedness of $85 by churchyard work. Fr. McClenaghan encouraged interchurch work with the Westside Neighborhood Center, and support of the Sister Diocese of Botswana.

Early in 1968, after much exploration, St. Paul's purchased the Bowen Ranch on Oakdale Road, nearer the center of population growth, as a new site. Abandonment of the old property, however, proved difficult. Severe strain resulted between parish and diocese. When finally resolved, Ralston Tower, quality apartments for low-income elderly, was built on the 17th Street site with the cooperation of several other churches. The park beside it proved to be an asset. "Stormy weather" for St. Paul's was not improved for St. Paul's by introduction of the first "trial liturgy" in May, 1969. By the end of the year, the parish budget was about $7,000 in arrears. The Vestry suddenly found itself in the ranching business with "18 acres of the most undesirable cling peaches in California." Leasing and selling parts of the ranch provided some solution. Zoning changes were finally made, and the old property was eventually sold in 1971.

On August 8, ground was broken for the new church on the former ranch site. It was an innovative design with the first "triodetic dome" on the West Coast. The building was to give people inside "a feeling of reaching out to the world." But the financial crisis continued. In December, with the church nearly built, Fr. McClenaghan announced his resignation, to be effective after dedication services on the Feast of the Conversion of St. Paul, 1972. Christmas services were held in the new building. The Rev. Robert Slocum was made Interim Priest for 1972. The old church building was deconsecrated; annexation of the new site by Modesto was voted, and many other regular church activities continued unabated.

In November, Fr. Thomas M. Foster was called from Grace Church, Westwood, New Jersey, to be Rector. He was instituted on December 31, 1972, officially beginning his Rectorship the next day. At the Vestry meeting of January 2, the new roof was reported leaking, in one of the wettest winters on record. Fr. Foster set about the revival of parish groups, from ECW to acolytes and ushers. On September 16, St. Paul's hosted a grand service for eight Episcopal churches in the area, called "Body Building Day." The Eucharist, fellowship, games, and entertainment enlivened the festal gathering. The financial picture at St. Paul's began to look better. From the old church many items were salvaged and distributed to other parishes and missions before its demolition.

Stress over issues in the National Church, created problems throughout the country. St. Paul's Vestry consistently held to the norms established by Scripture and Tradition, and instructed parish delegates to Convention to do the same. At the same time, St. Paul's was moving ahead with the mission work of the parish. The parochial mission in Ceres was encouraged to find property in 1974, and helped in that search by Fr. Foster. Interest in the services of the Church voiced in Patterson (near the west side of the valley) led to a weekday Eucharist and Bible study there, conducted by a retired priest. Fr. Albert Collins. At Easter, St. Joseph's Roman Catholic parishioners took part in St. Paul's Paschal Meal and warmly responded to the reverent occasion. In January 1975, the parish hosted a "Faith Alive!" weekend with very positive results. The warm parish family atmosphere and interesting programs have continued to attract new members to St. Paul's, so that the parish is now the largest in the diocese.

In 1976, St. Paul's hosted the annual Diocesan Convention; Presiding Bishop John Allin was the Guest of Honor. He told the Convention, "We're not going to be saved by our projects . . . They are only vehicles; we are saved by Jesus Christ. Our response to Him is what God judges us by." The parochial missions continued to develop; Charles Threewit was ordained and given charge of Patterson, and Fr. William Harvey was assigned to Ceres. Average weekly attendance rose from 200 in 1972 to 525 in 1976. Plans and fund-raising toward the Centennial in 1979 were launched. This enabled the building of a multi-purpose double classroom in 1977. The parish was deeply sympathetic at this time to those aggrieved by the stresses in the national Church and who felt it necessary to dissociate themselves from the actions of the 1976 General Convention in Minneapolis. The parish made a renewed commitment to seek "Jesus, the Truth."

Growth in the physical plant and programs, as well as spirituality have been evident over the years as Fr. Foster has striven to give the parish a "liberal conservatism" in the Anglican heritage. Donna Wilson, a parishioner, headed the establishment of a parish school in 1977, spanning pre-school to sixth grades. "Family Connections", an adoption agency, was headed up by Mrs. Audrey Foster, to meet the special needs of children. The parish also adopted two Vietnamese refugee families. Marriage Encounter, Cursillo, and other renewal programs have found wide acceptance at St. Paul's also. Marple Manor, a second unit of Ralston Tower, was built in 1984 by MACH Co., Modesto Affiliated Church Housing Corporation. Another fund drive raised enough to build a gymnasium which was nearly finished for the 1986 Diocesan Convention. Parish life has been anything but dull or stagnant under the dynamic leadership of Fr. Foster. He has now been Rector longer than any previous pastor of St. Paul's. The stability brought about by his long and resourceful leadership has done much for the congregation. It gives its membership the courage to "launch out into the deep" with Jesus.

ST. JOHN'S CHURCH, TULARE

"Tulare City" became a significant stop on the Southern Pacific Railroad through the San Joaquin Valley when the town of Visalia elected not to have the dirty, noisy locomotives pass through its neighborhood. The Rev. D. O. Kelley first held services in Tulare City Tuesday evening, February 17, 1880. Despite the fact that there was but one Church family in town, 70 people turned out for the service. For a time, further services were held in the home of Mr. and Mrs. Thomas Y. Sentell. This couple, and their three children, "a very intelligent and devoted Church family," were the sole basis of Church services in Tulare City for the remainder of the year. "St. John's Mission, Tulare County," was organized on February 19, 1880, but it should be noted that the entire county was embraced, including Visalia and Hanford. (Kings' County was not created until 1893.) When the Sentells moved to Hanford, early in 1881, services at Tulare City were discontinued for several years. When the congregation in Hanford chose the name,

"The Church of the Saviour," this became the name of the County Mission until D. O. Kelley resumed work in Tulare City, and a new St. John's Mission was organized on December 19, 1886. (Hist. of Dioc. of Calif., p. 402. District Journals list January 18, 1887.) The general County Mission no longer included Hanford, though the Vicar of Hanford served all.

In 1887, the Rev. C. S. Linsley was appointed Missionary for Tulare County, resident at Hanford. In his time the first permanent Episcopal church building was erected in Tulare City, on West King Street, on two lots donated by the S. P. R. R. In 1892, he was succeeded by J. H. Waterman. A parsonage was built beside the church, but at later times was rented out. By 1895, Linsley was back, with an added specific charge in Visalia. William Hart was in charge of both in 1898; C. M. Westlake, in 1899; Archdeacon Austin Scriven of British Columbia had charge of Tulare and Visalia in the winter of 1900. Henry Badger served here in 1901. The Rev. William Burns was Missionary in 1903. Hubert F. Carroll served from 1904 to 1908, although he build a rectory in Visalia and lived there, while Tulare's was rented out.

Carroll was followed by the Rev. Lee A. Wood, who stayed at Visalia until 1911, and had charge of Tulare, from Porterville until 1913, while another priest was assigned Visalia for two years. As Visalia had morning services, Tulare had evening services under Fr. Wood. This made for a long day, but "the horse knew the way" and could take a buggy home through the night without driver, while Fr. and Mrs. Wood slept. By morning, the horse had stopped in front of Visalia's vicarage.

The two missions were recombined under W. D. Williams, from September 1913 to September 1914. In 1915, Fr. Wood was again in charge, from Porterville, assisted by two clergymen, in covering all of Tulare County. His assistants were John Haymaker, September 1914 to March 1915, and Thomas Bell, 1915-16. R. A. Greisser held Tulare and Visalia from 1916, but Arthur L. Walters had Tulare and Selma from 1916, without Visalia, from 1920 to 1927. In 1923, Journals report that an epidemic among Tulare's children prevented the staging of a pageant written by Mrs. Walters. Near seven years was the longest charge to date, and began to give the congregation a sense of stability for a change. Evenso, during the Depression St. John's Church was closed; the few remaining communicants were served by F. D. Graves, Assistant General Missionary of the District, and E. J. Batty, Vicar of Visalia, for brief periods.

In 1943, after being closed for about 16 years, St. John's Mission was reopened, under the Rev. Norman E. Young, 1943-45. The Rev. Milton S. Kanaga served 1945-46, and the Ven. Joseph S. Doron, Archdeacon of the District, served from 1946 to 1952. At the same time he had charge of Lindsay and Delano. (At some time, a parish hall was built at the West King site, but the date remains undiscovered.)

The West King building served the congregation until 1957. During the time of Fr. John Wilcox (1952-58), the Warren family gave St. John's three acres of land at the corner of Prosperity and Laspina. In the same year, the present church was built and occupied. Mr. Herbert C. Evans, a skilled cabinet maker, then in his late 70s or early 80s, nevertheless did a major portion of the carpentry work of the new building, including pews, chancel furniture, and altar. Volunteer labor was given in considerable amount by the men of the Mission. In 1958, a Sunday School building was erected, and named in honor of Mr. Evans. A third building was added to the site by moving the old parish hall from King Street to the new location. It was given the name of Tex Rankin, another member of the mission, who established and ran a training school for World War II Army pilots. The cost for the moving and restoration of Rankin Hall was largely covered by the gift of Tex's widow, Shirley.

Fr. Ralph W. Jeffs was Vicar, 1958-63, when he left to study in England. Later he became a widely respected college chaplain. Thomas Masson was Vicar in 1963-64. He was followed by the Rev. John T. Raymond who served from 1964-72. In 1970, a fourth building was purchased from St. Aloysius' Roman Catholic Church for $500. It had been a Released Time school room; it now serves St. John's Kindergarten class. Douglas Judson was Vicar from 1972-75, and Shepherd Crim, 1976-77. Fr. Watson T. Bartholome served as Vicar from 1977 until his retirement in 1987.

The congregation made a valiant effort to become self-supporting and qualify for Parish status in time for their centennial celebration in 1986. Depressed economic conditions throughout the valley caught them and they were compelled to put aside their goal of self-support for the time being. The Rev. Robert Jordan was assigned as Vicar of St. John's in mid-1987.

That "miracles" sometimes do happen is evidenced by the fact that recently a legacy of approximately $400,000 was left to St. John's by a former parishioner. It will be interesting to see what develops at St. John's as a result of this bequest.

ST. PAUL'S, VISALIA

Visalia is located on the delta of the Kaweah River, which drains Sequoia National Park watershed. The dependable supply of water made it a choice and desirable location for settlement, both by Indians and whites. The first white settler was John Wood, who settled eight miles east of present Visalia in 1850, but was driven out a few months later. Nathaniel Vise and his brother came soon after, and in 1851, they gave a quarter-section of land for a townsite, named for themselves, with a mock-Spanish twist, Vise + alia. When the vast original County of Mariposa (encompassing most of the San Joaquin Valley) was subdivided, Visalia was selected as County Seat for Tulare County in 1853. At the time, it was the only Anglo settlement between Stockton and Los Angeles.

In 1855, the Kern River Gold Rush brought many from the north through the town, and some discovered that their farming skills could be put to good use more easily than they could extract gold at Havilah, for that required heavy machinery, not hand tools as at the Mother Lode. The remoteness of Visalia in those days was not conducive to industry; cattle were the chief product, until 1874, when farmers were given preferential rights by the "No Fence Law," making cattlemen responsible for keeping their livestock on the range. At first Visalia rejected the offers of railroad builders, who therefore bypassed the town and started Tulare; but a spur line was extended to Visalia in 1869. Visalia's prosperity began with that extension.

The first church services were held in the frontier town by W. C. Powell and Elias Birdsall on exploratory trips around 1876. When D. O. Kelley made his first journey through the valley in June, 1879, he spent the 15th and 22nd in Fresno, then went to Visalia and Tulare before going on to Bakersfield for the 29th. On Tuesday, June 24, he was in Visalia and conducted an evening service for about 20 people. By the Spring of 1880, when Bishop Kip visited all of Fr. Kelley's new missions, there was one Confirmation candidate in Visalia, and some 80 people attended on Wednesday, April 14. The "Tulare County Mission" (St. John's) was then organized, including Hanford and Lemoore, as well as Tulare and Visalia (Kings' County was created in 1893). Hanford soon became a separate mission, and the Tulare County Mission was reorganized in December, 1886. The Vicar of Hanford, however, was the priest-in-charge. St. Paul's traces its formal organization to February 9, 1887.

The Rev. C. S. Linsley, resident in Hanford, was in charge of Visalia from 1887 to 1892, and again from 1895 to 1896. Services were held sometimes in a former Presbyterian building, or the Odd Fellows' Hall, sometimes in private homes. The Visalians had an altar and lectern (from Trinity Parish, San Francisco), which were faithfully taken wherever the service might be held. John Waterman was Vicar of Tulare County from 1892 to 1895. During that time Mr. Elias Jacob donated a lot on North Church Street at North East Avenue, and the congregation collected funds to build a first church, completed in 1894. Waterman worked side-by-side with the carpenters until late the night before the arrival of Bishop Nichols, in order to finish the ceiling. The pews gleamed with fresh varnish the next day, but it was recorded that "many a new dress and suit received a lasting mark at that time. Certainly the adhesive quality of the Episcopal faith was clearly demonstrated!"

A quick succession of priests followed: William Hart, 1898; C. M. Westlake, 1899; Archdeacon Scriven of Canada, in the winter of 1900; H. L. Badger, 1901; William Burns, 1903. Despite his brief stay, Westlake had the church building moved to the corner of Encina and Center Streets. The Rev. Hubert C. Carroll remained from 1904 until 1908, and was followed by Lee A. Wood, Sr. They "did especially fine work" building up the congregation and facilities. A rectory and parish house were erected; the latter was opened by Bishop Nichols on January 16, 1910. The church size was nearly doubled in 1909. Seeing that Visalia's young people had no place of their own, Fr. Wood opened the parish hall to them for dances. At once the place was dubbed "The Episcopal Dance Hall" by scandalized Protestants. Fr. Wood later resigned Visalia to devote his efforts at Porterville in 1911.

Another period of rapid changes followed just as San Joaquin became a new jurisdiction: W. H. Webb, September 1911 to October 1912; W. D. Williams, September 1913 to September 1914; J. F. Hamaker, September 1914 to March 1915. More stable leadership was required, so Visalia was once again placed under the charge of Fr. Wood, assisted by two clergymen, covering all of Tulare County. It was evidently a depressing time. In 1916, the Rev. R. A. Griesser came. After two years, the mission listed 30 communicants in good standing out of 70 on the records. It was Fr. Griesser's opinion that, since the membership had hit rock bottom, it was a matter of necessity and pride for the members to strengthen the bonds that drew them together. Nevertheless, things continued to decline. In 1920, Bishop Sanford assumed the debt on the building. That brought about a response. The Vestry considered themselves morally bound to take care of the debt, as an example to their children and future generations. In twelve months the church was debt-free. Bishop Sanford had the satisfaction of consecrating the property. The Vestry then asked that he use the repaid funds to aid some other mission in need of assistance.

At the annual meeting of 1921, the Treasurer reported that St. Paul's Mission had been self-supporting for 1920. The Vicar then suggested that a request be sent to the Bishop asking that St. Paul's be accorded Parish status. On December 6, 1921, the Bishop responded favorably to their request. Griesser resigned in 1923. The Vestry then called the Rev. Dr. Philip Grouchy (sic) Snow of Troy, N. Y., to be the next Rector. Although he made many house calls (119 in three months), finances became a matter of grave concern once again. In debate, reducing the Rector's salary was suggested as a means to economize. Dr. Snow objected, and requested that other means should be investigated. The Vestry agreed to allow him to seek other methods to secure funds "as long as the dignity of the Church was not involved in the hunt." What means he found is not reported. By the end of 1928 he had retired to Long Beach. St. Paul's was returned to Mission status.

January 1, 1929, saw Edward Joseph Batty in the position of Vicar of both Visalia and Tulare. He retired in October 1931. For 1932, a Lay Reader, Mr. Vernon Brown, was the only listed person from Visalia in the Convocation Journal. In 1933, Duncan G. Porteous was listed as the Lay Reader; Mr. Brown had moved to Taft. On January 25, 1934, Porteous was ordained Deacon, to serve Visalia. Just a year later he was ordered Priest in Hanford. He served as Vicar of Visalia until February 1945, when he resigned to become Rector of St. Stephen's, Colusa.

Typically, the women of St. Paul's have always had a vital role in the maintenance of the church. Their position on the Vestry was debated and voted down with one dissent; ten minutes later, the Vestry thought better and reversed itself, electing two of the women to join the Vestry. An example of the many activities of the Church Service League (predecessor of the Women's Auxiliary and Episcopal Church Women) may be seen in 1934, in the depths of the Great Depression. They brought three new members into the Church, sent a Lenten box to Alaska and an Advent box to a retired priest, made ten shirts for the Red Cross, made eleven choir caps, purchased a burse and veil for the chalice, held four parish dinners, and decorated and furnished the kitchen in the parish hall.

In April 1945, the Rev. Victor Manuel Rivera accepted the position as Rector of St. Paul's. A native of Puerto Rico, the son of an Episcopal priest, trained at Church Divinity School of the Pacific, Berkeley, California, he spoke English heavily accented with his mother tongue, Spanish. An unlikely choice, one might imagine, nevertheless, he remained as faithful pastor and church-builder for one of the longest tenures in the history of this diocese. His energy is legendary and, equally as important, infectious. He succeeded in conveying his hopes and dreams for St. Paul's to its Vestry. Within two years he had Vestry approval to inquire about plans for a new church building. In March 1947, a new rectory was purchased on West Center Street, and in October, two lots at Center and Hall were purchased. Even before plans for the new building were completed, Miss Mettie Webb donated old stained glass windows from St. James' Church, Philadelphia. The Encina Street property was sold, and in 1948, trucks moved the parish hall to the new site. Brick by brick, the new building was raised; much of the labor being done by the Rector and parishioners. On September 11, 1949, Bishop Walters dedicated it.

Continued growth of St. Paul's and of Visalia made necessary the building of a new wing to the parish hall. This was done in 1953. A patio and arcade were added, joining these. The Baby-boom brought the parish hall facilities to bursting, and the parish to another building campaign. Additional property was purchased in 1961, and in 1962, the new Sunday School building was finished and dedicated to God and in memory of Henry White a devoted parishioner.

At this time, the clergy staff was increased when the Rev. John Wilcox became Associate Rector, in charge of Christian Education and college work at the College of the Sequoias. Not only was the physical plant increased, but the numerous organizations involved parishioners and non-parishioners in a great variety of programs for outreach and service. Many of the non-parishioners thus involved soon found themselves active churchmen.

Victor Rivera was also long-time Secretary-Registrar of the Convocation of San Joaquin, involved in all manner of District offices, and it was little surprise when he was elected Third Bishop of San Joaquin in 1968. He left St. Paul's in mid-summer to prepare for his consecration in September. Happily, his aged father was able to be present for this occasion.

Subsequently, St. Paul's Vestry called the Rev. Stanley Sinclair as the next Rector. He had served a number of posts in the Diocese prior to his call. He remained at Visalia until 1973 when he was called as Rector of the church in San Gabriel. Later he returned to his native Canada. After Fr. Sinclair, the Rev. Donald Cole was called from the Diocese of Nevada and assumed his duties as Rector in August, 1973. Additional property adjacent to the church has been gradually acquired for much needed parking space, and the fine facility designated as Rivera Hall. St. Paul's has continued to grow under Fr. Cole's able leadership, and has established a parochial mission of St. Barnabas.

ST. MATTHIAS' PARISH, OAKDALE

The founding of the Episcopal Church in Oakdale dates back to early 1884, making it one of the oldest churches in the city. It was not until 1887 that St. Matthias' was officially recognized by the diocese. The beginnings of the work there were laid in 1883 under the direction of Bishop Kip of the Diocese of California.

No sooner had the Mission begun than a group of women members organized "Saint Matthias' Guild" in a meeting held in the Union Church, Oakdale, March 31, 1885. The Minutes of that first meeting list the names of the ladies:

Mrs. A. Llewelyn	Mrs. Fannie R. A. Hunt	Mrs. Mary A. Lovell
Mrs. M. E. Stearns	Mrs. Anne Leuhrs	Mrs. Margaret Gilmer
Mrs. Green	Miss Hattie Woods	Mrs. Wyckoff

In 1900 and 1901 services were held in the rear of the old Lovell Building (east of the railroad) where a chapel was fitted up to meet the early needs of the church. "Through the thoughtfulness of Mr. Harry Ogle, the proprietor, the saloon in back of the altar observed quiet hours during the time of services." At other times meetings were held in the Union Church when the Rev. D. O. Parker of Saint James, Sonora, walked from Sonora to carry on the parish work and to conduct the services. The Rev. Jerome Trivett and the Rev. C. S. Linsley also served the church during this period.

The need for a more permanent place of worship was soon obvious, and a building was planned, built, and paid for within one year — the latter half of 1904 and the early part of 1905. The Rev. William Edgar Couper was in charge. The movement for the new church was begun by Deaconness Dorsey, cousin of Edward M. Dorsey of Oakdale, Mrs. C. G. Hoisholt, and Mrs. Dora Rodden. Deaconness Dorsey raised fund to purchase the lot, and through the combined efforts of the above ladies besides others whose names have been lost the money was obtained to enable the building of the new facility. So notable was the accomplishment of a church being built and paid for in one year that word reached the East where the Babies' Branch of the Women's Auxiliary of the Parish in Bishop Nichols' home town in Connecticut sent the lovely granite and oak font that stands in the church today.

The doors of the new church were opened to its first congregation on Sunday, January 29, 1905. It was consecrated June 3, 1907, by Bishop William Ford Nichols with the assistance of Deaconness Dorsey. The Venerable Archdeacon John Abbot Emery preached the Sermon from the text: "What hath God wrought?" (Numbers 23:23).

In January, 1911, the Missionary District of San Joaquin was formed. The Bishop was Louis Childs Sanford, with a jurisdiction that had fewer than two thousand members.

The Rev. G. G. Hoisholt, a native of Oakdale, was ordained to the Diaconate in 1917, and the Rev. E. I. MacNalty, also of Oakdale, entered the ministry from St. Matthias'.

The year 1914 marked the beginning of World War I and there followed several years of difficult times for the churches. A temporary period of recovery following the end of the war was soon wiped out by the stock market "crash" of 1931, and the years of the Depression were a time of retrenchment. Giving by the church members declined and grants from the National Council were slashed. The financial position of the Missionary District was grave, and it became necessary to close some churches. St. Matthias' was one of them.

In 1937, a young Public Works Administration worker came to Oakdale. He set about the challenge of reopening the church and contacted members to that end. A few responded and the church was reopened for worship. Mr. Price, the P.W.A. worker, was given permission by Bishop Sanford to hold services and to serve as lay-reader. Saint Matthias' Women's Guild was again organized and the congregation began to grow.

On May 27, 1938, a meeting was held to reorganize the church. James E. Price, seminarian in charge, assisted in the organization of a Vestry. In October, 1938, a budget of $12.00 per month was suggested for 1939. This was augmented by a rental of $42.00 per year from the Lutherans who also used the building. Mr. Price was followed by another seminarian, Mr. Richard Hartley, who served from 1942-1944.

At the March 5, 1944, Vestry Meeting, attended by the new Bishop Sumner Walters, he suggested that Oakdale was ready for a full-time priest. It was agreed that housing would be provided with a stipend of $1,500 per year. Half to be paid by St. Matthias' and half by the District. In June, 1944, a seminarian, Gerwyn Morgan, from C. D. S. P. was appointed in charge, and became full-time Vicar upon his ordination in December.

Fr. Morgan left in 1947 and Tom Turnbell, another seminarian, was appointed in charge and served for three years. During his tenure the construction of Tulloch Hall was begun. The Tulloch brothers, Dave and Jack, provided the leadership for the building of the hall, much of the work being done by volunteer labor from the members.

In January, 1951, the Rev. Arthur Beckwith and his family arrived from Burns, Oregon. It was hoped that an older more experienced priest might remain longer and bring some stability to the congregation. St. Matthias' became a parish in 1959 under his leadership and Fr. Beckwith was immediately elected Rector. During his tenure there was a need to expand the Church School facilities and classrooms were built in a record 38 days, most of the labor being volunteer. Dedication of the new facilities was held Sunday, November 20, 1955, with Bishop Walters officiating.

Upon completion of this project the Vestry, at the Annual Parish meeting in January 1956, appointed a New Church Building Committee, chaired by V. A. Rodden, son of one of the original founders, Mrs. Dora (Woods) Rodden. In August it was decided that a new church building was necessary. This was unanimously approved by the congregation and a five-year pledge plan was begun. In four months over 60% of the projected costs were pledged. The new building was dedicated a year later in October, 1957. The original cost of $54,000 was 25% paid for at the time.

The Rev. Mr. Beckwith retired and the Rev. Richard Henry who had been ordained Deacon and served with Fr. Beckwith until he was ordered Priest in December, 1961, became the new Rector. During his tenure record-breaking confirmation classes were held and the congregation grew. A new rectory was purchased on Oak Street. This was replaced by another on Poplar after Fr. Henry left in 1965 to become the Vicar of the new Mission of St. Mary's in Fresno.

The late Rev. Thomas Steensland succeeded Fr. Henry in 1965. He left in 1970 and was succeeded by the Rev. William Eastman who served until 1979 when he became Vicar of St. Paul's parochial Mission in Ceres. The Rev. Edwin Shakelford served for one year and left in 1981. Since 1981 the parish has been served by the Rev. Leon MacDougall.

St. Matthias' stands today in the downtown area not only as a monument to God and Jesus Christ, but to those pioneers who weathered the hard time . . . who kept the saving truth of God alive in this township.

ST. LUKE'S, SELMA

The history of St. Luke's, Selma, is one of many ups and downs, reflecting the changing fortunes of a small town in the Central Valley. In its time the mission has grown, dwindled, lost its building, worshipped in buildings of other denominations, often without a full-time priest, and in recent years begun to slowly grow again. The mission first grew out of services begun in the "Prairie School District" (Clifton) by D. O. Kelley of Fresno, in 1882, and continued regularily for some years. At one time, steps were taken to build a church in Clifton. Then the John R. Barid family, chiefly interested in the plan, moved into the town of Selma, and this, with other changes, made it seem best to transfer the work to the new locus.

Mr. George B. Otis leased a lot to the congregation and a rough board chapel was built on High Street, where Fr. Kelley held services. W. C. Mills and Octavius Parker served as resident clergy for short periods. Louis C. Sanford came as Deacon-in-charge in 1892, and a new location was secured on Sylvia Street, between Third and Fourth; the old building was moved there, and added to, much improved. This was consecrated on St. Matthias' Day, February 24, 1893. Sanford, later to be Bishop, stayed in Selma until 1897. The Mission was linked with St. Michael's, Fowler, at this time. In 1896, Mrs. Montroyd Sharpe gave six lots to the Mission, and a small rectory was built. William Higgs was in charge from 1899 to 1902; C. L. Thackery, 1903 to 1907. During this period the rectory burned down and a new, larger house was immediately erected. The Cathedral Staff in San Francisco had charge of Selma in 1907 to 1909. H. E. Dibblee was in charge from 1910 until 1912; W. H. Evans, 1913 to 1914; and W. B. Belliss, in 1914. These short-term tenures did nothing to give the congregation a sense of permanence.

In January 1939, the building was declared unsafe and the property was sold. The church was dismantled, and its furnishings were given to other churches in the District. Only the stained glass windows were kept, and they are still in storage. The processional cross has been recovered. During the Depression the congregation dwindled and no plans were made to relocate. The Rev. A. L. Walters was serving Selma at the time, and also had charge of missions in Reedley, Kerman, and Mendota. In April, 1940, St. Luke's Community House was opened by Miss Olive Meacham, a worker funded by the United Thank Offering. At first her work was at 2051 High Street; a year later it was moved to 2518 Logan Street, but soon thereafter it was also closed.

There followed a gap of twenty years, after which time St. Luke's Mission was reactivated on February 15, 1959, by the Rev. Max Drake, Rector of the Church of Good Shephered, Reedley. The initial meeting was held in the home of Mrs. G. L. Thompson, at 2047 Stillman Street. On the following Sunday, Fr. Drake celebrated the Holy Communion in her home. In the afternoon of the same Sunday, Bishop Walters met with the congregation. He authorized St. Luke's congregation to organize as a parochial mission of Reedley, and appointed Fr. Drake as Priest-in-charge. At the 50th Annual Convocation of the Missionary District of San Joaquin, held in Sonora on January 31, 1960, St. Luke's, Selma, was formally readmitted as an organized Mission.

From March 1959 through January 1977, St. Paul's Lutheran Church, Selma, was used for Episcopal services and other meetings on a rental basis. Fr. Drake and Canon Harold B. Thelin were the two long-term priests. In 1977, St. Luke's shared St. Andrew's Presbyterian Church in Selma. Canon Thelin and lay members organized and staffed a very successful Church School during the time at St. Andrew's. Unfortunately, this had to be disbanded because of lack of space when St. Luke's moved to another location.

In 1980, the Rev. Robert R. Richard came on a part-time basis, while working in the Diocesan office. The Selma Women's Club was used for services at first, then the congregation used a vacant house owned by a member of St. Luke's. Fr. Roger Jones, followed, working part-time at the Diocesan office and having charge of Selma. In 1985, a new location became available, in the "Pioneer Village" just off Highway 99. It is almost as old as the original work of St. Luke's Mission. The church building that has been preserved there is the old St. Ansgar's Swedish Lutheran Church, which was moved to the site from Traver. It was first built in 1884 as a school house, and acquired for St. Ansgar's in 1896. It was then moved to the corner of Manning Avenue and Bethel, northeast of Selma. In October, 1978, it was given to the Selma Historical Society and moved to its present location. In September 1985, following Fr. Jones' departure, Bishop Rivera appointed Fr. Bruce Kirkwood of St. James' Cathedral staff as Priest-in-charge. The congregation now numbers 31 communicants and is growing once again. A renewed commitment to responsible stewardship under the able leadership of Fr. Kirkwood is strengthening the work in Selma.

TRINITY EPISCOPAL CHURCH, MADERA

As of this writing, November 6, 1987, Madera has not submitted a parish history. Lacking that, the following is extracted from the Rev. D. O. Kelley's Reminiscences and from the notice in the Appendix to his History of the Diocese of California.

"The new County of Madera had been recently formed from that part of Fresno County lying north of the San Joaquin River, with the ambitious young "City" of Madera as its County Seat. (Ed.: "Madera" is Spanish for "wood"; the city was located at the end of a long loggers' flume from the Sierras.)

Though I had been through and about there somewhat it was not until the early part of 1890 that the way seemed clear for attempting any regular ministrations. It was on a weekday evening, March 27, that the first public service was held, in a hall, with an attendance of thirty-three persons, including several Church people or families — the Newmans, the Woolleys, the Goodens, and perhaps the Mordecais from several miles away in the country. I was now convinced that these made a nucleus for a beginning, and that there was a considerable promise of growth for the new town and County, and so determined to inaugurate a new mission district. And so from that time on regular services were held. From the start we were specially fortunate in having quite good and complete music, which soon resulted in a small vested choir.

"The first Sunday service was on the evening of September 14, with a congregation of 75! — and a baptism of a child. The latter part of November a Sunday School was started. On Sunday morning, January 11, 1891, the first public celebration of the Holy Communion was held, with nine persons receiving, and on the following Wednesday evening Bishop Nichols preached and confirmed a class of eight, including Robert B. Gooden, who afterwards entered the Holy Ministry. (Ed.: He was later consecrated Suffragan Bishop of Los Angeles, and lived to be 102. His funeral services were held at St. Mark's Church, Glendale, and he was interred in the family burial plot in Santa Barbara. His son, Heber, was also consecrated Bishop of Panama.) This was Bishop William Ford Nichols' (then Assistant Bishop) first Confirmation in my "jurisdiction", the next being in St. James' Church, Fresno, on Sunday morning, January 25th . . . The Church was packed with a congregation of 240, sixty of whom received the Holy Communion. That was the first time the new recess chancel was used. 'Trinity Mission, Madera,' was duly organized in 1890."
(From the History of the Diocese of California, p. 397)

"Services were begun here in 1890 by D. O. Kelley, and the mission was organized November 22, with James Gooden as Warden, J. E. Newman as Treasurer and Wm. Woolley, Clerk, all communicants. In '92 Octavius Parker was sent as missionary. Church built '93. W. M. Bours missionary in '95, and Dr. Geo. H. Jenks, Oct. 1, '98. Church consecrated Oct. 26, 1902. Nelson Saunders missionary, '04-'06. J. Nicholas, '07."

THE CHURCH OF SAINT JOHN THE BAPTIST, LODI

Lodi is the northern-most parish in the Diocese of San Joaquin. It is fertile agricultural land, and now rapidly growing as a virtual suburb of Stockton. Services were held here prior to 1896 by the Rector of St. John's, Stockton, or his assistants or lay readers. A first mission was named

"St. Matthew's" A hall was rented, and a cabinet organ and other simple furniture were procured; but after a time, services were discontinued and the furnishings were stored or loaned.

Archdeacon John A. Emery of California visited Lodi in 1899. He assigned the Rev. D. O. Kelley of the Cathedral staff in San Francisco to take charge. At this time, Stockton and Lodi were transferred to the Convocation of San Joaquin.

Fr. Kelley held his first service in Lodi on November 12, 1900, and arranged for a monthly visit thereafter. Services took place in the Odd Fellows' Hall, on the corner of Sacramento and Pine Streets. There were half a dozen Church families, with over a dozen communicants "of more than ordinary intelligence and loyalty to the Church." Mr. George H. Cowie of Stockton became Fr. Kelley's Lay Reader assistant. A Sunday School and guild were organized, and continued "without much effort or aggressive work" until 1906, when St. John's Mission was organized on September 15.

In 1909, Mr. Hobart J. Couper presented the mission with property for a church site, and funds were raised for a building. The town itself was growing rapidly, and help was given by Stockton friends of the Lodi mission, and a loan was granted from the Eastman Fund. Bishop Nichols laid the cornerstone on May 22, 1910. The building was of redwood. The first service in it was conducted by Fr. Kelley on September 25, 1910. In December of the same year his health collapsed, and Fr. Kelley was relieved of this charge. Mr. W. F. Higby served efficiently as Lay Reader for a year or two, and Mr. George Hoisholt was Lay Reader-in-charge for a year or more. The Rev. Wm. H. Hawken of the newly created Missionary District of San Joaquin then had oversight.

The Rev. W. L. Greenwood was the first resident Vicar, and served from 1913 to 1916. Bishop Sanford was able to consecrate the redwood church on St. John the Baptists' Day, June 24, 1914, with all debts cleared, demonstrating the vitality and commitment of the first congregation.

The Rev. Charles Verleger was Vicar from 1916 to 1918, and G. B. D. Stewart followed, from 1918 to 1922. During his time, a parish hall was built, in 1919. David Todd Gilmore was Vicar from 1922 until 1929, and the Rev. E. A. Shapland served from 1929 to 1945. In 1945, St. John's was received by the Annual Convocation of San Joaquin as a Parish. Norman Young served as Rector from 1945 to 1948, and John T. Raymond was Rector for 16 years, from 1948 to 1964. During his time, Sunday School rooms were built and the patio laid, in 1951. In 1955, a rectory was built. Following the Rev. Mr. Raymond's retirement, the Rev. Stuart Anderson was Rector, from 1964 to 1970. The Rev. Raymond C. Knapp became Rector in 1970 and served until his retirement in September, 1987.

During the years of growth, a parish hall with kitchen was added. A two-story office and classroom building was built, and a portable building was brought in to accommodate a growing Church School. A small adjacent house became "The Hut," a thrift shop that serves the community.

Stained glass windows were given as memorials over the years, and new pews and carpeting have been put into the church. The original church building is now too small; the congregation must be served by having three services on Sunday mornings. There are plans at present to expand to meet the needs in the near future. In 1986, during a 75th Anniversary celebration, the cornerstone was removed and opened; new materials were placed within it before it was relaid. Two grand-daughters of a man who laid the first cornerstone in 1910 are current members of the congregation and were able to take part in the ceremony.

In 1982-83, the Vestry allocated funds for a curate to assist the Rector. Fr. Stephen Wendfeldt and Fr. Gregory Waddington, both newly ordained, served in succession before moving on to other charges. The Rev. Bruce R. Bramlett, a graduate student at Graduate Theological Union in Berkeley, came as part-time assistant in March, 1986. Since Fr. Knapp's retirement he is continuing as Interim Priest-in-charge, while the Vestry seeks a new Rector.

The congregation has grown spiritually as well as physically, and St. John's, Lodi, is one of the stabler parishes in this diocese. An Outreach Program, youth choir, senior choir, lay reader-chalice bearers, prayer groups, active Church School classes, and the many other activities that evidence the vitality of a congregation are to be found at St. John's. There is room for everyone and St. John's has a reputation for being a "hugging Church" as its members welcome all who attend.

THE CHURCH OF THE GOOD SHEPHERD PARISH, REEDLEY

Good Shepherd Mission was organized on Saturday, May 8, 1908, by the Rev. D. O. Kelley, who had come down to Reedley from San Francisco. The initiative, however, was taken by Judge Otis D. Lyon and his family, who had moved to the town. Their earnest desire for services, and paying all his bills for travel, prompted Archdeacon Emery to make investigation, and on May 26, 1907, he conducted a service in the Lodge Hall, and directed the organization of a Women's Guild. He delegated Fr. Kelley from the San Francisco Cathedral staff to take special charge in the summer of 1907. Monthly visits were at once begun, the community was thoroughly canvassed, and a Sunday School was organized. There were four communicants. The Women's Guild met again on July 3, and allocated $25 to purchase a lot for a church — then the going rate for property in Reedley. At the time, the town was a new one of only a few hundred people, "made up largely of Dunkards, Baptists, and Roman Catholics, each with its own house of worship."

In a few months, the Sunday School, guild, and congregation grew in numbers and in favor with the community, and the Mission was organized on the eve of Good Shepherd Sunday, Easter IV. D. O. Kelley was particularily attached to this Mission, the last in which he had a part in founding. The timing of its organization, and its name, may well relate to a Sunday School Mission he had organized and supervised in Cincinatti, just after the Civil War, while he studied law, and before he came to California in 1867, when he was but 23 years of age. This was also named "Good Shepherd".

A sturdy Guild Hall was built in 1909 at Tenth and J Streets, then an excellent site to serve for a church. It cost $1,101.45, with only $400 left unpaid upon its completion. By now there were 12 communicants. W. H. Webb was appointed to the Mission in August, 1910, for about a year. On September 3, 1911, Walter H. Evans was sent by Bishop Sanford as Lay Reader-in-charge, he being a candidate for Holy Orders. He remained about two years. On Ascension Day, 1912, he helped organize a Women's Guild in Dinuba, from which grew a mission. He was ordained Deacon in the Guild Hall on St. Peter's Day, June 29, 1912. He was priested on Bishop Sanford's second anniversary of his consecration, January 29, 1912. During his second year, a parsonage was built, costing some $2,500, with a debt remainder of $1,500.

In September, 1913, Richard Whitehouse came as Missionary Priest-in-charge. He stayed until September 1919. During his tenure a chancel was added, and another Guild Hall with kitchen was built. Property owned had expanded from an original four lots to six. The church was largely furnished with items from the closing of St. Michael's Church, Fowler (c. 1915), and by gifts from friends of the Vicar. Frederick D. Graves (who carved the St. James' Cathedral altar) served from October 1919 to April 1923. He practiced his art of carving while at Reedley, making the credence table, lectern, and litany desk. The altar was a gift of the District's Women's Auxiliary, which had the provision of altars for new mission as a special project. The pulpit came from the closed mission in Dinuba. In January, 1922, Fr. Graves organized a Boy Scout troop and in July they camped in the Grant Grove. R. C. Jenkins served from October 1923 to May 1926. By 1928, however, Reedley shared its Vicar with Selma.

The Rev. Arthur L. Walters served for 21 years as Vicar of Reedley, from December 1926 to June 1947. During that period, he had charge not only of Selma, but also of Kerman, and Mendota. He was also Rural Dean of the Central Deanery. In 1933, a 25th Anniversary service was held with Bishop Sanford attending. Arthur Ernest Bello served from July 1948 to August 1949; Walter Malcolm Clarke, Jr. served from June 1950 until September 1956.

Camp San Joaquin, started in 1950 by Fr. Victor M. Rivera, then Rector of Visalia, has always had the active involvement of membership of Good Shepherd. Mr. Farris Lawand, Sr., and his brother Sam, graded the roads into the camp and levelled areas for tent cabins and other buildings. The "Schellbach Cabin" was built by volunteers from Reedley and named for a family active in the parish. Members have taken important positions at the camp each summer, from Camp Director, Fr. Max Drake; Camp Nurse, Mrs. Charles Huey; and Mrs. Ardzrooni, Head Cook. Fr. Bill Fay has served as Chairman of the Camp San Joaquin Committee for more years than anyone counts. Mr. David Rouff, former Senior Warden in Reedley, is now Camp Director on a year-round basis, and is heading up a campaign to build a Boosters' Organization.

Fr. Max L. Drake, baptized at Good Shepherd in 1920, was its priest from October 1956 to 1961; during his time, St. Luke's Mission, Selma, was reactivated, first as a Parochial Mission of Reedley. Five adjacent lots were purchased from Eitzon Estate in February 1957, at a cost of $10,750. In January 1958, Good Shepherd became a parish, and Fr. Drake, the first Rector. In May, the Vestry determined that a new location, nearer the center of the community, would better serve the needs. Mrs. Fannie McClanahan bought the old church and rectory site, and over 9 acres were purchased on Frankwood Avenue at a cost of $20,000. A Building Fund was opened for pledges to be paid over a 30-month period, to pay for the land and begin funding construction at the new site.

Fr. Harold Leroy ("Lee") Wilson served from June 1962 to October 1966. On September 1, 1965, a new building was completed at a cost of $73,148. Its architect was Noboru Nakamura, a graduate of Reedley High and Reedley College. It was planned for use as a multi-purpose Parish Hall until a new church could be built. A single laminated beam, 80 feet long, weighing nearly three tons, runs the length of the roof's peak. The furnishings of the old church were brought to the new one. Fr. Lee Wilson redesigned the original altar to fit the large space. The rectory was built at about the same time by another builder. In partial payment about four acres facing the Sierra-Kings Hospital were traded with them for residential development. Fr. Lee Wilson was followed by Harold M. Wilson, Rector from September 1967 to January 1971. Fr. Dwight T. Hansen served as *locum tenens* from February to July 1971.

Fr. William Merrill Fay came as Rector of Good Shepherd in August 1971. In 1975, Good Shepherd was the first church in the area to sponsor refugees from Southeast Asia for resettlement. Two Vietnamese men were housed by the parish, and assisted with English instruction and other needed help. Within six months, both were self-supporting. On Easter Day, 1984, one was confirmed by Bishop Rivera. On December 2, 1979, a Mortgage Burning was held at the Annual Parish meeting. The Rev. Walter Clarke, a former Vicar, was Guest Preacher. The three former Rectors were also present. On Easter Day, 1982, a series of stained glass windows was dedicated. On April 10, 1983, Bishop Robert Mize dedicated the new Butler Hall, and education building. This was made possible by the bequests of Marion and Patricia Butler, who died in 1978 and 1979, respectively. They left their entire estates to Good Shepherd, totaling some $80,000. The building cost was about $35,000, and the remainder has been invested as endowment for other major church purposes and improvements. In May, 1984, a 75th Anniversary celebration was held, and a fine commemorative book was written and published for the occasion. In February, 1985, Fr. Fay was called to St. Clement's, Woodlake, and in August, Fr. John Wilcox became Rector of Good Shepherd.

ST. JOHN'S CHURCH, PORTERVILLE

The Dean of the San Joaquin Convocation reported to the 1899 Convention of the Diocese of California that Church work had begun in Porterville. William Hart, Missionary at Visalia conducted this before leaving Visalia. Thereafter work in Porterville lapsed. When a Women's Guild begin meeting in 1908, this led to regular services of the Church being reinstituted and held in an upper room over a hardware store, from 1909 onwards. For a time Lay Reader Richard M. Trelease of Visalia, conducted services. He was later ordained. By the time of the first Convocation of the Missionary District of San Joaquin on May 9, 1911, the delegates of St. John's, Porterville, were seated, though no mention is made of "voice" or "vote", as they were still "passing through the regular procedure of organization." Official organization of St. John's took place on June 4, 1911, with Bishop Sanford's consent. At the second Convocation in Hanford, May 22, 1912, St. John's was formally admitted, but no delegate was present, only the Vicar.

The Rev. Lee Axtell Wood of Visalia conducted regular services in Porterville (as well as Tulare). In 1911, he was appointed the official Priest-in-charge, and soon moved his residence to town. Valuable lots were purchased on the corner of D and Thurman. A guild hall was opened, and dedicated by Bishop Sanford in May, 1913. This was later modified and is the present church. Under Mr. Wood's leadership the congregation grew. He remained until year's end 1929, when he became the first Student Pastor at Fresno State College and Vicar of the Church of the Holy Spirit, Fresno. He was succeeded by Fr. John Keble Burleson.

The early promise shown by the congregation withered during the Depression. In order to try to save a salary, Bishop Sanford appointed the Rev. Charles H. Powell, Ph.D., Vicar of both Porterville and Bishop! Needless to say, Dr. Powell found the assignment impossible and took the position in Bishop, where Inyo County employed him as Juvenile Probation Officer. Porterville was reassigned, and struggled along through the years of World War II.

After the war, the Rev. Charles M. Brandon came to Porterville as Vicar after 11 years as an army chaplain. It brought a new lease on life for St. John's. Under his leadership St. John's grew again and became self-supporting. Parish status was granted by the Convocation in 1948. Fr. Brandon retired as Rector in 1959. He continued to live in Porterville until his death.

The Rev. John Atkinson served as Rector from 1960 to 1963. Fr. M. Fletcher Davis was Rector from 1964 to 1968. Fr. Richard Warren was Rector from 1969 until his retirement in 1977. Fr. James C. Thompson succeeded as Rector in the summer of the same year. A program of repair and painting on the aging church building has been completed, and under Fr. Thompson's leadership the church is thriving.

The Bishop appointed Fr. Thompson as Dean of Sequoia Deanery in late 1987, following the resignation of Fr. Don Cole of St. Paul's, Visalia, from the position as Dean.

ST. JAMES' CHURCH, LINDSAY

A retired British Army officer, Captain Hutchinson, settled in Lindsay to raise oranges. He had assisted in forming the Pacific Land Company, which laid out the town of Lindsay. Capt. Hutchinson and his family were faithful Church of England members, and encouraged the faith of others. In 1896, Hutchinson appealed to Archdeacon John A. Emery of San Francisco for the services of the Episcopal Church. Emery, as Superintendent of Missionary Work for the Diocese of California, sent the Rev. C. S. Linsley, Rector of Hanford, to Lindsay to conduct services occasionally, but no record of these exists. C. M. Westlake officiated in Lindsay in 1899. Eventually the Hutchinson family moved to San Francisco to seek better schooling for their children.

Mr. Basil Prior, a Lindsay resident and friend of the Hutchinsons, continued the effort to secure an Episcopal Church. On April 23, 1899, Bishop William F. Nichols came to Lindsay, and evidently urged the formal organization of a mission. This date was thought "close to the Feast of St. James (the Less)" (May 1), and that dedication was chosen. The Diocese of California records the official organization on January 6, 1900. D. O. Kelley on the staff of the Cathedral in San Francisco had charge of Lindsay in 1901. Thereafter, care was irregular. H. C. Carroll had charge in 1906-07. L. A. Wood took up the work again on Sunday, September 24, 1911, when services were held in the old Waddell Building, now occupied by the Ben Franklin Store. It is recorded that $3.00 was collected in the offering, and the diary of Mr. Prior notes another Sunday service on December 10, with five attending.

The previous Wednesday evening, December 6, however, was the beginning of a subscription drive for the building of a church and the acquisition of land. St. James' Mission was formally reorganized on February 11, 1912. The Rev. Lee A. Wood, Sr., was Vicar of Visalia at the time, but after St. John's Mission, Porterville, became the first to be admitted into union with the Convocation of the new Missionary District of San Joaquin.

On April 10, 1912, Basil Prior spoke with Captain Hutchinson who sent a check for $750 to pay for the property. On the 27th, Prior recorded Articles of Incorporation with Bishop Sanford. At the same time, certificates of Title to three lots were sent to Bishop Sanford. On October 17, 1912, Fr. Wood showed plans for a church building to Mr. Prior. On March 7, 1913, the lumber for the building was delivered, and by Easter Day, March 23, the first service was held in the new building, with 73 present. It was a "Guild Hall", a multi-purpose room. Here on April 26, a reception was held for Bishop Sanford and his wife. On the following day, Rogation Sunday, April 27, the Dedication Service, with Communion and Confirmation, was conducted by the Bishop.

Unfortunately, within three months of the dedication, the new Episcopal Guild Hall burned to the ground, on Wednesday, July 9. Only the piano and a few benches were saved. Mr. Prior was absent at the time. For the remainder of 1913 and 1914 the diary says little. On April 18, 1914, he notes that he sent a check to the Adventists for the hire of their building for eight Sundays.

The first building was insured for $800, and the contents for $500, but damage was $2,000. By 1915, a second church was built and still stands. Its first pews were benches without backs; after services, they were pulled up around tables, and the nave was transformed into a parish hall. Two of the old benches are in the patio today.

No Service Register survives from before the days of the Rev. Mr. Young.

The separate Parish Hall was begun when the Rev. Milton S. Kanaga was Vicar after World War II. Archdeacon Joseph S. Doron covered Lindsay and Delano from Tulare, from November 1952. During his time, construction of the Hall was completed, and a new Wurlitzer organ was bought to accompany services. The same organ was badly damaged in 1977, when St. James' Church was vandalized.

Mrs. Charles Mills left her home adjacent to the Church as a vicarage. The congregation was growing, and needed a Sunday School building. In 1958, additional land was purchased from the School Board. Work began at once on the new facilities. In the next year, an addition was built onto the vicarage. Improvements and furnishings were made in the church; these, too, suffered at the hands of vandals, but were lovingly restored. Help in this was provided by many in the community, not just Church members.

Fr. Robert Rible served the mission in 1969. He was succeeded by Fr. Robert Ransom who served a short time and was followed by the Rev. Lyle A. McBee who served until 1971. The Rev. H. Lee Wilson served from 1972 until 1979. The Rev. Raymond Reid came in 1981 and served until 1983. The Rev. Stephen Wendfeldt was then appointed Vicar and served until 1984. His successor, the Rev. Gregory Waddington was appointed to St. James' as of September 1, 1984.

During Fr. Wendfeldt's brief tenure a rose window was cut into the wall above the altar, and a fine collection of vestments and hangings were made locally. Fr. Waddington, in addition to his responsibilities as Vicar has served the diocese in a variety of capacities. Among other things he continues to work with the Youth Commission, has served as Camp Director at Camp San Joaquin and has done a splendid job of handling the logistics and arrangements for the annual Diocesan Convention for the past several years.

ST. PHILIP'S CHURCH, COALINGA

The Southern Pacific Railroad established two coaling stations, labelled "A" and "B". Coaling-A became the nucleus of a town. Oil and agriculture have been the economic foundation, and a college has added diversity and breadth. Although located in Fresno County, St. Philip's has chosen to be a part of Sequoia Deanery for reasons of distance.

In 1909, a small group of Coalinga's pioneer women formed a St. Cecilia's Guild as a vehicle to further their religious life. Sunday School classes began in February, 1909. Sometime later the ladies assembled a cookbook and these were sold in town to raise money to purchase 100 Prayer Books. By 1911, services were being held once a month in the Presbyterians' hall, by a priest from St. James', Fresno. Beginning April 10, 1911, services were also held in the club rooms of British Consolidated, Ltd., later to be the Shell Oil Company Camp, nine miles from Coalinga. The Rev. R. W. Rhames conducted services from September 1911 to May, 1912.

Christ Church Mission was formally organized on March 7, 1912. The first resident clergyman was the retired Bishop of Nebraska, the Rt. Rev. Anson Rogers Graves, who arrived in October. He remained only to May, 1913. By then a new but abandoned building of the Christian Church was bought and converted into a chapel-guild hall. In 1919, a corner lot was purchased at 4th and Durian Streets for $900, and the chapel was moved onto it, to serve for another 36 years. In March, 1935, the title of the mission was changed to St. Philip's, "the reason being that there were several religious organizations in the community bearing the same name, causing confusion and inconvenience."

The Rev. James C. Caley came to St. Philip's in 1955, and motivated the people to build a larger, more appropriate church building. William Keck of Superior Oil Company donated a new site on Coalinga Street. Materials were donated by various members, and labor was volunteered by many. The old church building was sold, and the new church and parish hall were erected. First services were held during Christmasstide 1956. The new St. Philip's was consecrated ten years later, in 1966, by Bishop Walters.

Over the 75 years of its existence, St. Philip's has reflected the fluctuations of a typical oil and agricultural community, but has stood steadfast in spirit, with the Bishops' support and encouragement, and the dedication of its members. The earthquake on May 2, 1983, cracked the walls and toppled the steeple. Most of the crockery in the kitchen was broken as well. Had the earthquake occurred a day earlier, St. Philip's Day, many parishioners might have been inside at the time. Bishop Rivera made a special visit to the devasted town immediately after, being allowed through police barricades, to inspect the damage. Parish faith, and the great outpouring of concern, with gifts from other churches in the diocese, and across the State and Nation, saw St. Philip's repaired and refurbished. For a few years St. Philip's was in the status of an "Aided Parish", but has rebounded under the leadership of the Rev. Donald Kroeger, its present Rector, ordained to both the Diaconate and Priesthood in Coalinga. People from many religious backgrounds in Coalinga came together for these services, showing the spirit of cooperation engendered as a result of the community's unified efforts to rebuild physically and societally after the devastating earthquake.

ST. TIMOTHY'S CHURCH, BISHOP

The city of Bishop, near the north end of the Owens Valley floor, takes its name from Bishop Creek, named in turn for Sam Bishop, a 49er, who drove a herd of cattle through the region in 1861 from Fort Tejon, settling long enough to name the creek and the pass that leads into King's Canyon.

Bishop William F. Nichols of California visited the town by railroad from Carson City, Nevada, in mid-June, 1901. Bishop Sanford visited in June, 1912, conducting services in the facilities of the Presbyterian Church. In the winter of 1913-14, he heard a "Macedonian cry" from the isolated Eastern Sierra community and began regular visitations. In October, 1915, Deacon Alfred G. Denman was made Vicar, with charge of Lone Pine and Randsburg as well. Services were held in upstairs rooms over the school house, or the Lutz Grocery.

After Fr. Denman returned from World War I, having been injured, "St. Paul's Guild Hall" was constructed. This served as the church until decline of population, due to the bitter and protracted "Water War" with Los Angeles, led to its purchase by the local undertaker. Los Angeles set out to eliminate the town altogether, by pumping it dry, but was halted by court order. In 1928, Dr. Charles Powell became Vicar of Bishop, Lone Pine, and Porterville, with services also at Cartago (in 1929), in an effort to hold down the missionary budget of the District of San Joaquin. The impossibility of such an assignment soon became apparent and Dr. Powell accepted employment as Inyo County Probation Officer, and was relieved of responsibility for Porterville. After his death in January, 1942, priests from Tonopah, Nevada, served Bishop about three times a year during World War II.

By the end of the war, Bishop Walters was anxious to have the work back under his control, as he considered the clergy from Nevada "too High Church", even if they came but three times a year. On June 17, 1945, the Rev. Leslie C. Hill was inducted as Vicar of St. Paul's, but no suitable housing could be found, so he moved to Coalinga. In 1946, Bishop Walters himself took the Easter Day service, and the Sunday after Ascension.

On July 13, 1947, Bishop Walters escorted the newly ordained Deacon Paul E. Langpaap to Bishop, where they lodged in the motel. After Sunday services, they drove to Inyo-Kern, where St. Michael's Mission had begun. Langpaap would have charge of both, since Lone Pine was still involved in a Concordat made earlier with the Methodist Church. At Bishop, Fr. Langpaap held services in the Mortuary Chapel until St. Timothy's Church was built a few blocks away on land leased from the City of Los Angeles.

St. Timothy's was largely designed by Fr. Langpaap's Basque landlord, who was an architect. Its distinctive Romanesque features, however, came from a famous Black architect friend of Larralde's in Los Angeles. (The evidence suggests Paul Williams, who has several impressive mansions to his credit.) The church itself was built by parishioners, assisted by other local labor, between March, 1950, and December, 1951. By then, Fr. Carleton Sweetser was Vicar, and his father, an executive with the South Pacific Railroad, obtained a bell from one of the locomotive engines that served the standard-gauge line in the Owens Valley, just in time for the dedication. In 1954, a Hall was built, and named for Dr. and Mrs. Charles Anderson, early supporters of the church.

The Rev. William Landless Shannon became the next Vicar in September, 1955. The memory of his tenure still rouses strong emotions "pro" and "con". During his tenure the congregation became so divided, in any case, that Bishop Walters authorized the establishment of a separate chapel under a Lay Reader. Shannon finally left in late 1957 for Arizona, where he died of a brain tumor.

Dr. Horatio Nelson Tragitt, Jr., retired, was called to Bishop in February, 1958, and did much to effect healing among the congregation. An expert horticulturist, he bred prize iris and peonies, and landscaped the churchyard. He purchased a house from a former Churchwarden as vicarage, and later sold it back to the congregation. (He lived to be well over 90, and died in 1986.) In 1959, the Bristlecone Pine Altar and Cross were made by Al Larralde, from timber cut before the Ancient Forest atop the White Mountains was set aside in 1954. The trees providing this wood may well have been flourishing at the time of the Resurrection. Dr. Tragitt retired again at the end of May, 1961.

He was followed immediately by the Rev. John F. Putney. In his time, the post-war Baby-boom peaked. Sunday School attendance at times topped 100, with classes stuffed into the tower chamber, the attic, and every possible nook. Fr. Putney also began holding regular services in Mammoth Lakes, some 45 miles distant. In 1967 he reported 11 Eucharists, 11 services of Evening Prayer, four confirmations, and 12 communicants there. Fr. Putney left in March, 1969.

His successor was the Rev. James C. Thompson, a former Congregationalist minister, who later also served as Vicar of Lone Pine while still in Bishop. He became the Vicar at Bishop in July, 1969. At the time the Church was beginning to go through the process of Prayer Book revision with unsettling effect upon congregations nation-wide. It produced some negative effect in Bishop as well. Nevertheless, the mission was able to clear all its debts. He held regular services at Mammoth Lakes, from 1971 to 1976. He accepted a call to become Rector in Porterville in 1977.

There followed a brief interim period under the Rev. Virgil Evans, who left the Episcopal Church to enter the Roman Catholic Church. His successor the Rev. Christopher P. Kelley, came in August, 1978. A great-grandson of the famous and indefatigable, Douglas O. Kelley, who established numerous congregations in this diocese. Fr. Kelley, an ardent admirer of the Orthodox faith, and authority on church history, was able to inspire the members to decorate the church with banners depicting saints from every age, carved Stations of the Cross, needlepoint cushions showing the life of St. Timothy, and outlining Apostolic Succession. The Chapel of Our Lady and the Nativity was beautified, and the garden restored. In 1981, as the building's 30th anniversary was observed, Bishop hosted the 21st Convention of the Diocese, the first to be held in the Eastern Sierra.

During Fr. Kelley's tenure, popular annual festivals, like St. Andrews' Day, complete with bagpipes and Scottish dinner, were begun; and the Liturgy of Holy Week as outlined in the

Prayer Book was observed with meticulous care, as the focal point of the entire Church Year. Despite the ancient origins of these observances, there were those who came from congregations where, typical of the Episcopal Church, such observances were either ignored or deemed "Romish". The result was to produce division and some dissension in the congregation.

Fr. Kelley's active involvement with the water issues of Mono Lake and groundwater pumping, and alcoholism, won approval outside the church itself, but many members felt he was too much pre-occupied with such issues. In spite of this unrest, St. Timothy's was able to become self-supporting for four years and applied for probationary Parish status in April, 1984, in the faith that "nothing ventured, nothing gained". They were able to continue self-support and built a capital reserve for major maintenance in 1985.

Fr. Kelley left in early 1985, and was succeeded by the Rev. Philip Swickard, who had previously been an assistant to the Dean at St. James' Cathedral, Fresno. Fr. Philip quickly won the support of the membership, and has himself taken an active role in the local community. Not being a "strict contructionist", he permits those at the Andrewmas Dinner to skip the haggis — provided they pay a small fee for the privilege!

An economic downturn in the Owens Valley as the result of the closure of Union Carbide's tungsten mine and mill, the cutbacks in the federal budget for the Forest Service and other agencies, computerizing and centralization of the telephone service, with the consequent removal of a number of church families have caused St. Timothy's to postpone their request for full Parish status, but they continue to be self-supporting, and are wisely remaining a strong mission, for the present deeming it more prudent to do so than to become a weak parish.

TRINITY MEMORIAL CHURCH, LONE PINE

Trinity, Lone Pine, is favored with the most magnificent scenery of any of San Joaquin's churches. From the steps one looks upon the craggy eastern escarpment of the Sierra Nevada, dominated by Lone Pine Peak and Mount Whitney. Its outdoor chapel of the Transfiguration at Whitney Portal, elevation 8,300', is reputed to be "the highest church in the Diocese".

In 1901, Bishop William F. Nichols, of California, visited the Eastern Sierra by narrow-gauge train, making a stop for services at Lone Pine and Keeler, then an active port on Owens Lake. The Bishop also held services at Independence, the County Seat. After his consecration, Bishop Louis C. Sanford visited the Owens Valley in 1912. In October, 1915, Alfred G. Denman was appointed Vicar of Bishop, with responsibility for Lone Pine and other small communities in Inyo and eastern Kern Counties. It appears that he first held services in Lone Pine in November, 1915.

On November 5, 1916, the cornerstone was laid for the church, to be built in a Swiss style "in keeping with the mountainous character of the country." This was built at the expense of Mrs. E. H. Edwards, as a memorial to her husband. Townspeople fitted the church with other memorials. Mr. Edwards had been a pioneer in developing silver mining, and the very first bar of silver bullion mined in the county was donated for the building and beautification of the church. It was "debt free" upon completion.

Following service as a Red Cross Chaplain in World War I (in which he suffered permanent damage in a mustard gas attack), Fr. Denman was assigned in 1920 to cover Porterville, as well as Lone Pine and Bishop! It is small wonder that by 1924 his health broke.

The City of Los Angeles began its Owens Valley aqueduct's drain on the Owens River in 1913. After a drought in the early 1920s, the City began pumping groundwater. Soon, the City began buying out local ranches, farms, and water claims, to send more water south. The late 1920s became the era of the fierce "Water War". Mining activity declined in this period as well. Many families were forced to leave Lone Pine as a result. Trees along the highway at Manzanar were once so thick it was described as "like driving through a tunnel". It was not long before Owens Lake was a dry spot on the map, and caustic dust clouds, like thick fogs, were kicked up by the winds and rolled through town.

To solve problems created by the Water War and the Depression, Bishop Sanford entered into a novel "Concordat" in 1934 with the Southern California Conference of the Methodist Church. The Episcopal Church retained ownership, and the Book of Common Prayer was used, while a Methodist minister, licensed by the Bishop, served the congregation. A curious list of pastors, named Miller, Pancake, Bacon, and others served, but reports indicated that only the first, Mr. Mounts, abided by the Concordat's terms. Finally, Bishop Walters was forced to end the experiment when the new Methodist Superintendent refused to cooperate. In 1949, Trinity was returned to full Episcopal jurisdiction.

In 1950, Fr. John Pickells, affectionately known as 'Dad', became Vicar, and brought many of those who had been Methodists into the Church by Confirmation. He was killed in a tragic accident at a rodeo.

Shell Oil Company bought the church's property on Main Street in 1950, and the church and vicarage were relocated to a larger location at Locust and Lakeview. This allowed room for the building of "Walters Hall". The church was extensively remodeled at the time. Quite recently, the land on which the church is located (which belongs to Los Angeles Water and Power) has been offered for sale at a price of $30,000, and the congregation is working with the diocese to raise the money to purchase the land.

Trinity has seen many short-term Vicars, and long-term faithful service by local Lay Readers. Fr. Richard Beaumont, a retired priest, has served perhaps the longest of any. In addition to Episcopalians, Trinity Church serves many "associate members," as it is the one "mainline" non-Roman Church in Lone Pine.

ST. FRANCIS' EPISCOPAL CHURCH, TURLOCK

In October, 1919, a group of Episcopalians led by Mr. Coburn Cook, Mesdames Kerfoot, Weldon, Beardsworth and Taylor were instrumental in a mission being formed in Turlock. A residence on East Main at Thor was secured as a Mission House and Deaconess Willis was in charge. She organized a Sunday School and a Guild and the mission was named St. Francis'. The group was active for a few years and then disbanded.

Some time later, the Rev. Harold Brewster of St. Paul's in Modesto, held services on Sunday afternoons in the Dr. Julien Building. The Guild became active again and did mission work. The services, however, were again dropped when Rev. Brewster moved away.

On January 10, 1934, a group of women met at the home of Mrs. Foster Ivy to reorganize a guild to work in connection with St. Paul's church. The Guild grew in membership and several money making projects made it possible for them to contribute $50 to St. Paul's on their new lot on April 13, 1935. They were able to assist with a pledge as well. The first service was Vespers, held in the Lutheran Church with Bishop Sanford officiating. A reception followed the service at the Albert Julien home.

By this time the group felt they were ready to be a new mission. Subsequently, at a lunch in the E. B. Leduc home, the men of the church met with Bishop Sanford who gave his consent for forming the Mission. In October, 1939, the first seminarian came to St. Francis', William Lankford, from the Church Divinity School of the Pacific. He was later followed by Mr. Maxwell Brown. During this time a beautiful carved altar was made and presented by the Rev. Mr. Graves in memory of his daughter. Bishop and Mrs. Sanford gave the Mission its first silver communion service. The chapel location, at the time, was upstairs in rooms in the Dr. Julien Building.

The year 1943 was the year when the first ordained man was appointed to serve the Mission, the Rev. McMurdo Brown. Under his leadership the Mission grew rapidly and became a parish. He had a vision of building a beautiful church, and a generous check given at a Christmas midnight service by Wilton and Winifred Olson made it possible to start a building program. Mr. Coburn Cook was appointed chairman for the program. However, due to World War II, the project was delayed. On August 2, 1944, a lot was purchased on East Main and Pioneer Streets with money given by the Guild from their many projects.

Fr. Brown was forced to resign because of ill health and a seminarian, Ralph Stevens, supplied until the Rev. Gordon Reigler arrived. Ground-breaking for the new church at last took place November 7, 1948. The building was finished and dedicated July 31, 1949, with Bishop Sumner Walter officiating. Fr. Brown, unfortunately, did not live to see his dream come to fulfillment.

The first Rector was the Rev. Gordon Reigler. The members of the first Vestry were: Coburn Cook, Senior Warden (later Chancellor of the Diocese); Edward Leduc, Junior Warden; Messrs. Charles Cook, Herman Hanston, Gerald James, Milton Olson, John Orth and Russell Peterson, and Mrs. Foster Ivy, Clerk.

In 1951, the Rev. James Trotter became Rector and served for seven years. During this period many of the memorial gifts were received, including the windows. St. Anne's Guild was organized with Mrs. Wesley Anderson serving as the first President. The outstanding event of the period was hosting the 43rd Convocation, January 25-27, 1953. Bishop Walters proclaimed it the most outstanding Convocation in the history of the diocese. At that time the mortgage was burned. The pipe organ, a gift of Winifred and Milton Olson was made. The first organist was Mrs. Eleanor Moon.

Plans had already begun on a new Sunday School building which was much needed. The Rev. Jerry Skillicorn (1958-1962) was the new Rector, and on May 16, 1960, the new building was used for the first time. During his tenure youth work flourished.

Following Fr. Skillicorn, Fr. Richmond served as Rector from 1962-1965, when he left to serve as chaplain in the U. S. Navy. He was succeeded by the Rev. Ronald Swanson who served from February 1, 1965 to April, 1966, when he left to serve at St. James' Cathedral, Fresno.

The Rev. David Wilson served from July, 1966, through June, 1969, when he was succeeded by the Rev. James Trotter, who returned to serve as Rector on November 27, 1969. He served until his retirement in January, 1976. He was followed by the Rev. Paul Levine who came in 1977 and is currently serving St. Francis as one of their longer tenured clergy.

ST. ANDREW'S EPISCOPAL CHURCH, TAFT

Oil was located on the "West Side" in 1910, by the blowout of Lakeview 1 Well. "Siding Two" and its cluster of tents and false-front saloons was incorporated with a population of 750 and named Taft for the incumbent President. It was a rough, shanty town for many years, although the wealth meant fine schools could be erected at once. Wild car races, "Oildorado" celebrations recalling the significant population of prostitutes, well blowouts and burning gushers character-ized the town for years. Drinking water had to be brought in by railroad. The stories and legends are related in William Rintoul's book, OILDORADO.

It was not until the Fall of 1922, that Episcopalians in Taft were able to arrange for services to be conducted by the Rector of Bakersfield, W. A. Cash. In the following Spring, Archdeacon Hawken visited from Fresno. He visited around for two days, but received a negative response to his suggestion of forming a mission. The following year, the Archdeacon visited once again. Newly arrived Episcopalians encouraged him to establish frequent ministrations, "not every Sunday, but as often as possible." By then, Taft's 5,000 people called the place "The World's Biggest Little City", a title also claimed by Reno, Nevada, at the same time. A Church School party went to a hilltop overlooking Taft and counted over 1100 oil derricks in sight. The city itself was still shacks; windows were of canvas over screen; glass was a rarity.

On September 14, 1925, Judge Cassius G. Noble was elected the first Warden, a Committee and Church School were also formed. St. Andrew's Mission was formally admitted to the District Convocation on January 27, 1926. For several years the Archdeacon and Canon Frederick Graves came from Fresno to hold services. These were located in the Odd Fellows, Masonic, Knights of Pythias, Boy Scouts, Music Hall, and sundry other places too numerous to list. "Some of the old timers say that the only way they could find the services was to get up early and stand around Fourth and Center Streets until they saw Judge Noble going by with the Altar on a truck, and follow him." In 1926, a lot was purchased from Standard Oil Company. An old oil field cookhouse was moved onto it. This seated about 40 people. Buying and moving took all the available funds; renovation of the building was put on hold. But the Archdeacon was a carpenter and rallied the men to achieve the necessary remodeling.

On Wednesday night, November 24, 1926, heavy rains turned the bed of Buena Vista into a muddy lake, seven miles from Taft. The barley and maize fields began to disgorge thousands upon thousands of mice, which made their way to higher ground: Taft. The harvester reported that when he set the blades low, they became so "choked with fur, flesh and blood" they resembled "a sausage mill." Men were taken off the derrick and pressed into digging ditches around all installations, filling them with poisoned grain. As many as 50,000 mice a day were killed this way. Cats were sent in from around the country, but were soon gorged; two cats were even reported as found sleeping with sixteen mice under them. The invasion let up for Christmas services, but resumed in greater numbers in January. They even killed penned sheep, feasting on their meat. Mice outnumbered the people of Taft by many thousands to one. On January 22, 1927, a federal poisoner from Colorado arrived, one Stanley E. Piper, a serious man, offended by references to Hamelin. He and his crew estimated as many as 44 million mice still on the floor of the lake, in several species. Suddenly, over 1,000 Mono Lake gulls appeared, followed by owls, ravens, hawks, turkey vultures, falcons, herons, roadrunners, shrikes, and at least two golden eagles were reported, joining in the counter-attack on the mice. The mice began cannibalizing each other, and an epidemic mouse disease suddenly spread through their ranks. By mid-February the "Great Mouse War" in Taft was over, with over 30,000,000 mice dead.

Alfred Denman, disabled in a mustard gas attack during World War I, served very briefly in Taft; and for eleven months, Michael Louis Daly was the first official Vicar, from November 29, 1925 to October 31, 1926. In 1930, Bishop Sanford appointed the Rev. J. Elmer Darling as the first resident Vicar of Taft, with care of Coalinga. He worked with such intensity that he died after a year and half. The Bishop appointed his son, Gordon Darling, as Lay Reader and Minister-in-charge of the two missions; he successfully carried on the work for more than a year. In September, 1933, the Rev. Mr. Aubrey Bray, just out of seminary, was appointed to Taft as Deacon, and Mr. Darling was left at Coalinga. Bray took up residence in the Savoy Hotel.

By Spring of 1934, Sunday School enrollment was up to sixty, many of whom were from homes of no religious connection. Average Sunday attendance was fifty; the cookhouse had to be replaced. In the Fall, a meeting took responsibility for building a larger facility, facing realistically their limited resources and money.

Mr. Clarence Cullimore of Bakersfield was engaged as architect, and adobe was decided upon, since soil on the lot was ideal. The American Church Building Fund came up with $800 to be used as a last payment. Initial work was done as a "class project" by students and instructors from Taft Union High School and the Junior College. R. Rose, Instructor in Surveying, had his class lay out the ground plan. Mr. Geoffrey B. Noakes, an Englishman and Instructor in Carpentry, superintended the actual building. Adobe bricks were made and dried on the site. The cornerstone was set on St. Andrew's Day, 1934. Children of the church made drawings and watercolor paintings to sell to finance the work, but most labor was volunteered. "Hardly any businessman in Taft did not make a contribution. Some of the oil companies were also liberal in the donation of money and materials." Friends of the Noakes in England also gave generously. Trinity Sunday was celebrated in the building on June 16, 1935; the coolness inside was much appreciated during the summer.

Canon Graves, a woodcarver noted throughout the Valley, designed an Altar for the new building, which Church Service League (precursor of the Episcopal Church Women) paid for; the work was done by Cathedral communicants, Mr. and Mrs. Homer Hoyt. The original work incorporated symbols of St. Andrew and the Blessed Virgin Mary. Later, one Vicar had the symbol of Mary effaced. Consecration of the Church and Altar was done by Bishop Sanford on Sunday, May 3, 1936. In one, five months, and three days, the church was built and paid for — this at the depths of the Great Depression!

Fr. Bray remained in Taft until the end of January, 1943. It was not until August that Leo M. Brown came as the first Rector. He stayed about two years, leaving just after V-J Day, in September, 1945. Cyril H. Boddington was Rector of Taft from November 1, 1945, until his death on June 18, 1950. Another lengthy period followed before John Atkinson, from St. Andrew's, Nogales, Arizona, became Rector in mid-January, 1952. During his tenure numerous memorials were given the church. Mrs. Boddington gave a silver baptismal shell in memory of her husband. In 1955, a rectory was build adjacent to the church, replacing the adobe "Annex", which now became the office. Much work was again done by parishioners, holding the cost to $8,800. Widowed, Fr. Atkinson left Taft in November, 1958, to become Assistant at St. Paul's, Bakersfield.

Charles A. Sunderland became Rector on January 15, 1959. In February, moves were made to replace the old cookhouse that had served as church, then parish hall. Based on some earlier sketches and plans, bids were opened in October, 1960. The building was finished and ready for occupancy on September 1, 1961. The debt on it was retired and the building dedicated by Bishop Walters on March 17, 1968, as the Aubrey O. Bray Memorial Hall.

In the meantime, Fr. Sunderland left on June 15, 1961, and the Rev. Lester Mather came as Rector on August 1 of that year. Taft's economy collapsed on September 30, 1971, when Standard Oil of California closed most of its operations. Many families moved away. St. Andrew's was forced to become an aided parish on July 1, 1972, and then had to revert to Mission status. Parishioners continued to do as much for themselves as possible, with a sense of humor. "The Painting and Sanding Society of Upper Woodrow Street" took care of needed building mainten- ance, calculating what they had saved as "donated labor" at a wage of $0.1815 per hour, "just slightly less than the pay of Ham the Astronautical Chimpanzee." A history booklet was put together by St. Andrew's for its 50th Anniversary, edited by Fr. Mather.

Fr. Mather retired from Taft at the end of June, 1977, and was followed at once by Fr. Paul Lambert. Fr. William Wight served as Vicar from early 1979 to 1981. His deep interest in the Orthodox East, and connections with a gifted ikon-painting monk in Oklahoma, procured for St. Andrew's a fine ikon of the patron Apostle. Coming in great personal pain, the good people of St. Andrew's were able to give Fr. Wight support and time for some healing. He resigned from Taft to become a military chaplain. Fr. Wight was succeeded in July, 1982, by Fr. Thomas C. Barnett, formerly assistant at St. Paul's, Bakersfield. During Fr. Barnett's time, St. Andrew's once again became self-supporting, and much needed repair work was done. The Bishop's Committee adopted the title "Vestry". Endowment funds were surrendered to the diocese for safe-keeping. Plans to acquire land for a future parking lot were not approved by Diocesan Council because of the precarious state of Taft's economy and the uncertainty of their being able to meet the commitment. Fr. Barnett taught classes for the Junior College in philosophy and religious subjects. He remained until the end of August, 1986, when he became Rector of a parish in St. Louis, Missouri, closer to Sewanee where he was working on a doctorate. Since his departure St. Andrew's has been without a resident priest. The oil industry took another down-turn in 1986 due to the OPEC Oil Cartel; as a result over 1,000 people left Taft to seek work elsewhere. At the time of this writing the Economic future of Taft is uncertain.

ST. THOMAS' MISSION, AVENAL

Avenal advertises itself as "an oasis in the sun". The small community sits beside Highway 33, west of some hills pierced by many oil wells. Recently, the State has built a prison facility there, which the locals believe will bring in a number of new residents who will be employed at the prison itself (inmate population not counted!).

St. Thomas' Episcopal Church was accepted by the Convocation on February 11, 1940, the result of the work by the Avenal branch of the Coalinga Episcopal Women's Guild. The Rev. Harold Jenkins served as Vicar of both congregations. The Guild had organized itself in October, 1939, with Mrs. T. C. Preuss as President, Mrs. W. L. Piguet as Vice-president, Mrs. E. F. Staugaard as Secretary, Mrs. E. A. Carlson as Treasurer & Altar Custodian, and Mrs. Charles Engstrom as Offering Custodian. The women met twice a month, working toward regular services in Avenal, and the establishment of a local mission.

Bishop Sanford appointed Charles F. Worthy as Bishop's Warden, Edwin Staugaard as Junior Warden, and Frank Dean, W. W. McFadden and W. L. Piguet as Bishop's Committee members. By June, two had moved and only one replacement was found. Services and Sunday School were held each Sunday evening, except on the second Sunday of the month, when the Holy Communion was held at 11 A.M.

Typical of most of the small missions they have had a rapid turn-over in the clergy serving them. In 1968 the Rev. George Swanson was Priest-in-charge. The Rev. James Marner served from 1969 to 1970, when he was succeeded by the Rev. Harvey DeWitt Smith in 1971 who served Corcoran as well. The Diocesan Journal does not indicate anyone for 1972, but the 1973 Journal shows the Rev. Robert M. Santry as serving Avenal, while residing in Corcoran. He resigned as of July 31, 1977, to become a chaplain in the Armed Forces. The Rev. Brian Endicott was licensed in this diocese and appointed to serve as Vicar of Avenal. He continued in that position until 1985. The Rev. Donald Kroeger who was Deacon-in-charge at Coalinga and ordained Priest there and became their Rector has also been responsible for services at Avenal since 1985.

ST. MARK'S MISSION, TRACY

In 1938, a devout Church of England family moved to Tracy, then a community of about 3400. The John Robertsons were disappointed that there was no local parish church, but drove faithfully to Stockton and attended St. John's. There they discovered some neighbors doing the same. The Rev. George Pratt, Rector of St. John's, suggested that those from Tracy advertise and hold a meeting there of all Episcopalians. Ten to fifteen families responded. Fr. Pratt offered to hold services in Tracy every other Sunday evening. Arrangements were made with St. Paul's Lutheran Church on E. 10th Street to hold services there. These flourished for a time, but "several disappointments occurred" and as a result regular services were discontinued.

Infrequent and irregular services were held in the homes of various members during the years of World War II. In spring, 1946, remnants of the original group approached the new Bishop Walters and voiced their frustrations concerning a church in Tracy. The Bishop encouraged them to try again, and on March 7, a meeting was held in the home of Mr. and Mrs. Manuel Rico.

Reports were heard concerning a survey of Episcopalians in Tracy. There was sufficient interest to organize a mission under the sponsorship of St. John's, and services were begun soon after. Bishop Walters conducted their first service in the American Legion Hall on March 24. Some 50 people were present. The Bishop appointed Wardens and a first Bishop's Committee. The first Sunday School class was held on Palm Sunday, April 14, with four children and the first Easter celebration was held on the 21st, conducted by Dean Henry Shires of Church Divinity School of the Pacific.

Little time was lost in starting a Confirmation class, and organizing the first Women's Auxiliary, with Bemis Grant as President. The men did not formally organize, but nevertheless set about making furnishings and appointments to transform the Legion Hall into something more like a church. During the spring and summer, visiting clergy, assisting clergy from St. John's, and Bishop Walters covered the services at Tracy. In November, the Bishop appointed the Rev. Waddell Robey to serve the new mission as part-time Vicar for a few months. On December 2, 1946, the Tracy Mission was officially given the name "St. Mark's." On January 19, 1947, the Convocation accepted St. Mark's Mission into union.

In June, 1947, the Bishop placed Morgan Sheldon part-time at St. Mark's while still a seminarian at C. D. S. P., until his ordination in 1949, when he became St. Mark's first full-time priest. By the fall of 1947, lots were bought on the corner of Emerson and Wall Streets for $1,750. Ground-breaking was held the afternoon of Easter Day, March 25, 1951. Bishop Walters also officiated at Baptisms and Confirmations in the morning. That same month St. Mark's first vicarage was purchased at 1331 Madison.

The first service in the new building was held on September 9, 1951. The dedication was conducted by the Bishop on November 18, 1951. A year later, Fr. Sheldon left St. Mark's, at the end of December, 1952. Deacon-seminarian, William T. Halstead, then commuted to Tracy to take Sunday services until his graduation in June; when priested in September, 1953, the Bishop placed him at Los Baños. The Rev. Wilbur Caswell, a retired priest living in Patterson, served St. Mark's from September, 1953, to November, 1954. He was followed by another seminarian, Lester L. Westling. During his time, a new vicarage was purchased at 1423 Wilson; it served many a clergy family until the spring of 1980, when it was sold. Fr. Westling left in June, 1955. He was succeeded by the Rev. Wayne Parker who came in December.

During Fr. Parker's time the congregation continued to grow. The Sunday School, Women's Auxiliary, youth fellowship, youth choir, boys' choir, men's club, several social groups, a Boy Scout Troop, all developed and grew. It became apparent that more space was needed. An ambitious building fund drive began on September 27, 1957, with a goal of $30,000 to be pledged over 3 years. In three weeks, pledges of over $35,000 were received. Ground-breaking for a new parish hall took place on May 15, 1958. The new hall was dedicated on December 28; Bishop Walters presided on both occasions.

While founders and newer members joined in divers efforts and fellowship, their children were also brought into the many activities. The Sunday School grew from four to over forty by the time the new building opened. The first wee disciples grew into an active youth group and brought in friends from outside to enjoy their activities. Some of these also became church members in time.

Fr. Parker left St. Mark's in June, 1957, to found St. Mary's in Fresno. The Rev. Roger Strem came as the new Vicar. He was most active with the youth groups. Many of their programs were accelerated under his direction. Fr. Strem left at the end of December, 1963. An interim period from January to April, 1964, was filled by the Rev. Arthur Beckwith of Oakdale. Canon Fred J. G. Kepler was appointed Vicar of St. Mark's and served until his retirement in 1967. St. Mark's people considered themselves fortunate to have this older priest of great wisdom and wide experience. The Vicar contributed his expertise as the buildings and grounds were improved by many additions, inside and out. Fr. Kepler was much loved by parishioners and other townspeople of Tracy.

The financial situation at St. Mark's became strained, and Bishop Walters arranged that Fr. Thomas Corrigan, Vicar of St. Mary's, Manteca, should serve Tracy part-time. In October, Fr. Tom became full-time Vicar of St. Mark's and he remained until the winter of 1975, when he left Tracy for San Andreas.

During his time a large bell was given to the church by Karl Boos, a retired Southern Pacific Railroad man, this was installed. More stained glass windows were added to the sanctuary, and the building refurbished.

In December, 1975, the Rev. Douglas Judson came to Tracy and served until spring, 1977. His family's studio, Judson's of Los Angeles, executed the remaining stained glass windows which he designed. The last of the 12 windows was not installed until early 1981. At the dedication, five of the original members were able to be present: Richard Alcock, Ray and Rhetta James, Gertrude Newbury, and Dorothy Robertson.

The Rev. Paul Snider came from Colorado in September and remained through May, 1984. In October, 1978, St. Mark's hosted the Diocesan E.C.W. convention, most successfully. Tracy celebrated its centennial in 1979, and St. Mark's was proud to be a vital part of this growing community.

The Rev. E. James Kingsley, a retired Air Force Chaplain (Col.), doing doctoral work at C. D. S. P. served St. Mark's on a part-time basis from July, 1984, to June, 1985. His resignation was brought about by his need for serious surgery. It is of interest that the first Vicar, Morgan Sheldon, brought a friend at C. D. S. P. to visit his mission 37 years before, this same Fr. Kingsley! Fr. Kingsley was succeeded by the Rev. John Burk who came from Clovis.

ST. MICHAEL'S PARISH, RIDGECREST

In earlier years a thriving mission once flourished in Randsburg, during the gold rush there in the first decades of the 1920s. Its Sunday School was so lively that "the denominational churches despaired of setting up a rival work." Mr. H. H. Nagle, a hardware merchant, formerly of Mokelumne Hill, set up the school on his arrival in 1896-97. He inspired Alfred G. Denman to go into the Priesthood, but by the time Denman finished at Church Divinity School of the Pacific in 1915, Randsburg's Rush was spent, so he was assigned to Bishop, with oversight of all the missions east of the Sierra. So Randsburg got an occasional visit. Abandoned property was held there until after Bishop Walter's time, when notification reached the Diocese that the Kern County Sheriff had finally auctioned it for back taxes.

Ridgecrest is located in the bottom of the Indian Wells Valley, a sink in the Mojave Desert, about 20 miles from Randsburg. All that is left of Pleistocene Searles Lake is the dry, white bed of China Lake, location of an important naval testing center, since World War II. St. Michael's was started in conjunction with the Base Chapel in 1946. During the first year, no priest was assigned, but Bishop Walters and Fr. Joseph Doran visited about every other month. From 1947 to 1948, Fr. Paul Langpaap, Vicar of Bishop, was assigned to the mission.

For the next two years the mission was served by Fr. John P. Christiansen (who was ordained there, in the Chapel Annex on Base, then used for the mission services), and by Fr. Stephen Green. In 1950, the Rev. Frederick Stillwell was assigned to St. Michael's. He and his wife were a team, and the mission grew in strength under their devoted ministry.

In 1955, a directed canvass launched the move toward the building of a church off the Base at 200 Drummond Drive (now "Avenue"). The building program was supervised by Maurice Clifton. The first buildings were the chapel, with an adjoining kitchen, sacristy, choir room, Sunday School room, and restrooms, and the rectory. A large curtain was used to screen off the altar and sanctuary from the nave, so it could serve as the parish hall. This was dedicated on April 20, 1958.

Following Fr. Stillwell's retirement in 1959, The Rev. Robert Harvey was called. Under his leadership, St. Michael's continued to grow in spiritual strength and physical plant. Additional Sunday School rooms and the parish hall were added. St. Michael's was accorded parish status by the Convention in 1964. Fr. Harvey and his family remained until 1966.

The Rev. H. Lee Wilson was called to serve at. St. Michael's from Good Shepherd, Reedley, and served with love and devotion during the years of the Viet Nam War and its associated unrest, something felt keenly in a military community. He was succeeded by the Rev. C. Bruce Spencer who came from St. Mark's, Shafter, in 1971. Under his direction the appearance of the Altar, sanctuary, and nave were modified extensively. A new altar front was carved in wood by Jack Durk, depicting St. Michael slaying the dragon. Pews were installed, and Eleanor Lotee took on responsibility for interior decoration. Fr. Bruce coped with the difficulties of the introduction of the proposed Prayer Book revision with compassion and compromise. He left in 1977 to go to Oregon.

The Rev. John Patterson (who had served in British churches in Africa) was recruited by Bishop Rivera from Ashton-under-Lyne, near Manchester, England, and called to St. Michael's in March, 1978, with his wife, Olive. Under his pastoral care, St. Michael's has continued to grow in strength and outreach. Priest and parish took part in a city-wide evangelical crusade in 1983, in partnership with nine other churches, and special ties have been developed between St. Michael's and other churches in the Indian Wells Valley. The appearance of the church has been enhanced by the addition of stained glass memorial windows, designed and installed during 1984 and '85 by Robert Burrows, a member of the church.

(Information supplied by R. G. Sewell and F. Plain, Feb. 1985)

CHURCH OF THE REDEEMER PARISH, DELANO

Under the leadership of Archdeacon Joseph S. Doron, after some preliminary organization meetings, the first service of the congregation which was to be known as "The Episcopal Church of the Redeemer" was a service of Holy Communion at 11 A.M. on Sunday, November 14, the 25th Sunday after Trinity, in 1948. Thirty people were present, and the offering was $19.65. That service, as was true of all subsequent worship services until the completion of a multi-purpose building four and one-half years later, was in the Delano Mortuary at 12th and Kensington.

Church of the Redeemer was accepted into the Missionary District of San Joaquin in the Convention on February 7, 1949, and, for its first two and one-half years of existence, had Morning Prayer conducted by a Lay Reader on all but one Sunday of each month. For the most part, Archdeacon Doron returned once each month to celebrate Holy Eucharist.

In July, 1951, Deacon Robert H. Cochrane, now Bishop of Olympia, became Redeemer's first Vicar, and continued with the same worship practice until November 4 of that same year when, following his ordination as a Priest, Fr. Cochrane celebrated his first Eucharist at Redeemer. During Fr. Cochrane's cure the congregation grew and 3 large lots of land were purchased on the East edge of town. Fr. Cochrane left to take another cure in October, 1952, and beginning with a ground-breaking on December 14 of that same year, Archdeacon Doron became Vicar.

Easter Day, 1953, was an especially glorious one since it also marked the first service in the new building, where worship and fellowship continued under Archdeacon Doron's leadership until January 17, 1954, when Fr. E. Leslie Rolls was called as Vicar. During his cure, Fr. Rolls celebrated the 40th anniversary of his ordination, the congregation built the vicarage next to the Church (1955) and the Church School building (Wilbur Hall-1957). Fr. Rolls was called to eternity with the Lord on August 22, 1958.

Fr. Charles W. C. Leel served as Vicar from January 1, 1959, until mid-June, 1960, and Lay Readers led the worship until November 27 of the same year, when Fr. G. S. Scovell served as Vicar until December 3, 1961. Lay Readers were again called upon to lead the worship until August 12, 1962, when Fr. William H. Hogshead was called as Vicar. Fr. Hosghead, under whose leadership the congregation achieved Parish status at the Diocesan Convention January 24-26, 1965, remained until April 30, 1966, when he left to become Associate to Fr. Victor M. Rivera at St. Paul's, Visalia. He was replaced, in September of that same year, by Fr. Ray Knapp, who served as Rector until October 31, 1970, when he left to become Rector of St. John the Baptist in Lodi.

In March of 1971, the parish called Fr. Ellsworth "Butch" Wayland. During Fr. Wayland's cure the parish continued to grow until the small multi-purpose building was no longer able to accommodate the worshippers. Planning and fund-raising began, and, on January 14, 1973, the first service was held in the new church. Fr. Wayland left Redeemer on February 29, 1976, to become Rector of the Church of Our Saviour, Placerville. Visiting clergy and Lay Readers conducted worship services until December 5 when Fr. Maurice Turner was called as Rector. Fr. Turner served until July 30, 1978, and was quickly replaced by Fr. John D. Spear, now Rector of St. Paul's, Bakersfield, as interim Rector. He remained until Fr. Sylvan Law arrived on April 1,

1979. Fr. Law remained until May, 1981, when he left to become Vicar of St. Paul's, Cambria, in the Diocese of El Camino Real.

Once again, Lay Readers and visiting clergy were called upon to lead the worship until the arrival of Fr. Maurice Furlonger from England in September 1981. Fr. Furlonger served as interim Rector for a year and then returned to England. Concurrent with the scheduled departure of Fr. Furlonger, a Postulant and Seminarian from this Diocese, Edward J. Renner, Jr., married Dee Draper a member of Redeemer Parish. At Bishop Rivera's suggestion, the parish called Mr. Renner as "Resident Seminarian in Charge," in September, 1982, at the beginning of his last year of seminary at C. D. S. P. In early 1983, Fr. Lee Wilson became the regular "Visiting Priest," celebrating Holy Eucharist on all but the last Sunday of each month. That worship schedule was followed through the ordination of Mr. Renner to the Diaconate in August, 1983, until September, 1984, when Fr. Renner was ordained Priest. At that time Fr. Renner was called as Rector of the Parish.

ST. ANNE'S CHURCH, STOCKTON

St. Anne's Church began as Emmanuel Church, Terminous, in 1930. Until 1941, Emmanuel was an active mission. During World War II the mission was closed. In 1949, when plans were completed by Fr. Pratt and the Vestry of St. John's to open a mission in North Stockton, the old mission building was moved from Terminous by May, 1949. Property for the new mission was given by the family of the late Alfred Benjamin Holt, Lincoln Properties, Inc., and Sims and Grupe Development Company. The mission was named "St. Anne's" by Bishop Walters in November, 1949. St. Anne was the wife of St. Joachim (San Joaquin), and they were the parents of the Virgin Mary, Mother of our Lord. St. Anne's was admitted into union with the Convocation on January 23, 1950.

The first Vicar to be appointed was the Rev. C. T. Abbott. In 1950, the present parish hall was built; in 1953, the church was extended. From its early years, St. Anne's established a strong liturgical tradition, including the para-liturgical services, such as Benediction of the Blessed Sacrament, much to the scandal of Bishop Walters. Fr. William Richmond and his family were the first occupants of a new rectory at 1020 Lincoln Road, in August, 1955. He was followed by Fr. Ellis E. Peterson, who was soon called to be Rector of St. John's, Oakland. The church school premises were built in 1960, during the tenure of Fr. James Caley.

The Rev. John Smedburg came to St. Anne's in 1964. During his time the Senior Youth Group made several trips to Bluff, Utah, to help with construction of St. Christopher's Mission there among the Navajo.

For a time, St. Anne's was served by seminarians from Church Divinity School of the Pacific. Then, in 1970, Fr. Frank Williams was the Rector. Fr. Roger Jones was Rector from 1977 through 1982, until forced to resign due to a chronic illness. Following Fr. Jones, the Rev. Connor Lynn, former Superior of the Order of the Holy Cross, was called to be Rector in February, 1983. He left in 1985 to accept a call to mission work in the British West Indies. The current Rector, Fr. Steve Ellis, was called from St. Paul's, Modesto, where he had been an assistant, and has served St. Anne's since 1985.

ST. COLUMBA'S CHURCH, FRESNO

Located near the busy intersection of Shaw and North Palm in northwest Fresno, St. Columba's began as a small mission in 1952. Initially, it was just a hope in the minds of Bishop Walters and the young man he was to make Vicar of the Mission in 1952, the Rev. George Woodgates. The Bishop resided in Stockton, but his committee of six, with the help of others who followed, by working industriously and praying fervently, "What wilt Thou have me to do, O Lord?", managed by April, 1952, to hold an Easter service within the rising walls of the church, with the new Vicar, Fr. Woodgates, assisting and preaching.

Within a few months, there were 60 children in the Sunday School, and about 100 families lending support of all kinds. An Esty organ and Baptismal Font were purchased with donations of Fresno's supportive citizens in loving memory of Neal Haig, Sr.

Growth was such that by 1956, the architect, Robert Stevens, was called upon again to design a much larger structure. In 1958, Bishop Walters dedicated the new $77,000 building which is in use today. At the same time, he instituted Fr. George R. Turney as the new Rector, to succeed Fr. Woodgates, who had been called to Christ Church, Winnetka, Illinois. These ceremonies were attended by 20 Episcopal clergymen from the District, and Fr. N. Pappas of St. George's Greek Orthodox Church.

St. Columba's was named for the great Celtic missionary pioneer, who worked in Scotland prior to the arrival of St. Augustine at Canterbury (597 A.D.). The Celtic Cross standing now before the Abbey which St. Columba established on the island of Iona, in the Inner Hebrides groups, is the model for the cross adopted by the modern St. Columba's in Fresno. It stands facing Palm Avenue, reminding everyone who passes that God's work goes on down through the centuries, from one part of the world to another, as the result of courageous missionaries in the past who labored to bring the Gospel to those who had never heard it. A stone from Iona rests in the brick wall near the east entrance of the church. The zeal for Christian work manifested by the historic St. Columba was emulated by Fr. Woodgates, who believe that "great things for Him do not happen by chance. They are willed by prayer, stewardship, and decisive action." He felt strongly that "Christians everywhere must be alert to the needs of the community, and care that spiritual values are not lost."

St. Columba's continued to grow under the ministry of Fr. Turney, who was called to St. Paul's, Visalia, in November 1968. Fr. Turney brought the parish into line with the liturgical movement by exercising sensitive pastoral care. Fr. Lyle McBee was the curate, and filled in after Fr. Turney's departure, until the Rev. M. Fletcher Davis came in January, 1969. Other curates who have assisted at St. Columba's include the Rev. Mssrs. R. Rible, L. Mann, R. Stevenson, B. Samson, C. King, J. McDonald, and J. Short. Fr. Davis left St. Anne's in November, 1978, to accept a call as Rector of St. Anselm's, Garden Grove. St. Aidan's Day School was formed to provide Church-based education; it operated in St. Columba's School building. In April, 1979, the Rev. James Short resigned as Curate at St. Columba's to become Vicar of the new Diocesan Mission of St. Aidan, which, in effect, made it independent of St. Columba's. The school did not work out as had been hoped, and the location proved to be a handicap, forcing the closure of the mission after valiant effort to sustain it had been made by sacrificial giving on the part of a number of lay people.

In April, 1979, the Rev. Bernard Flynn, a former Roman Catholic priest, became Rector of St. Columba's. He has played a leading role in the Fresno community in the work of Alcoholics Anonymous (A.A.). St. Columba's also maintains a strong outreach program which includes Valley Social Service, World Impact, Poverello House, Marjorie Mason Center, Santa Margarita Mission, and the Episcopal Asian Center. Fr. Flynn is assisted on a part-time basis, by the Rev. Fred Johnson, a retired priest of the Diocese of Navajoland.

The Church of St. Columba stands today with its high-pitched roof and warm and interesting architecture, as a symbol for the spirit of Christ in the midst of a burgeoning commercial center that has steadily grown up around it. It stands as a highly visible witness to the community of the efforts of a dedicated congregation, past and present, who have been led by able clergy.

ST. ALBAN'S CHURCH, LOS BAÑOS

Prior to the arrival of European culture in the persons of the Spanish, Native Americans had healing spas in the west side of the Valley, giving the area the reputation for its therapeutic baths, so that the Spanish named it "Los Baños". The town itself is just south of the Kesterson Wildlife Refuge, a swampy area used by millions of wildfowl, but now dangerously polluted by the concentration of naturally occurring selenium, washed from the soil by agricultural runoff. Various government agencies are working to correct the situation; but the crisis has put Los Banos on the national map, as it were. The National Geographic Magazine dramatized the situation with pictures of deformed birds caused by genetic altering from the heavy metal poison. Los Baños has become, willing or not, the symbol of mankind's need for careful stewardship of God's created order.

In 1951, a group of interested residents of Los Baños met with Fr. John Christiansen, Rector of St. Luke's, Merced, to discuss the feasibility of establishing a local mission. There is no extant record of that meeting, but St. Alban's was admitted to union with the Convocation on Monday, January 28, 1952.

St. Alban was Britain's first martyr, bravely facing execution as a Catechumen in 209 A.D., rather than betray to Roman soldiers a fugitive priest in his home. Early services in Los Baños were held in the home of parishioners, then in the old city library, the Seventh-Day Adventist building, and the local funeral chapel.

In 1953, the Rev. William Halstead came to serve Los Baños as first resident Vicar. He was much loved by the congregation and the community at large. In 1954, ground was broken and the present church building was put up. Fr. Halstead served faithfully for three years, during which time the congregation grew in communicant and financial strength. He was succeeded by the Rev. Ernest Phillips, who served Los Baños for one year.

In 1958, the Rev. Walter Clarke was appointed Vicar of St. Alban's. During the next few years, the Mission experienced steady growth, and became a Parish in 1961. The church also acquired and installed a 13-rank pipe organ during his tenure. It is probably the only instrument of its kind in the area. Fr. Clarke became St. Alban's first Rector.

In 1965, Fr. Robert Adams was called as second Rector, and served for five years. Financial reverses, however, led to a reversion to Mission status in 1970. Fr. Edward Wicher came as Vicar, and under his leadership the Parish Hall was built. It was dedicated by Bishop Rivera in October, 1971.

In 1973, James Conrad, Jr., as a new Deacon, was appointed Vicar. During his six-year tenure, the Mission saw much growth and vitality. Lay Readers were trained and licensed, and a Church Library was created. Unfortunately, he had to leave under a cloud. Fr. Philip Swickard served as interim Vicar from 1980 to early 1982.

In October, 1982, the Rev. Leland Peterson came from the Diocese of San Diego. Under his leadership the Mission continued to grow in numbers, and was self-supporting for 1983 and 1984. The grounds were improved, and additions made to the church plant. Links were fostered, too, with the Cathedral and Abbey Church of St. Alban's in England. In 1985, St. Alban's hosted the 26th Annual Community Prime Rib Dinner, with over 500 in attendance. The Shrove Tuesday Pancake Supper is a local institution; and a Seder-type supper was held Maundy Thursday. In Eastertide, an outdoor service and parish barbecue is a regular feature of parish life. As part of Venture in Mission, St. Alban's was one of the few congregations in the Diocese to produce a plan for local mission, even though, in the end, the plans did not materialize due to lack of local support from other churches. In 1986 Fr. Peterson went to St. Paul's, Modesto, as an assistant.

The Bishop appointed the Rev. Dr. George Mullins, a priest of the Archdiocese of Melbourne, as interim. Fr. Mullins was on leave from Australia to do special study in the U. S. on Church Growth principles. The congregation was sad to see him and his wife leave at the end of May, 1987. In late summer, the Bishop appointed the Rev. Mark Hall to Los Baños. Fr. Hall had served St. Alban's briefly as an interim several years before, and the congregation had asked for permission to call him as their Vicar.

THE CHURCH OF ST. STEPHEN, DEACON & MARTYR, STOCKTON

As a result of mission outreach by St. John's Church, Stockton, St. Stephen's came into being in 1954. The Rev. Max Drake, curate at St. John's, became the first Vicar. Property was acquired by St. John's, before the freeway route for I-5 through Stockton was known. The entire west side of Plymouth Road was residential housing. It was even considered for a time that St. John's Church itself might relocate there from the then declining inner city.

The first service was held on October 10, 1954, in the home of Mrs. Inez Henderson Pond. For the next year, the Eucharist was celebrated weekly in her home until the church building was finished in 1955. During the first year, the children remained at St. John's for Sunday School, and only a small group of adults attended these Sunday services. Bishop Walters, who lived in Stockton, was present for the first Christmas Eucharist in the temporary quarters, and lent his moral support to the mission.

In 1955, the 3 acre oatfield site was given by St. John's to the new mission. A "temporary building" was purchased from the U. S. Government and refurbished for opening services in October, 1955. On the day before the first service, an old organ from St. Timothy's, Bishop was brought in and hastily assembled. Seventy-nine communicants were transferred to St. Stephen's from St. John's to form the nucleus of the first congregation.

The year 1956 saw a wing added to the north, which served as social hall and class rooms for several years. Fr. Laurence S. Mann came as second Vicar in October, 1956, and the mission grew rapidly, so that in 1961, 260 baptized, and 190 communicants were listed. A vicarage on Country Club Boulevard was built, then the present Parish Hall, and an electronic organ was installed.

When Fr. Harry Leigh-Pink became Vicar in 1964, the vicarage was not large enough for his family, so it was sold, and the present one built on church property. The Altar and its furnishings were given to St. Stephen's as a memorial of his wife by Malcolm Cuett. The pews were purchased as gifts by church members.

From May, 1968, to October, 1971, Fr. Kenneth Schildt was Vicar, and there was a good deal of activity with the young people, as the "Post-war Baby Boom" peaked. Fr. Jerry Roberts was Vicar from January, 1972 to September, 1974. He was followed by Fr. Richard Williams, from October, 1974, until forced to retire by ill health in February, 1977.

From February to September, St. Stephen's was without a Vicar, and the laity were called upon to work together to keep St. Stephen's going. When the Rev. James Stanton was called it resulted in a "new lease on life" for St. Stephen's. A building program was instituted, and optimistic plans drawn for a new church to be located on the rear of the property as far from the freeway as possible. Fr. Stanton left in December, 1981, to accept a call to a church in the mid-West. Plans for the achievement of Parish status were postponed and eventually shelved.

For the next eight months St. Stephen's was again without a Vicar. Once more it was the laity who held things together. The Rev. James Sanford came as Vicar in September, 1982. He remained until May, 1984, to return to his former mid-western diocese.

Following another lengthy interregnum, Fr. Donald Seeks was appointed Vicar in late 1985, and under his leadership there is once more a hopeful spirit, the parish is engaged in outreach to the unchurched around them, and there is good reason to hope for growth both in numbers and in spirituality under Fr. Seeks' able leadership.

ST. LUKE'S PARISH, BAKERSFIELD

St. Luke's began early in the Fall of 1955, when a group of 12 families from St. Paul's Church met to organize a new Mission on the hill in East Bakersfield. It was there that Fr. Francisco Garces proposed a mission in May, 1776, when he saw the bluffs above the Rio de San Felipe (now the Kern). He was the first of the European "boat people" to visit what is now Kern County. The Native Americans welcomed him gladly. By the 1950s, this area was now being subdivided and Bakersfield City College was relocated to the hilltop.

Bishop Walters appointed the Vicar of Delano, Fr. E. Leslie Rolls, as Priest-in-charge; he was assisted by Fr. John Keester, then Vicar of St. Peter's Church, Arvin. Fr. Keester actually conducted the first service for St. Luke's on October 2, 1955, in the Knights of Pythias Hall.

In 1956, the small congregation secured a three acre site on Mt. Vernon Avenue beside the freeway route. By August, 1957, the first full-time Vicar had come, in the person of Fr. Luther Williams a former Church Army Captain. A double-barracks building was used for worship. The present Parish Hall was built in 1959 and served as "church" for a number of years. The barracks became church school rooms.

St. Luke's grew rapidly and attained Parish status in the early 1960s, under the leadership of Fr. Gordon Ashby. He was elected the first Rector. Fr. John D. Spear came as Rector in May, 1967. In August, 1970, he left to become Dean of St. James Cathedral, Fresno.

Fr. Spear was succeeeded by Fr. John Wilcox. On January 28, 1973, the church building was finished and dedicated. Under Fr. Wilcox's leadership, the parish grew lively in spiritual renewal. Fr. Wilcox resigned in May, 1981, to go as Vicar of St. Dunstan's, Modesto.

The Rev. John Galagan was called from Wyoming as the fourth Rector. He remained until June, 1984. For a time he served as Chaplain-Director of Kern Hospice. He was then called as Vicar of St. Jude's-in-the-Mountains, Tehachapi.

In September, 1984, Bishop Rivera appointed Fr. James B. Denson from Chicago as Priest-in-charge. With some independent means he was able to accept a salary less than the diocesan minimum which enabled St. Luke's to struggle along during a period of reduced income and some internal division. Fr. Denson was called as Rector, against the Bishop's wishes, and as a result was never instituted. In 1986, Fr. Denson suffered a massive stroke and was forced to retire on permanent disability. Local clergy served as interim supply.

In late 1986, the Rev. Duane Thebeau was called as Rector. He had for many years been Rector of St. Anne's, Oceanside.

ST. MARK'S CHURCH, SHAFTER

The town of Shafter was created by the Santa Fe Railroad and Kern County Land Company in 1911. It was named for a celebrated Spanish-American War General. This was where the Santa Fe tracks crossed the Lerdo Highway, the county road. Potatoes, onions, and other root crops were the first economic base. The Shafter potatoes refrigeration requirement, together with nematodes and other soil pests have changed that. Almonds and grapes, but more especially cotton, now dominate the agricultural scene. In early days a Mennonite colony settled in Shafter. Dust Bowl refugees came in large numbers during the Depression years. Nearby oil fields have both accelerated and destabilized Shafter's growth and economy. City fathers chose a slow growth policy in building several years ago, which is now regretted. There is a deep sense of "old families" in charge in the town of Shafter; some feel they "haven't made it" into those ranks after 20 years.

A few dedicated Episcopalian families lived in Shafter in the early 1950s, commuting to St. Paul's, Bakersfield, for services. Mrs. Eleanor Kelly approached Bishop Walters about establishing a church in Shafter and he gave tentative approval. Mr. and Mrs. William Arnold and Mrs. Genevieve Cooper asked Fr. Leslie Rolls of Delano to begin holding services for about a dozen people. Meetings and services were held in homes. Fr. Rolls came from Delano in the evenings, first conducting only Evening Prayer. Later, he began to come on Sunday mornings after services in Delano. Bishop Walters met with the Shafter group, and perceiving that nothing would deter them, he gave his blessing to their plan of a Shafter congregation and promised to work with them closely. At that time Fr. Rolls suggested they adopt the name of "St. Mark's" for the new mission. This was accepted unanimously. (Fr. Rolls was involved at the same time in starting St. Luke's, Bakersfield.) St. Mark's was admitted into union with the Convocation on January 22, 1956, in the motion preceding that for admitting St. Luke's.

By early 1956, the congregation grew so that it could no longer be held in a private home. For a time, the guest house of the Ed Browns at 340 Mannel Avenue was used. The mission rented a building for a few months and outgrew it, and so rented a larger space at 135 Shafter Avenue, which came to be known affectionately as "the tin building." The first service was held there on October 7, 1956. Members from Wasco, 8 miles north, and Buttonwillow, on the west side of the Valley, began to swell St. Mark's numbers.

Bill and Maud Arnold made the trip each weekend from their mountain cabin, 82 miles away, to help set up the altar for services. Fr. Rolls celebrated the Eucharist once a month. Bill Arnold meanwhile hand-crafted many of the items for the services, such as altar rails, processional Cross, candlesticks, hymn-number boards, lectern, and so forth. Various other furnishings, the first organ, kneelers, etc., were generously donated by members of the founding families, and by St. Luke's, Bakersfield, as well as by St. Therese's Roman Catholic Church in Shafter.

Plans were soon in motion for a permanent building; the Episcopal Church Women were unstinting in their efforts to raise money for it. St. Mark's E.C.W. was first organized in 1955, with Mrs. Marjorie Brown as first President. By 1959, 38 families were listed at St. Mark's. In July, 1958, Edward L. Key came as first resident Vicar; he was ordained Deacon in September, 1958. Previously, he had served as a pastor for three years in the Congregational Church. Bishop Walters ordained him Priest in the Tin Building in March, 1958. He served until June, 1963.

Enthusiasm for the new church was growing apace, fund-raiser affairs were held, and the Ohanneson family donated a piece of land on Beech Avenue, two lots of which were later sold for further funds. The ground-breaking ceremony was held on Saturday, July 30, 1960, attended by the Bishop, Dean Lee of Fresno, and others. Work began in early August, scheduled for three phases. Phase I was the building of a parish hall as a temporary church, to seat 120, with two school rooms, office, and kitchen. Phase II was a series of classrooms, separated by accordion screens, that open into one large room. Phase III was to be a permanent church, which has not yet been done. The present "temporary" church was occupied in early 1961.

In September, 1963, the Rev. John D. Spear came into the Diocese as Vicar of St. Mark's, and served there until April, 1967. During his time, the Christian Education Building (Phase II) was completed. Ground-breaking was in October, 1965, and dedication took place on January 30, 1966. It was designated by the Bishop's Committee as a memorial to the late Marjorie Brown, as much of the funding was given in her memory. Fr. Bruce Spencer followed Fr. Spear in September, 1967. He served until he was called to Ridgecrest. Fr. Spencer is remembered by many as a firmly orthodox teacher of the faith.

Fr. Boardman C. Reed was St. Mark's fourth Vicar, from November, 1970, to February, 1973. He was a Prayer Book traditionalist, opposed to the novel liturgical "trial uses".

Dana O. Howard, originally of Taft, was ordained Deacon at Shafter in August, 1973, then ordered Priest the following year. He remained at St. Mark's until August, 1979, when he left to test a vocation in the Order of the Holy Cross at its Mother House in New York State. His was the longest tenure to that date. The church was given a definitely "High Church" veneer: a figure of the Risen Christ, carved in Italy, replaced the altar cross; a figure of the Blessed Virgin Mary was placed in the entry alcove, with votive lights. An ikon of the Virgin painted by a priest of Holy Cross, with its lamp, was put on the wall. "The Mass" was made the standard Sunday service, and incense was used regularly. Fellowship in the church was accented with numerous parties at the Pine Street vicarage and elsewhere, and on occasion police were called by scandalized Shafterites to investigate the observance of Shrove Tuesday/Mardi Gras. Some people journeyed from Bakersfield, attracted by Fr. Howard's dramatic sermons, liturgical style, and the smaller congregation. Those who disapproved were invited to leave. As a consequence, intense feelings of loyalty and disaffection were generated. Fr. Howard died in 1986 after a lengthy bout with Lou Gehrig's disease.

Fr. J. Frederick Johnson became Vicar in December, 1979, and served until April, 1981. He had a difficult time following in Fr. Howard's popular footsteps. The vicarage was sold and income was used for clergy housing. Fr. Mark Lawrence came on a "temporary basis", but served from August, 1981, until September, 1984. The church was packed for his farewell service. He sought to bring a strong consciousness of the Bible and its direction for the Church today, but left feeling very frustrated. During his time, however, St. Mark's people pledged more than their alloted share to Venture in Mission, and took on a measure of support for SAMS (the Anglican South American Missionary Society.) His departure left many in the congregation depressed and angry.

Recognizing the need for stability, Fr. Christopher Kelley came as Vicar in February, 1985. He tried to cultivate the artistic talents in the congregation, supervising the creation of several processional banners. One was to be a replica of the banner brought by Fr. Francisco Garces on his trip to the San Joaquin Valley in 1776. Some church members, however, thought it was "too Roman Catholic." Fr. Kelley also endeavored to encourage the Wasco members to become the nucleus of a new congregation there, since Wasco is considerably larger than Shafter. This proved to be premature.

For the church's 25th Anniversary service there was a large congregation with Fr. John Spear, now Rector of St. Paul's, Bakersfield, and Rural Dean, preaching for the occasion in February, 1986. Several friends of the congregation assisted financially with interior repainting and exterior refurbishing. This helped provide a needed morale boost, but the economic decline in oil and farming have continued to take their toll. Fr. Kelley, having been recently married, accepted an appointment as assistant at St. James' Cathedral in 1986.

In September, 1987, an English priest, Fr. Robbins, former Dean of the Cathedral in Panama City, Panama, was appointed Vicar.

ST. MATTHEW'S CHURCH, SAN ANDREAS

Calaveras County, famous for its annual jumping frog contest, is part of the California Mother Lode history. An Episcopal Church at Mokelumne Hill was pioneered by hardware merchant and active layreader H. H. Nagel, who, virtually single-handedly, constructed St. Paul's Church there in 1895. It would seat 30, and had a steeple over the entrance. When the boom at "Moke Hill" went bust, Mr. Nagel moved on to Randsburg in the Mojave Desert, where he did the same thing again, and so quickly that other denominational churches despaired of setting up any competing work among childen. As Moke Hill's economy crumbled, the church was left to ruin. Any who wanted spare parts took whatever they needed. A stained glass fragment was salvaged, however, and now adorns St. Matthew's, San Andreas, the gift of Goldia Shuck. The Mokelumne Hill property on Chilicita Street was sold by Bishop Sanford in 1940.

In 1955, two women, Betsey Metzger and Herchse Allen, agreed that the County needed an Episcopal Church. On November 27, Mr. and Mrs. Robert Allen opened their home to a meeting of local Episcopalians. The Rector of Sonora, the Rev. Leonard Dixon, and his wife were in attendance. A first service was held on December 11, at 5 P.M., in the Fire Hall at Murphys, a town in the Gold Country. Fr. Dixon, his wife, and three children came from Sonora every Sunday, regardless of the weather, to conduct services and Sunday School. Average attendance was 22. In February, services were transferred to St. Basil's Serbian Orthodox Church in Angels' Camp, because it was more centrally located. In March, 1956, the Bishop's Committee was appointed, and plans were made for becoming an organized mission. On Easter Sunday, April 21, Bishop Walters came, and the Episcopalians made use of the Seventh Day Adventists building in Altaville. Location and more space made this attractive.

During July and August, 1956, the Bishop placed a seminarian in Calaveras County to do a survey of active and potential members. He conducted Morning Prayer, at least on Sundays, at 9 A.M. On September 17, a meeting was held and the Women's Auxiliary was formed. They undertook to provide hymnals, cassocks and cottas for the boys ready to become acolytes, and kneeling cushions for the pews. Mr. O. L. Kenfield, having been a licensed Lay Reader in Nebraska, conducted services, and was chairman of the Bishop's Committee. On January 28, 1957, St. Matthew's Mission, was received into union with Convocation. Services up to the first Confirmation, March 3, 1957, were held in the Adventists' building. From March 10, 1957, to April 10, 1960, they were held in the Gardella Mortuary Chapel; Sunday School classes met in other parts of the chapel, or in the Boy Scout Hut across the street.

In June, 1957, the Bishop appointed seminarian Edward Murphy to conduct regular Morning Prayer services, relieving Fr. Dixon. A year later he was ordained Deacon, and in December, 1958, he was priested; both ordinations were at St. James', Sonora. He de-emphasized the Episcopal connection in an attempt to build a "Community church". This proved quite success-ful; the Sunday School doubled in size, and 63 communicants in "good standing" were listed.

In June, 1958, St. Matthew's purchased land from Jack and Blanche Lodato in San Andreas, on Oak Street, overlooking the northern part of the business district. Serious planning for construction began in February, 1959. On Friday, November 5, 1959, the ground-breaking ceremony was held with Bishop Walters and some 55 people present. The San Francisco firm of F. W. Johnson was engaged as architects. Construction was supervised by Charles Bloom of

Shepherd and Green Contractors in Stockton. The building was erected for the modest sum of $40,273.55. Mr. DuPont Vincent created the mosaics on the front of the building. The materials were purchased for $500. The first service was conducted in the new building on Easter Sunday, 1960, with a few pews in place and many temporary chairs. Bishop Walters dedicated it on Sunday, May 22, 1960.

A second building campaign was launched in 1962, to put up a hall and rooms. This was built and dedicated on April 2, 1963. Fr. Murphy left in August, 1963, and was followed by Leon R. MacDougall (October 20, 1963-June 30, 1967). Under the leadership of Carl Persall, the vicarage, on adjacent property was purchased from Alfred and Judy Whited at the end of 1963 for $11,500. Fr. Robert P. Slocum served as Vicar from November 16, 1967 to December 7, 1969. The Memorial Funds allowed for the purchase of an Allen organ in July, 1969, at a cost of $8,700. It replaced an antique reed organ on loan from the diocese.

The Rev. Ronald W. James was Vicar from May, 1970, to January 4, 1971. The Rev. Robert L. Stevenson was Vicar from April 1, 1971, to March 1, 1975. The Rev. Thomas Corrigan was Vicar from April 1, 1975 to January 31, 1979. The Rev. Robert Downs, Jr. with his new bride from Holland, arrived September 1, 1979, and served through September, 1984. During this time the E.C.W. improved the kitchen facilities under direction from Milligan Hereford. Extensive repairs were done on the mosaics because of weathering.

The Rev. James G. Bingham, formerly on the staff of the National Church in New York, became interim Vicar from January, 1985, through July, 1986. Under his able leadership there was a renewal of spirit in the congregation and new members were added. The last debts on St. Matthew's were paid off, and on St. Matthew's Day, 1985, the mortgage was burned and a church cornerstone was laid with the assistance of local Masons in the congregation. A set of beautiful eucharistic vestments and a cope was made by Ruth Clyatt. Fr. Bingham was succeeded by the Rev. Randall Rainwater, formerly on the Cathedral staff in Fresno. Newly married, he and his wife, Susan, have continued the good work begun by Fr. Bingham and the congregation continues to thrive under Fr. Randy's ministry.

ST. MARY'S CHURCH, MANTECA

Manteca ("butter" in Spanish) is near Stockton. For some time, Episcopalians resident in Manteca attended St. John's, Stockton, for services. In 1956, Fr. Paul Langpaap, Rector of St. John's, with the help of Mrs. Ed (Carolyn) Fatzer, and Evelyn McFall, was instrumental in forming the mission. In the late Spring, Fr. Langpaap, assisted by a number of Deanery clergy and several Manteca laity, made a survey of about 2800 homes in Manteca. As a result, it was decided to establish a mission work in the city. Mrs. Fatzer is credited with naming the Mission for St. Mary the Virgin, daughter of St. Joachim (San Joaquin) and St. Anne. A Bishop's Committee was appointed, and St. Mary's was received into union with the Convocation on January 29, 1957. Robert T. Fortna, on the faculty of Church Divinity School of the Pacific, was the first Deacon-in-charge, taking services on weekends.

Before the church was built, services were held in various locations, requiring much moving of books, the organ, and altar supplies. None of the places used had storage space available for these things. Ronald Swanson, a seminarian at C.D.S.P., was assigned to take Sunday services in

January, 1958. The building project was begun in June. By September, 1960, the building was ready for dedication. September 4, the Sunday nearest to the Feast of the Nativity of the Virgin (September 8), was chosen for this event. By this time, Fr. John Wilcox was Vicar. He, Mrs. Fatzer and Mrs. McFall, with others, labored energetically to raise money for the church to have a home.

Fr. B. Stanley Moore followed Fr. Wilcox as Vicar, from 1963 to 1967. During this time a vicarage and parish hall were built. Fr. Thomas Corrigan served at Manteca from 1967, then was given the added charge of St. Mark's, Tracy. He became Vicar of Tracy in 1969. After Fr. Corrigan, Fr. Gordon C. Ashbee became Vicar until his retirement on December 31, 1971. In 1972, the Rev. Percy Jerkins took the Mission, until he was forced to retire due to failing health in summer, 1983. He was followed by Fr. Maurice Furlonger, a priest from England. His wife, June, became organist and choir director. For a time, Fr. Furlonger has assisted at St. John's, Stockton, on a part-time basis, to relieve St. Mary's budget. Over the years, this has been reduced as financial stability has been achieved in Manteca. At this writing, he assists at St. John's one day a week, although St. Mary's now feels capable of supporting him full-time.

CHRIST CHURCH, LEMOORE

In 1880, Lemoore was larger than Hanford. Some people in Lemoore invited the Rev. D. O. Kelley to visit from Fresno. He came on Wednesday night, February 18, and held a service in Lemoore. At the time, not much more happened in Lemoore, but two sets of English brothers had come from Hanford for that service, and invited Fr. Kelley to celebrate the Holy Communion for them the next morning in Hanford. "St. John's Mission, Tulare County" was organized on February 19, 1880, to embrace Tulare City, Lemoore, and Hanford. (King's County was created by taking the west end of Tulare County in 1893).

By 1946, Lemoore was again being considered a suitable site for a chapel of Hanford. There were about 20 Episcopalians known in the "trading center . . . of about 3,000 people." Before long, 40 families were being counted who had some sort of "contact with the Episcopal form of worship" but were "largely an unchurched group, and did not draw from any other Christian body."

An organizing meeting for Christ Church Mission was held on September 20, 1956. The first service was held on Sunday, February 24, 1957, in the Alpha Clubhouse, 320 B Street, a 100 year-old building, originally the Santa Fe Railroad Station House. John Hancock, Rector of Hanford, officiated at Morning Prayer. Two weeks later, Bishop Walters celebrated Holy Communion on the first Sunday of Lent.

In 1957, the Pentagon announced that a Naval Air Station would be built at Lemoore, confirming years of rumor. It was expected that 5,000 men and their families would be brought to the area, and prospects for growth were seen to be excellent. Bishop Walters assigned several Church Divinity School of the Pacific seminarians to take Sunday services. These were Eugene Harshman, Andrew MacDonald, and Hugh Miller. Upon ordination as Deacon, Hugh Miller became the first full-time Vicar of Lemoore. The Mission was accepted by Convocation on January 27, 1958.

The Alpha Clubhouse soon became too small for the growing congregation, and plans were made for a building. By 1960, a vicarage and land for a building site were bought, and $10,000 was granted from the 1959 Church School Missionary Offering towards construction of the first unit. Another survey in 1961 showed excellent prospects for continued growth. Average attendance was about 70 per week, with three Sunday services. The congregation had five licensed Lay Readers. By November, 1961, the Rev. M. Fletcher Davis was Vicar; however, in 1963, he accepted a call to Porterville as their Rector.

The Rev. Stanley R. Sinclair, came in 1963, and surprised the members by designing a building himself. On December 8, 1967, that structure was dedicated by Bishop Walters. Two days later, Evensong was conducted by a combined Deanery and interdenominational service. A month later, Bishop Arnold Lewis, Suffragan Bishop for the Armed Forces, visited and dedicated the nave in honor of the men lost in Viet Nam. This was an auspicious beginning for a fledgling mission that served many members from the nearby Naval Air Station. Fr. Sinclair left in 1969 to succeed the Rev. Victor M. Rivera as Rector of Visalia, Fr. Rivera having been elected third Bishop of San Joaquin.

The lack of space for a Christian Education program was soon felt; a small building was moved onto the church property and remodeled to serve as a Sunday School building. Playground equipment and fencing were added, and a Project Head Start Center was located at Christ Church to provide pre-school education to minority and disadvantaged children. Lawn and trees were added to make the area more attractive.

The Rev. Roger Jones became Vicar of Lemoore, and served from 1974 to 1976. An acolyte once asked him about an observance in the Church, and Fr. Jones told him it was in memory of the men who had died in the service. The startled boy asked, "Which one? The 8' or the 10'?" Fr. Jones left to become the Rector of St. Anne's, Stockton, and was succeeded by the Rev. Terrell Hamilton who began serving while still a Deacon. He was subsequently ordered a Priest in December, 1980. He left to become an Air Force chaplain in 1985. His successor, Fr. E. James Kinglsey, a retired Air Force chaplain, served for one year and left to become an Assistant at St. James' Cathedral, and part-time chaplain for the Fresno Veterans' Administration Hospital. At the time of this writing Lemoore is being served by the Rev. William Burberry and other clergy as supply priests.

THE CHURCH OF THE EPIPHANY, CORCORAN

Corcoran is located in eastern King's County, about 13 miles west of Highway 99, and beside Highway 43. It is a farming community with a small amount of industry on the east edge of town along the Santa Fe Railroad line. A geological feature of importance to the whole Central Valley is the "Corcoran Lake claybed," several hundred feet below the surface, which seals the watertable below from the chemical pollution above. In ancient times, "Corcoran Lake" covered the floor of the Valley.

On December 18, 1956, a meeting was held in the home of Mr. and Mrs. Allan Smith to discuss the establishment of an Episcopal Church in Corcoran. The meeting was led by Fr. John Wilcox from Tulare. Present were Mr. and Mrs. Gary Frame, Mrs. Allan Smith, Mrs. Bea Kelton, Mr. Richard Schallhorn, Mrs. Dorothy McDonald, and Mr. Robert House. With the blessing of Bishop Walters, the first Eucharist was conducted on the Feast of the Epiphany, January 6, 1957. This was the anniversary of Bishop Walters' consecration in 1944, and was also related to the discovery of El Rio de los Reyes by the Spanish, on the same date, which gave King's County its name. Fr. Wilcox held the service in the Bledsoe Mortuary Chapel on Waukene Road. Thereafter, services were held every other Sunday for a year.

The Mortuary relocated into town, and the services moved with it in 1958, although by fall of 1957, talk of a separate building was well advanced. A Sunday School had begun, meeting in a dentist's office. The Diocesan Investment Trust granted a loan of $13,500, and ground was broken on May 25, 1958. Bishop Walters was assisted in this by Fr. Wilcox and Fr. Caley of Coalinga. Construction began in July, 1958, and the building was completed and dedicated on November 15, 1958. Pews were loaned to Epiphany by Our Lady of Lourdes Roman Catholic Church. For four months these pews were moved over every Saturday night and returned on Sunday, until the present pews were put in.

The Rev. Mr. Edward Shankland, a perpetual Deacon, was sent to serve the mission until June, 1959, when the Rev. Ronald Swanson became Epiphany's first full-time Vicar. During his time the Birthday Thank Offering gave $5,000 toward a classroom wing, named in honor of Bishop Sumner Walters.

In 1967, the Estate of Guy and Rose Bliss designated a sizeable sum both to the District of San Joaquin and to the Church of the Epiphany. This was enough to pay off all debts on the building, and the church was formally consecrated by Bishop Walters on the Feast of the Epiphany, 1968. The rest of the Bliss Estate made possible the creation of Bliss Grove on 40 acres at Oakhurst.

Since that time, the Mission has known its triumphs — one of the star Sunday School programs in the Diocese, and about the highest per capita pledging, even though most of the congregation are employed in service-related jobs, or teaching, none of them highpaying positions. The Mission has also known its down times as leaders moved from the community, and long periods went by without a resident Vicar.

Various clergy have served the Church of the Epiphany since Fr. Swanson. These include Fr. William Tumbleson, Fr. Edwin Shackleford, Fr. Richard Vaggione, and Fr. Dana Howard, who came to them when it was known that he was dying of "Lou Gehrig's Disease" at the time. Capt. Herman Buck of the Church Army also served the mission for a time, functioning as a layman.

ST. MARY'S PARISH, FRESNO

Under the direction of Bishop Sumner Walters, the Rev. Wayne Parker, Vicar of St. Mark's, Tracy, came to Fresno one day a week in early 1958 to do survey work for a new mission in Southeast Fresno. Fr. Parker was assisted and encouraged by the Rev. George Woodgates, then Rector of St. Columba's, Fresno, and by Mr. and Mrs. Bert Taylor, Communicants of St. Columba's, who subsequently became members of the new mission.

Thus, Grace Mission, Fresno, was founded in 1958, and Fr. Parker became the first Vicar. The inaugural service was held on May 4, 1958, in what was known as the "Marion Nine Hospitality Room" on East Kings Canyon Road. It was the only place then available in the neighborhood for public meetings. Services continued there until March 1, 1959, when the congregation rented Hagopian Hall (formerly Locan School) at Temperance and Kings Canyon.

Some members of the congregation were dissatisfied with the name of Grace Mission. They believed that this would lead to confusion since there were so many denominational churches named Grace Church. From a list of names submitted to Bishop Walters, he chose St. Mary's, and the church was admitted as an organized mission of the Diocese of San Joaquin in 1959 under that name.

The first Bishop's Warden of St. Mary's Mission was Dr. Fred Havrilla, a dentist, and the second was Dr. A. W. Pearson, a dental surgeon, who continued to worship in, and support, St. Mary's until he moved out of the city in the late 1970s. With St. Mary's from the beginning, including the organizational meeting, until now, is William B. Aukerman. He was on the first Bishop's Committee and has served as Lay Reader, Chorister, and in many other ways all through the years. Other pioneers: the late James Kunkel, organist and choirmaster for many years; Martha Paliwoda, the Jack Knutsen family, the Bennett Levinsons, the Dorsey Elgins, Mrs. Dorothy Gonzales, and of course, the Bert Taylors.

As with most new missions, the early years of St. Mary's were marked by a hard struggle to meet its budget and to recruit members from the Sunnyside, and other likely areas, including Sanger. 1960, after one full year as an organized mission, saw a communicant strength of 43 in the congregation, with 40 financial pledges.

In the Vicar's Report to the congregation at the Annual Meeting in January, 1960, it is noted: "The purchase of land which took so much time and energy and discussion this past year, has been made. This is a significant accomplishment. We paid perhaps the highest price ever paid for land by a new mission in San Joaquin's history, but we have the best church site in our valley in relation to our community." Six acres of land has been purchased at the corner of Kings Canyon Road and Burgan Avenue, two acres of which were sold for enough to halve the cost of the whole. Financing for the remainder, and also the building costs, was arranged through the Bishop's office. The present building, an all-purpose, classroom-type, building was dedicated on June 15, 1963. It contains an altar of native granite dedicated in memory of Margaret Bundy Parker, the wife of Fr. Parker.

In March, 1965, Fr. Parker suffered a stroke and had to retire from the active ministry. In June, 1965, the Rev. Richard Henry was appointed the second Vicar of St. Mary's Mission.

The struggle was not yet over, financially. But January, 1970, reports show 124 Communicants in Good Standing and a budget for the year of $19,684.

By 1976, however, St. Mary's had reached the self-support stage and, after serving one year's probation, was admitted as a parish of the Diocese of San Joaquin in February, 1977. Fr. Henry was immediately elected Rector.

In 1984, St. Mary's maintained a mailing list of over 200 members and interested friends in the community, buildings and land were free and clear of debt, and record attendance and income were reported for the year.

In the effort to affirm our belief that a parish church should be a lighthouse to the world around it, St. Mary's opens its doors to a number of religious and community organizations. The congregation, in 1985, had just completed a three year period of sharing facilities with a local Baptist congregation, an arrangement which proved to be an interesting and growing experience for both groups.

St. Mary's is also involved in outreach to the community. It has participated in initiating the first ecumenical St. Vincent de Paul Society program in the community, involving the Episcopal, Methodist and Roman Catholic parishes in the neighborhood. Rector and members are involved at the diocesan level in Hispanic Ministry and Asian Refugee Ministry, both of which are located in the area.

Playing no small part in the growth and success of St. Mary's in the last two decades is the Rev. Dr. Richard Henry (D. Min.). Under his direction and guidance, a 1984 goal-setting meeting endorsed and applauded plans looking toward expansion of facilities within the near future to more adequately serve the community and better provide the needs of our present and projected membership.

ST. CLEMENT OF ALEXANDRIA MISSION, WOODLAKE

St. Clement's began its life as an Episcopal congregation on February 22, 1959, as the "Shepherd of the Hills Church" in Lemon Cove, with a service of Holy Eucharist celebrated by the Rev. Victor Rivera of St. Paul's, Visalia. Regular services of Morning Prayer were conducted by St. Paul's Lay Readers, with a monthly communion service by one of St. Paul's clergy. The first meeting place was the Lemon Cove Women's Club House. In March, 1960, at a congregational meeting chaired by Father Vic, the decision was made to move to Woodlake, and the first Woodlake service was held in the home of Ned and Karyll Baker, who are still active members of the congregation. It was decided to purchase the Jobe Home on Valencia Blvd. and to remodel it as a church building. The congregation was renamed St. Clement of Alexandria, in honor of the priest and theologian.

In January, 1961, Sister Anne Harrison, Church Army, arrived and served for one and one-half years as Missioner-in-charge. During her tenure, numerous surveys of the community and surrounding areas were made. In October, 1962, she was succeeded by the Rev. Sheldon Rankin as Vicar. Extensive renovation of the building was undertaken. The second story of the house was removed, and a 26 foot extension was made to form the nave of the church. A brick veneer was added to the outside, to give the building its present appearance. Growth continued, and one month after dedication of the church building, construction began on a parish hall to serve the church school and other purposes. It was completed in October, 1965.

In November, 1966, the Rev. William K. Morrison was appointed Vicar of St. Clement's, having formerly served as a priest in the Anglican Church of Canada. During his three-year tenure, the congregation made many advances, particularly in the areas of education and community life.

On June 1, 1969, another person instrumental in the mission's beginning, became its Vicar, the Rev. Lyle A. McBee. He had formerly been in the printing business in Visalia, and was one of the

Lay Readers of St. Paul's who conducted the early services at Lemon Cove. Fr. McBee was appointed Vicar of St. Clement's and of St. James, Lindsay. Despite the need to divide his time, the Woodlake mission experienced a sustained period of growth. In his address to the 1971 Convention of the Diocese, Bishop Rivera noted that St. Clement's had shown "the greatest percentage of growth among all the churches of the diocese." In 1972, Fr. McBee accepted a call as Rector of St. Phillip's, Coalinga, and the Rev. George Turney was appointed Vicar, having previously been Rector of St. Columba's, Fresno, and Associate Rector of St. Paul's, Visalia.

In 1976, "Father T" again made the decision to retire, and the Rev. Donald Seeks, a non-stipendiary priest from the Diocese of Los Angeles was called as the new Vicar. He remained at St. Clements' longer than any of his predecessors, seven and one-half years, until December, 1984. During his tenure, the mission began to gather funds to establish a Day Care Center to bring the love of Christ to the little children of Woodlake Valley. An initial $7,000 was raised to provide the required funds for equipment and remodeling necessary to meet State requirements. St. Paul's, Visalia, enthusiastically supported this project of its daughter mission. Their E.C.W. sponsored a benefit luncheon, and was able to present Fr. Seeks with a check for $10,000 to provide continuing support for the new Center. It opened its doors in September, 1980, and St. Clement's thus became the first diocesan mission to have an established school program.

In 1985, the Rev. William Fay was appointed Vicar, and the congregation celebrated its 25th Anniversary in October, 1985, with a dinner attended by Bishops Rivera and Mize, and former Vicars Turney and Seeks. The Day Care Center's popularity was such that there was need to enlarge the parish hall to accommodate more children. Ground was broken in July, 1987, for a 3,000 squre foot addition which should be completed by the end of 1987.

At the Diocesan Convention of 1988, St. Clement's will have completed their 3-year probationary status and have hopes of being admitted as a full-fledged Parish in the Diocese of San Joaquin.

ST. DUNSTAN'S CHURCH, MODESTO

Modesto has rated as one of the fastest growing cities in California for the latter part of the 20th century. The idea of forming a second Episcopal congregation in Modesto was first seriously discussed with Bishop Walters in December, 1961. The impetus came, at least in part, from stress in St. Paul's congregation during the tenure of Fr. Charles Williams. The Vestry of St. Paul's voted that parish staff could not be involved in the effort and that the new mission would have to be a diocesan project.

With Bishop Walters' tentative permission, an initial meeting was held December 26, in the home of Dr. and Mrs. Ken Powers; fifteen were present. On January 4, 1962, Bishop Walters met with these and others. He urged the group to reevaluate motives and consider carefully the momentous task they were undertaking. One said, "It looked like a miracle would be required to obtain the Bishop's permission." On Sunday, January 21, it actually snowed in Modesto; that afternoon four men from the planning group met with the Bishop and received his permission to form a mission.

On January 31, the official organizational meeting was held in the M. I. D. Auditorium. The name of St. Dunstan, Archbishop of Canterbury (d. 988) was selected, and the first Bishop's Committee was nominated to the Bishop. It was determined that three of the nine members had to be women. Forty attended the meeting. Mr. Gordon Jeroch, a founder member, owned the Modesto Mortuary, which was used for the first service, Sunday, February 4: Morning Prayer followed by a sermon. Fr. Arthur Beckwith, recently retired from Oakdale, served as supply priest once a month. Lay Readers took a prominent role, conducting the other services.

From the second Sunday onward, services were held at the Sylvan Club until property was bought and a multi-purpose building was put up in 1965. Many churches contributed hymnals, cottas, cassocks, altar rail and lectern, and other appointments. Bishop Walters personally conducted the first Easter service. In May Fr. Beckwith was asked to take on weekly services. Inquiries for a permanent site began by June. Sunday School classes began with 9 teachers and 32 students. The entire Thanksgiving Offering at St. Paul's was given to the new neighbor mission for land, $341.56.

On May 13, 1963, a representative from St. Dunstan's met in Berkeley with Norman Van Walterop, then completing his studies at Church Divinity School of the Pacific. This had been suggested by Bishop Walters. On ordination, he became St. Dunstan's first full-time Vicar, with a monthly salary of $350. In the same month, a purchase agreement was signed for $13,000 to buy property. $10,000 of this was a grant from the Bishop. The site was selected in cooperation with St. Paul's. A no-interest loan for erection of the first building was from a fund ear-marked for missionary work in mainland China. The building was dedicated in 1965; members helped with the construction in many ways. Fr. Van Walterop continues to live in Modesto, but chose to make his living as a pharmacist after this time as Vicar of St. Dunstan's.

On March 22, 1967, Bishop Walters appointed R. W. James the next Vicar, while still completing his seminary studies. Beginning his ministry that summer, he saw to it that the building was air conditioned, and the parking lot was surfaced. On August 16, 1970, Bishop Rivera appointed Charles C. Carman the third Vicar. By September, 1972, there was interest in seeking Parish status from the next convention, but it was decided that the time was not yet ripe. Fr. Edward A. Wicher, Jr., became the fourth Vicar on Sunday, July 1, 1973. The Committee on New Parishes and Missions recommended St. Dunstan's admission as a parish that October; this recommendation was subsequently withdrawn before the Convention met in November.

On Sunday, July 21, 1974, ground was broken for the church building. Bishop Rivera celebrated and preached for the occasion. Construction of the unusual building took longer than expected, but costs were kept within the estimate of $95,000. The building was completed in March, and dedication took place on April 27, 1975. By 1985, the loan was entirely repaid and the mortgage burned. At the end of 1974, the Parochial Report showed 238 communicants and 55 church school pupils; property was valued at $97,000, and pledges for 1975 totalled $27,801.

Fr. Arthur Cunningham, a gifted preacher from Carmel, became the fifth Vicar in the fall of 1978, but resigned in 1980 for personal reasons. Fr. Tod Ewald, later to become famous as Rector of Holy Innocents' Church, Corte Madera, who provoked Bishop Pike's denunciation of the exercise of "charismatic gifts" in the Episcopal Church, became interim Vicar.

The Rev. John Wilcox, called from Bakersfield in 1981 as the sixth Vicar, served several years. Fr. Wilcox encouraged spiritual renewal through Cursillo and other avenues, although meeting with resistance from some members. He was called to Reedley as Rector of Good Sheperd in 1985. The Rev. Brian Endicott served as interim priest while the search was undertaken for a successor to Fr. Wilcox.

The Rev. Zealand Hillsdon-Hutton came from Sacramento in March, 1986, to be seventh Vicar. His wife, Valerie, has served with Church Army and has been active in diocesan and national affairs. Together they form a very effective team ministry and there is great hope of St. Dunstan's growing in numbers as well as spiritually through their ministry.

ALL SAINTS' CHURCH, BAKERSFIELD

By the mid-1960s it became evident that the open areas to the south and west around Bakersfield were ripe for development. In 1965, Bishop Walters and the Diocesan Council decided to buy three acres of land on the SE corner of Ming and New Stine from the Kern Land Company, anticipating future growth. At the time it was the home of kit foxes, squirrels and burrowing owls, and grazing land for sheep. The nearest building was the new West High School, half-mile away. In 1966, Bishop Walters appointed Fr. George Woodgates to head up the new work. He had established St. Columba's, Fresno, and was, at the time, on the staff of the National Church in New York.

The Woodgates moved to Bakersfield and in August, 1966, an organizational meeting was held in the Park Stockdale Club House. Bishop Walters attended and commissioned the new membership of nearly 50 people. The first service was held on September 11, in the cafeteria of St. Francis' Parochial School. Fifty attended. St. Paul's transferred to the new mission many of its parishioners who lived in the vicinity. It was soon necessary to find another location. In February, 1967, the new Valley Plaza Town Hall became the worship place, inspiring thoughts of a "Church in the market place." Visions included a child-care center, counselling services, and Chapel of Ease for weary shoppers; but the directors of Valley Plaza decided not to "mix religion with business" and All Saints' was asked to leave.

The next move was to an Adventist facility, available on the Lord's Day. Neighborhood groups were formed for prayer, study, and pastoral care. Semi-annual meetings were scheduled to establish continuing goals. There were dreams of "a parish without expensive buildings." The Adventists found that they needed their facility, so the congregation looked to the three acres set aside for it. A loan was secured from the Diocese to erect a 3,000 square foot multi-purpose building. This was dedicated in June, 1969, by the newly consecrated Bishop Rivera.

The building soon proved too small. In 1973 "a miracle" was seen as the church received an interest-free loan from the Nat'l. Church to put up a 5,000 square foot educational building, which would be used both as a 100-student Day Care Center during the week, and for parish activities in evenings and on weekends. The "Tackett Building", named in memory of a faithful layman, opened in February, 1974. In 1975, All Saints' won the Kern Deanery Banner for Church School Excellence.

The congregation was active in community service as well. Mrs. Sylvia Woodgates worked with other members in a county program to help adult illiterates. The Diocese contributed financially. By 1970, 45 tutors worked with over 100 students. Mrs. Woodgates was elected President of the Kern County Council and national Vice President. "Friends Outside" was another program. It was designed to help the families of prisoners in the county jail, and assist prisoners upon release. Camp San Joaquin, and the Cursillo movement were also supported by All Saints' members. A special ministry of Spiritual Healing was also carried on by Fr. Woodgates and some gifted laymen, centered on a regular Wednesday evening prayer service. Giving outside the congregation was seen from the beginning as necessary for the spiritual health of the members. Within months of the first organization, a minimum of $25 a month was given; it has grown to over $650 a month for projects and persons around the world.

In 1977, All Saints' was received into Parish status by the Diocesan Convention. On May 1, Fr. Woodgates was instituted as first Rector. At that time, a Purpose Statement was published:

The People of All Saints' are committed to:
-Jesus Christ
-His Church
-Calling Persons into His Church
-Ministering to the World, near and far.

Fr. Woodgates retired as Rector in December, 1979.

The Rev. John C. Keester accepted the call to become second Rector in March, 1980. He began work in the parish on May 15, and was instituted as Rector on June 29, Feast of Ss. Peter and Paul. His first assignment had been St. Peter's Mission in Arvin. Some of All Saints' people had been his parishioners before. He came to Bakersfield from Claremont, where he had established a reputation as a "Charismatic" Episcopalian.

In July, 1981, a surprise came. A buyer approached the Vestry with the idea of purchasing the land for a shopping center development, offering a handsome price. After much prayer the offer was accepted. The sale was consummated in October, 1982, and new land was purchased, one and one-half miles west, on Gosford Road. On November 28, 1982, Bishop Rivera presided at the ground-breaking service on the new site. On May 1, 1983, the new Tackett Building, a combined parish hall and Day Care Center, was ready for occupancy. Work on a new church building of unusual design began in December, 1984. It was first used for services on Palm Sunday, 1985, which was also Fr. Keester's last Sunday as Rector. He had accepted a call to St. Timothy's, Catonsville, Maryland.

After a lengthy interregnum, during which Fr. John Galagan served the congregation well as Interim Priest, the parish issued a call to Fr. Edward S. Little. He arrived in late Summer, 1986, as third Rector. Fr. Little had previously established a reputation as a "charismatic" Priest in his ministry at St. Joseph's Church, Buena Park. Under his able leadership All Saints' continues to be a center of spiritual renewal and teaching, offering the Diocese and Deanery programs with well-known speakers. There is every indication of continued growth under Fr. Little's leadership.

ST. ANDREW'S CHURCH, MARIPOSA

St. Andrew's was accepted into union with the Diocese at the Convention meeting February 6, 1970. It was the first mission in a lengthy list of missions established during Bishop Rivera's time as Bishop of the Diocese of San Joaquin. Its beginnings, however, were a decade earlier when on the first Sunday in Advent of 1960, a group of people interested in forming an Episcopal congregation had their first service in the American Legion Hall.

Evenso, services were held in Mariposa much earlier. The Rev. John Christianson, then with St. Lukes', Merced, held occasional service on Sunday evenings at the Tiscornia Chapel in Mariposa as early as 1949. Because San Joaquin was then a party to a comity agreement with the Methodist Church, Bishop Walters would not sanction a mission in Mariposa. Nevertheless, a group of people formed to meet as St. Peter's Episcopal Church at the old Bear Creek Lodge, Midpines (about seven miles east of Mariposa), but after a few years this effort was discontinued.

Several Episcopalian families traveled to Merced for a few years during which time the comity agreement expired. It was decided to form a church in Mariposa as an unorganized mission under the sponsorship of St. Luke's, Merced. The name, St. Andrew's, was chosen by Bishop Walters.

Soon after the beginning of the mission in 1960, the Rev. Jack Livingstone, Rector of St. Luke's, was involved in a train-car accident and could no longer function. He had been instrumental in supporting the Mariposa Mission.

The original "Chapel Committee" was headed by Warden, David C. Foster, and included Elizabeth Evans, Barbara Nichols, Gus Eastman, Vern Peter and Herb Davis, with Ruth Massey as clerk, and Fay Covert as treasurer. This group held the little congregation together and carried on the work begun by Father Livingstone. For several years the congregation met in the American Legion Hall in Mariposa, and was served by Lay Readers: David Foster, Vern Peter, Coyt Hackett, Herbert Davis and Mid Massey. A visiting priest or occasionally the Bishop came to celebrate the Holy Communion from time to time.

St. Andrew's had a small Church School and even a Junior Choir. Mrs. Carol Davis was one of the first teachers. The first confirmation class was presented to Bishop Walters in May of 1961.

Holding services in the American Legion Hall was always something of a trial. Chairs had to be set up, kneeling benches unstacked and placed, the organ removed from its protective case where it was kept locked during the week — all this after first sweeping the floor and, in winter, setting up small electric heaters to take the chill off the building. The altar was simply a turned-around desk and a dossal curtain was hung to hide a rifle case.

The year 1960 saw not only the purchase of the portable organ, but also negotiations with Judge Thomas Coakley of the Superior Court of Mariposa County for the purchase of 1.3 acres of land for a future building site. A building fund was started and members purchased "bricks" toward eventual construction of the church. The "bricks" were pictured on a large poster diagram and offered for sale.

Tiscornia Mortuary Chapel became available and the congregation moved there for Sunday services. During this period they were served by priests from Merced. This was never a convenient arrangement, however, and at one time the congregation was left without Holy Communion for six months. Bishop Rivera, newly consecrated, decided that a resident priest was needed.

During Fr. Clarke's tenure at St. Luke's, a special program was inaugurated in which the mission at Los Baños contributed $2,500. St. Andrew's was able to use $2,500 from their building fund and Mr. David Foster contributed an additional $2,500. These funds were used to commence the building.

Father Murphy, then at San Andreas, and Father Clarke came to Mariposa each Monday evening to lead discussion groups. This practice continued for several years. During these years St. Andrew's was having its struggles. With lay leadership not always available, and the availability of priests for Sunday services uncertain, progress was slow.

The Bishop's Committee decided that it was possible to proceed with the erection of a building on the site purchased earlier. This decision was urged along by the fact that Tiscornia Chapel was no longer available, and it became necessary to rent the use of the Seventh Day Adventist Church for about a year while the building was being erected.

The new building was dedicated February 18, 1973. Bishop Rivera presided, assisted by the lay leaders of the congregation. The Bishop's Committee petitioned for change from the status of unorganized mission to organized mission and this was approved.

Finding a resident priest was difficult, and it was not until November 4, 1973, that one was secured. The Rev. Robert Griswold served as Vicar until January 2, 1976. Up to this point in time, the congregation had never received any diocesan assistance. It was only with the coming of a resident priest that Bishop Rivera offered financial assistance for his support.

Following Fr. Griswold's departure the church was without a priest until April 17, 1977, when the Rev. Ellis Peterson came. He served until March 26, 1978. The Rev. Edward Parrot, Dean Harry Lee (then retired, but former Dean of St. James' Cathedral) and seminarian Robert Richard served the congregation. From January 21, 1979, until December 27, 1979, Fr. Thomas Corrigan, Vicar of St. Nicholas', Atwater, served both congregations.

The Rev. William L. Richmond, retired priest from Visalia, began serving on January 6, 1980, but was forced to leave after four months because of health reasons. The Rev. Kenneth German then came on July 7, 1980, and served until December 27, 1981. Fr. Richmond was able to resume his ministry and returned on January 1, 1982.

He continued to serve until poor health forced his resignation in 1983. There followed a period in which St. Andrew's was served by various priests as they were available, with Lay Readers taking the services for the most part. The Rev. Albert Walton and his wife Florence came in January, 1984. During their time pews were purchased by the Bishop's Committee, and the interior seating arrangement of the church was changed so that the congregation surrounded the altar on three sides. A mobile home was moved onto the property and was used as a residence by the Waltons. The E.C.W. was activated by Florence, and Bible study was instituted. A number of community seminars were held that proved to be quite successful. St. Andrew's celebrated their 25th anniversary in 1985. A Prison ministry was begun with the CYA Mt. Bullion Camp. Florence Walton died, a victim of cancer, in 1986, and Fr. Walton resigned on January 31, 1987, to take courses to prepare him for a hospital chaplaincy.

The Rev. Robert L. Stevenson and his wife Mimi had recently retired from St. Jude's, Tehachapi, and purchased a home in Mariposa. Following Fr. Walton's departure Fr. Bob was asked to assume the ministry as Vicar in Mariposa. Fr. Bob and Mimi were an immediate "hit" with the congregation and the community and there was great hope for the future of the congregation when tragedy struck. Fr. Bob was diagnosed as having cancer in a very advanced stage in mid-1987 and died shortly afterward. Since that time the congregation has been served by lay leaders and occasional visiting clergy. At the time of this writing the Venerable Wayne Williamson, recently retired as Archdeacon of the diocese is taking services on the first Sunday of the month.

CHURCH OF THE HOLY FAMILY, FRESNO

In the summer of 1970, Fr. Lee Wilson began a survey of northeast Fresno, where the Diocesan Mission Outreach felt there was a need and opportunity for the founding of a new mission. Door-to-door calling and aerial photos were part of the survey. Enough people expressed interest, and services began on February 14, 1971, in a children's theatre, Cinema 70, now a hardware store, at First and Barstow Streets. Fr. Wilson sometimes gave sermons in slides, showing God's glory in pictures and images as well as words. Music was played on a portable Army field organ, which sometimes collapsed on the organist, thereby adding a sense of expectancy to the services!

In August, the Rev. Laurence S. Mann replaced Fr. Wilson as priest-in-charge. In October, he arranged the use of the Sanctuary Hall at San Joaquin Gardens, 5555 North Fresno Street. Fr. Mann was a retired priest, and so in January, 1972, the Rev. R. Bruce Kirkwood was sent by the diocese to take charge on a part-time basis. Attendance grew, and in late April, 1972, the congregation of 38 adults met, selected the name, "Holy Family", and began a Bishop's Committee. Church School classes had also begun.

For Christmas services, 1972, the College Congregational Church across the street from San Joaquin Gardens was "borrowed'; from mid-January, 1973, the space was leased and used an hour earlier than the Congregational service. This meant much scurrying afterwards to put away the altar vessels and equipment. An Altar Guild, Choir, and EYC were formed. Thirty-nine family units now comprised the congregation, and the church school had grown to more than one class.

In September, 1976, the Rev. Robert Lucent arrived as Vicar; mid-week services were begun, and the Eucharist was celebrated each Sunday. Acquisition of property was given top priority, and by the end of December a place had been found on East Alluvial Avenue and was in escrow. The site included a 2500 square feet house on two and one-half acres. Due to problems in fulfilling City requirements, the move to the new location was delayed until May 1, 1977. A great deal of work went into the transformation of the house, as the chapel was enlarged, an organ was installed and office space was provided for Fr. Lucent.

Holy Family continued steady growth in size and service to its members and the community. Bible study, congregational dinners, and work parties enhanced the sense of being a true family of God. A mid-week Eucharist was offered at San Joaquin Gardens, where elderly residents often had problems getting to the church. An ECW and a Mission Council were formed. From July, 1980, to August, 1981, Mark Lawrence served as Deacon-in-training; he and his wife helped particularly in Christian Education.

A grant from the United Thank Offering for a Child Care facility made it possible to construct a multi-purpose building for a Day Care Center. Groundbreaking was on September 20, 1981, and by April, the building was occupied. It was formally dedicated on September 19, 1982. This building was designed as a parish hall, to be used for Sunday services and for day care during the week. The first students began classes on August 25, 1983. Mrs. Moina Lucent was the first Directress; she had been instrumental in its founding. It has grown to 60 children.

The church was soon "bursting at the seams," so it was decided to start another building; this one is a classroom Christian Education wing. The generous and hardworking "family" came through again, and ground-breaking was April 1, 1984. Dedication was on September 23, 1984. In the span of three years, the congregation erected two buildings and started a burgeoning Child Care Center. Furthermore, many are involved with work among Asian refugees in Fresno.

Holy Family Church has, at the same time of its rapid growth and building, fully supported the Diocese in development of the Episcopal Camps and Conferences-Oakhurst (E.C.C.O.), and in the funding of Venture in Mission. Their per capita giving and support is among the very highest in the diocese.

ST. PETER'S CHURCH, KERNVILLE

High in the upper reaches of the Kern River drainage, near the top of Kelso Valley is a strange and ancient pictoglyph. An eminent authority of such inscriptions, Dr. Barry Fell, Emeritus of Harvard, believes it was left by North African Christians perhaps before the 8th century! It contains a series of crosses and words meaning "Consecration, Elevation, Communion are the Ritual of the Mass" in the Libyan script used before the Arab invasion. Perhaps a Sunday School class was conducted there over a millenium ago! (1)

More recently, white explorers and trappers entered the upper Kern in the early 1800s. Gold seekers came in a rush in 1855, and Havilah ("where there is gold", Genesis 2:11) was the County Seat for 11 years. Lake Isabella was created for flood control and electric power in the 1940s. It rapidly became a water-sports center for the dry end of the San Joaquin Valley, and is increasingly popular as a retirement area, generally above the winter fogs of the Valley. The lake required the relocating of old Kernville to higher ground.

On Sunday evening, August 16, 1970, 14 people gathered in the home of Mr. and Mrs. James Crow of Kernville with Fr. Richard N. Warren of Porterville for a celebration of the Holy Eucharist. Thereafter, Fr. Warren would drive over Greenhorn Summit to Kernville on the second and fourth Sundays, a round-trip of 140 miles. When snow blocked that route, he would go by way of Bakersfield, a distance of 178 miles. At first the mission was named for St. Andrew,

Patron of Fishermen. From January 3, 1971, services were held in the recreation hall of the River View Trailer Park.

On February 21, Sunday morning services were commenced, with Church Army Sister Jeanette Kastorff in charge. Priestly visits were reduced to one a month. The same hymns were used as at St. Paul's, Bakersfield, and Sister Jeanette would record them at St. Paul's choir practice on Friday night to be used Sunday to help boost the Kernville singers. It was 110 miles round-trip to Bakersfield in those days, all on the old Kern River Road, before the upper section was made freeway; very few women would undertake to drive that road then. On April 19, 1971, it was decided to change the name of the mission to St. Peters' (another fisherman), since there were already two other missions named for St. Andrew in the diocese. On July 25, 1971, Bishop Rivera made his first visitation to the mission.

An organ was loaned to the mission early in 1972, and Dorothy Shaw volunteered to play. The ECW was organized, and on December 2, 1972, the first Rummage Sale was held in the Odd Fellows Hall to start a building fund. Before Christmas, two needy families with four children each, were chosen to receive a Christmas hamper and toys.

On September 30, 1973, St. Peter's welcomed Fr. Harold Wilson from Onancock, Virginia, a retired priest, as their first full-time Vicar. On November 3, Bishop Rivera flew to Kernville with Fr. Warren to discuss with Fr. Wilson and the people the building of a church on land already acquired.

On Sunday, April 7, 1974, Fr. Woody Peabody became the second Vicar. On June 30, Bishop Rivera, Fr. Warren, and Fr. Peabody officiated at the ground-breaking for the new church on Sierra Way, southeast of town, overlooking the lake. The church was raised entirely by volunteer labor. When finished it was entirely paid for. On St. Peter's Day, June 29, 1975, Bishop Rivera led a congregation of 91 through the door of the new building.

Former college drama professor Fr. Frederick Johnson was appointed Vicar on August 8, 1976. A diocesan music weekend was held at Kernville with Christian Education specialist, the Rev. Edgar G. Parrott in charge, preparing for an exciting celebration of Palm Sunday, 1979. In that same year a used double-wide mobile structure was purchased. In August it was moved to the property and became the "parish hall", for fellowship, education and assorted meetings.

On April 13, 1980, Fr. (Harold) Lee Wilson became Vicar. The noted bird-watcher and artist was compelled to leave the area for health reasons, and on September 26, 1982, Fr. David Graham, a retired priest, became officially the "part-time" Vicar. For a time it appeared that the mission might become bankrupt, but the people rallied in September, 1984, and the future of St. Peter's "is looking very good now." The Rev. Byron McKaig, a real estate agent with his wife Gladys Erickson McKaig, assists with services although he is canonically resident in the Diocese of Los Angeles.

(1) Fell, Barry — SAGA AMERICA, Times Books, NYC, 1980/83: p. 174.

ST. RAPHAEL'S CHURCH, OAKHURST

St. Raphael's Church met for the Holy Eucharist for the first time on the First Sunday of Advent, 1972, with its founder and organizer, the Rev. Canon Enrico C. S. Molnar as the celebrant. He had come to Oakhurst seeking a location for his new monastic community for married and single people, the Order of Agape and Reconciliation. The church met in the residence of the Vicar until his departure for Visalia in April, 1974.

St. Raphael is one of the Archangels and he is mentioned in the biblical Book of Tobit; in particular, he ministers the healing gifts of God, which is the meaning of his name. He is named in the hymn for the Feast of St. Michael and All Angels.

Oakhurst, located at the south end of Highway 49, marks the southern tip of the California Mother Lode. In late Gold Rush days, Oakhurst was known as Fresno Flats, despite its location in Madera County (created in 1893); it is beside the Fresno River. Church work began when a young school teacher from St. James', Fresno, came into the district. She found the one family in the vicinity who knew anything at all about the Church, around 1886. Consequently, she brought two children 50 miles to Fresno for Baptism. A year or two later, the parents came down for Confirmation, and D. O. Kelley added Fresno Flats to his circuit of preaching stations for regular services. The family was put in touch with the Women's Auxilliary office in San Francisco, and much interest was generated.

After D. O. Kelley left Fresno in mid-1891, veteran missioner, the Rev. James C. McGowan settled in Fresno Flats and opened several other preaching stations, at Raymond, Coarse Gold and O'Neal. At Fresno Flats, a church was built in 1893, and dedicated "Christ Church" in 1894, the only house of worship in town. McGowan continued successful work until 1900. Jonathan Nichols followed him, arriving May 5, 1900. In 1904, he was residing in Raymond, but by 1907, he was Vicar of Madera, with oversight of unorganized missions and stations in the Gold country. As the gold finds waned, so did the local population.

The missions of Christ Church, St. Thomas' (Raymond), and preaching stations at Coarse Gold and O'Neals were transferred to the care of the cathedral clergy in 1917; it appears that Nichols retired in Madera, and was made an honorary Canon of St. James' in that year. In 1919, Bishop Sanford reported that the dilapidated building in Raymond, used only occasionally in the last 15 years, was sold as second-hand lumber for $60, but the name was left in the Journal for three more years. The four were no longer listed as unorganized missions in the Journal of 1922. In the early 1950s, Fr. George Woodgates conducted services occasionally for a handful of people in Oakhurst. Bishop Walters instructed him to deconsecrate the building. It was sold to a civic group for about $2,000, who moved it across the road to the cemetery and restored it, where it is to this day.

Under the direction of St. Raphael's second Vicar, Fr. Peter van Hook, the church services moved to a building located on the property of one of the members. They were held there until late Spring, 1975.

The Rev. Peter Barker was the third Vicar. In his time, services were moved to an area behind the Sierra Sky Ranch, the former location of the Vicar's residence, and the original meeting site.

Later, a joint-use structure, a triple-wide modular building, was assembled at the same location to serve the needs of the congregation and the newly created Sumner Walters Conference Center.

In April, 1977, the Rt. Rev. Robert H. Mize, Jr., retired Bishop of Damaraland (Namibia), became Vicar and served for four years. He made it his plan to visit every home in the community whether churched or not. During that time Bishop Mize and a building committee began to plan for the construction of a regular building at the intersection of Highway 41 and Road 632, across from Sierra Sky Ranch. This is on property at the west end of a strip along the road into E.C.C.O., which was moving toward realization at the time. Bishop Mize became Assisting Bishop of San Joaquin, and moved to the Diocesan office in Fresno before St. Raphael's plans could be completed.

The Rev. Canon David W. Lueck was called back into pastoral ministry from the Bishop's Administration to become fifth Vicar in 1981. The present building was designed in 1983. The church is on a ground-level floor reached by a bridge from the parking area, with offices and rooms below. Construction was essentially complete in time for a first service on Ash Wednesday, 1984. The building was consecrated by Bishop Rivera on the Third Sunday of Easter, 1984. Located at the entrance to E.C.C.O., St. Raphael's is used not only by its regular congregation, but frequently by weekend conferees as well.

CHAPTER THREE

NEW BUILDING BEGINS

ST. JUDE'S-IN-THE-MOUNTAINS, TEHACHAPI

St. Jude's was born early in 1974, when Bishop Rivera met with a group of families who were interested in having an Episcopal congregation in Tehachapi. A. E. 'Buck' Waterstradt, project manager of the development of Stallion Springs found that he had something in common with the civil engineer working on the project — both were Episcopalians. Charles Karoly was studying for Holy Orders, and hearing Buck's feelings about having a church in the area, brought the matter to Bishop Rivera's attention. The Bishop's response was immediate, and a meeting at the lodge at Stallion Springs was arranged. The Holy Eucharist was celebrated and an entire family received the sacrament of Holy Baptistm. At the meeting following, though there were only five or six families, the enthusiasm was so great that Mr. Waterstradt was appointed Bishop's Warden and things were underway.

To assist in organization and growth, Sister Jeannette Kastorf of the Church Army was sent. She officiated at the office of Morning Prayer with intermittent assistance from area Lay Readers. Fr. Brian Endicott celebrated the Eucharist frequently, and from the latter part of 1976 officiated at services when Sister Jeannette had been given another assignment. The congregation through this period remained small, but faithful. Its life was literally from week-to-week. By arrangement with the Sams family, the local mortuary became the Sunday morning home of the congregation. Other meetings were held in homes of the people and local restaurants.

The group chose the name of the Apostle Jude after considerable discussion. As the patron of lost causes? No; but as the patron of the despondent and lonely, yes. They at no point considered the mission a lost cause; but have always had a sense of mission and ministry to the community.

By the middle of 1977, the Bishop sent Fr. Robert L. Stevenson to meet with the nucleus congregation. He celebrated the Holy Eucharist at the home of Spencer and Lillian Lees, and following the liturgy discussed with them their hopes and dreams, and what they felt they needed in a priest. The signal was sent to the Bishop of their desire to have Fr. Bob as their first priest and Vicar, and the appointment was made. Keeping a high visibility in the community, visiting in many homes, counselling and comforting people, he carved a significant niche in the affections and loyalty of the people of the Tehachapi area.

Early in 1980 the Episcopal Church Women of St. Jude's were formed for a three-fold purpose: Christian Fellowship, Christian Devotions, and the development of projects contributing to St. Jude's church. In April, a Men's organization was formed for fellowship, idea sharing, and working toward a useful and productive church in the community. By mid-June Spencer and Lillian Lees contributed a parcel of land nearly two acres in size located on South Curry Street, a main thoroughfare. It was becoming obvious that the mortuary location was only for a Sunday morning congregation, and that a permanent building was needed and desired.

The building committee was formed and began its difficult task of getting congregational input, arousing interest, developing plans, investigating avenues of finance, and the many things involved in having a building. Many gifted and devoted individuals worked together to do the work involved.

Ultimately the congregation raised some $45,000 in building pledges, and were supported and encouraged by a diocesant grant of $10,000 and a $20,000 United Thank Offering grant. A loan from the Diocesan Investment Trust of $35,000 is in the process of being paid off, with excellent progress.

Ground-breaking for St. Jude's Church was held in September of 1983; and, with a large congregation of local people and clergy and laity from the deanery and diocese, Bishop Rivera dedicated the building on November 4, 1984. St. Jude's has a parish hall which serves as a worship area, and offers the people a setting both aesthetically appealing and at the same time functional.

The Tehachapi area has a population of some 16,000 people. It is a scattered community, and has experienced a significant population increase recently, due largely to the expansion of the California Correctional Institution and the resulting influx of many families who serve the needs of the prison.

Fr. Stevenson retired as Vicar of Tehachapi mid-1986, leaving a community which loved him as missionary, pastor and counsellor of all. Bishop Rivera appointed the Rev. John M. Galagan to be Vicar of St. Jude's in January of 1987.

The congregation has goals and plans for the future which involve developing an informed and committed core of communicants, reaching out into the community for Christ in terms of attracting new members, forming a responsible church school program for all ages, and increasing our facilities as growth begins. We seek growth, not survival; and we look to the Lord for His guidance.

ST. NICHOLAS' MISSION, ATWATER

Atwater is located north of Merced, just off Highway 99, and is the location of Castle Air Force Base. The community has all the strengths and weaknesses that come from such a relationship. Efforts to form an Episcopal congregation were made as early as 1960, but met with no permanent success. Movement of military personnel, who comprise such an important part of the congregations membership, made it impossible at the time.

In January, 1979, another beginning was made, with the encouragement of Bishop Rivera and the Rev. Edward Murphy, Rector of Merced. Others had encouraged this project, too. At the February 27 Vestry meeting, three men, members of St. Luke's, who lived in Atwater, resigned in order to become a part of the nucleus of the new mission. They were Mike Bogna, Tom Dandy, and Norman Vaughn-Hulbert. St. Luke's donated vestments and altar linens; members gave money to help; when the church was finally built, St. Luke's also gave pews. This was the third mission St. Luke's has helped start. It was about a year before St. Luke's own budget was restored, but it was seen as "investment in mission", not a loss.

Fr. Thomas Corrigan had left San Andreas and was available to take the position at Atwater, where a thriving Sunday School could be started. Sister Jeanette Kastorff of the Church Army came from Bakersfield to help with a survey of Atwater. On Sunday, February 18, the first Eucharist was celebrated at the Bloss Home, Second and Cedar, in Atwater. On February 25, Bishop Rivera celebrated and Fr. Corrigan assisted. Following this service, the congregation met with the Bishop and named the mission for St. Nicholas, Bishop of Myra, Patron of Children and Sailors. A year later, in 1980, the Convention admitted St. Nicholas' Mission into union. Fr. Corrigan also had charge of Mariposa, and commuted each Sunday morning between his two charges.

From February, 1979, to August, 1980, the congregation met in Bloss Home, a historic building at the corner of Second and Cedar, given by the Bloss family to the city and used by the Atwater Chamber of Commerce during the week. Each Saturday, members of the congregation would move office furniture from one room to another and set up an altar and chairs for the Sunday services. After the service everything had to be restored to its usual place. The altar was made of two doors; one cut in two and hinged was set on edge in a "V" and the second door was laid on top. A piano, slightly out of tune, was among the home furnishings, and it was pressed into service. On the first Sunday, it was discovered that no one could play the piano. Usher Mike Bogna asked that numbers be taped to the proper keys, 1 to 4. When the first hymn was announced, he struck key #1, the first note of the melody. By the following Sunday there was someone found who could play the piano!

By August, 1980, the congregation had outgrown Bloss Home and moved into the old Library Building at Third and Cedar. There they were able to have pews and kneelers, given by St. John's, Lodi, and an altar rail from St. Luke's, Merced; St. Stephen's, Stockton, gave an organ.

In 1982, three acres were purchased on Shaffer Road. At first a search was made for a building that could be moved onto the site. St. Anthony's, Patterson, and the old Chapel at Castle A.F.B. were considered. Neither proved feasible, and sights were set on a new building. During this period, $16,000 was raised by the congregation, should moving St. Anthony's be possible. This sum was used to start the building fund, and a three-year pledge period was undertaken.

After necessary consultations and permissions, ground was broken by Bishop Rivera on November 25, 1984, for the church-parish hall building. The church is 2400 square feet, the hall is 900 square feet, and the vestibule joining the two is 192 square feet. The building was completed in time for Easter services in 1985, and a new organ, given by St. Raphael's, Oakhurst, was used.

St. Nicholas' was assisted by a $25,000 grant from a special fund established as one of the Venture in Mission diocesan projects for assisting new missions. This has helped them greatly in their development. Still, the ever-present reality of transfer in the military has meant that St. Nicholas' loses significant numbers of their congregation almost every year. In spite of having one of the highest per capita giving records in the diocese they have to struggle mightily to maintain their current expenses. There is, nonetheless, a strong determination on the part of the congregation to keep the mission solvent and hopefully to grow.

CHURCH OF THE RESURRECTION, CLOVIS

The proximity of Clovis to Fresno has been a significant factor in the development of an Episcopal Church in Clovis and has, in some ways, hindered rather than helped. In the closing decade of the 19th century and the first decade of the 20th, the relatively few Episcopalians living in Clovis traveled to Fresno for Sunday worship at St. James' Cathedral.

By 1911, shortly after the formation of the Missionary Diocese of San Joaquin, Clovis Episcopalians had formed their own congregation. In 1912 they were formally received into the Diocese as St. Mark's Episcopal Church. Sunday services were conducted in a Guild Hall in Clovis by clergy from St. James', Fresno.

Services were conducted regularly at St. Mark's for seven years, but in 1919 the congregation was disbanded, possibly as a result of the hard times following World War I and the epidemics of 1918-1919. For the next 60 years Clovis Episcopalians reverted to the earlier practice of traveling to Fresno for Sunday worship.

Then, in the summer of 1979, Bishop Rivera, appointed the Rev. Albert W. Majkrzak, a newly ordained Deacon, to the task of organizing a new congregation in Clovis. The first public worship of the new mission was held on Sunday, September 30, 1979. For several months, Sunday services were held in the Parish Hall of Our Lady of Perpetual Help Roman Catholic Church in Clovis.

At the 1980 Diocesan Convention, the Clovis congregation was formally recognized as the Church of the Resurrection. On Easter Sunday, April 6, the congregation began holding services at 6833 Sunnyside Avenue, in a house made available to the church through the generosity of Dr. Fareed Nader, one of the founding members of the congregation.

Under Fr. Majkrzak's gifted leadership, the new congregation grew rapidly and became known as one of the leading charismatic churches of the diocese, a distinction which it has maintained to the present. Fr. Al and his wife, Karen, were instrumental in bringing Cursillo to San Joaquin in 1980. Members of the Church of the Resurrection continue to play a significant role in the leadership of the Cursillo community.

In July, 1981, Fr. Majkrzak left Clovis to accept a call as Rector of St. Mark's, South Milwaukee, Wisconsin. In September, Bishop Rivera appointed the Rev. Michael Hinton from England, to serve as Vicar. Fr. Hinton was a forceful and effective preacher and he continued the forward momentum of the new mission. Unfortunately, because of visa complications, Fr. Hinton found it necessary to return to England at the beginning of December.

Beginning in December, 1981, and continuing through June, 1982, the Rev. James McDonald, a non-parochial priest resident in Fresno, served as Priest-in-charge. This was a period of continuing growth for the Mission, with significant lay leadership working together wtih Fr. McDonald.

In July, 1982, Bishop Rivera appointed the Rev. John Burk, a priest with significant parish and administrative experience in Utah and New York, to serve as Vicar. The growing congregation had, for some time, been aware of the limitations imposed by the house in which they were meeting. After discussion with the Memorial United Methodist Church of Clovis, an agreement was reached to allow the Church of the Resurrection to conduct Sunday services at 9 A.M. and to share the Methodist Church building during the week. A joint Methodist-Episcopal Sunday School was established; a joint Bible study meets weekly; and other joint activities speak to the success of the shared-ministry concept of two congregations meeting under one roof in Christian love and fellowship.

Fr. Burk and his wife, Anne, served, the congregation with distinction for more than three years. He was known for his scholarly teaching and his emphasis on increased service ministries to the community. Fr. Burk left at the end of July, 1985, to begin serving as Vicar of St. Mark's, Tracy.

In August, 1985, the Rev. John T. Rollinson, a newly ordained Deacon, was appointed Vicar. His wife, Shirley, a seminary graduate with a vocation in lay ministry, was licensed as a professional by the Bishop. Under the Rollinsons' leadership, the Church of the Resurrection has maintained its evangelical and charismatic emphasis, at the same time rejoicing in the richness of its catholic and apostolic heritage.

The Church of the Resurrection looks to the future with high hopes, anticipating the time when it will have a church home of its own. For the present, emphasis is on building up the congregation through evangelism, discipleship, and service. The purpose of the Church of the Resurrection is to glorify Christ through our worhship, witness, and work.

ST. THOMAS OF CANTERBURY MISSION, MAMMOTH LAKES

Mammoth Lakes traces its life back to a goldrush town and legends of the "Lost Cement Mine", at around the turn of the century. Old Mammoth became a virtual ghost town until Dave McCoy leased a tract of land on the north face of Mammoth Mountain from the U. S. Forest Service, and began to build an industry around skiing. The present resort community has a year-round activity, but still is largely dependent upon winter snow bringing the skiers. Population stays at about 4,000, except on a good ski weekend, when it may soar to over 27,000 persons, who have come to ski the slopes.

Bishop Nichols visited Bodie in 1901, but not Mammoth. As far as recorded, Fr. F. C. Benson-Bellis, Vicar of Bishop, first held services out-of-doors at Mammoth in July, 1926, on the 4th, 11th, 18th, and 25th. He recorded that 75 people attended a service at Bridgeport, Mono's County Seat, in November, 1925, and that services would continue "as long as weather permits" on alternate Thursdays. These were apparently the last local services until Fr. John F. Putney became Vicar of Bishop in 1961. In his report for 1967, Fr. Putney tells of 11 Eucharists and 11 Evening Prayer services held in Mammoth, and says there were 12 communicants. Fr. James C. Thompson, Vicar of Bishop from 1969, held Holy Communion services monthly on a Sunday afternoon in the Community Hall, weather permitting. In October, 1975, these had become bi-monthly, but ceased by September, 1976.

On October 13, 1978, immediately after his return from Turin, Fr. Christopher Kelley, the new Vicar of Bishop, celebrated the Eucharist in the home of Bob and Joanne Stanford. Publicity and other committees were set up, and services started every other week, weather permitting or not. The name, St. Thomas of Canterbury, was chosen in December, as he had a feast day both in winter (Dec. 29) and in summer (July 7), and Mammoth Lakes was seeking to emphasize its 'year-round' activity. Official recognition came on July 7, 1979, and the congregation was admitted to Convention in 1980.

In July, 1980, Bishop Rivera appointed Charles Karoly as Lay Vicar, while Fr. Kelley continued to supply priestly services. The Mission began using the new Lutheran Church for services, at a "significant" rental. After a few years of this, and an attempt to get the old building of St. Joseph's Roman Catholic Church, the new St. Joseph's was opened to the use of St. Thomas', rent free. Fr. Karoly was ordained Deacon at Mammoth in July, 1981, and Priest January 30, 1982. Under his leadership, the congregation showed encouraging growth. He chose to be non-stipendiary, earning his living as City Engineer of Taft, until Taft found this arrangement inconvenient. Karoly was appointed Engineer for the newly incorporated Town of Mammoth Lakes several months later. He subsequently found the work load too taxing to continue effectively as Vicar and resigned the position. After a few months the Rev. Milton Holmes from Idaho was appointed Vicar late in 1986.

SANTA MARGARITA DE ESCOCIA MISSION, FRESNO

Following a one year attempt by a Cuban-born priest to establish an independent Spanish-speaking congregation at St. Mary's, Fresno, the Rev. Efrain ("Jeffrey") Gonzalez, a Puerto Rican, began a full-time mission effort in 1980 to establish a Pan-Hispanic mission in Fresno. Services were begun in his garage; after a few months they were transferred to a store-front location at Orange and Butler. Assisted by a subsidy from the National Hispanic office, the early work focused heavily on trying to set up a local outreach center, emphasizing distribution of food and clothing, and working as an advocacy center on issues, such as immigration.

Congregational development was sufficiently successful to enable Santa Margarita Mission to be formally accepted by the Convention of San Joaquin in 1981. "St. Margaret of Scotland" represented a dual emphasis on family life and social outreach, hallmarks of this mission church. Several congregations of the diocese helped support the mission in special ways, both with tithes of legacies, special offerings, and personal presence.

The Rev. Keith Brown succeeded Fr. Gonzalez as Vicar on January 1, 1985. He had had business experience in Latin America and prior Hispanic work in the Church. He describes himself as a "multi-cultural Anglo functioning with multi-cultural Hispanics." Under his leadership, Santa Margarita continued to evolve along the more traditional pattern of a congregation, rather than as a social agency. Santa Margarita moved to a shared arrangement with Sierra Vista Methodist Church, at Illinois and Maple, in September, 1985.

This move enables Santa Margarita to use the excellent facilities of Sierra Vista and to be more centrally located and visible within the Hispanic community of Fresno. While food and clothing distribution was continued, a far greater emphasis was placed on networking, particularly in order to take advantage of existing community agencies and to increase the visibility of Santa Margarita in the community. A greater emphasis was placed on assisting with immigration problems, and job placement.

The congregation continues to grow steadily, with a gradual shift from mono-lingual recent arrivals and farm laborers, to bilingual members engaged in a broad range of occupations, and with greater income and job stability. In many cases the same individuals have made these transitions. This demonstrates the important role Santa Margarita has been able to play in their fuller integration into the local society.

Under Fr. Brown's able leadership, Santa Margarita has achieved a greater visibility within the diocese and encouraged greater interchange with other congregations. Theirs is a dual mission: To establish a permanent Hispanic congregation, and to serve as a test and model for the development of Hispanic work elsewhere in the diocese as its population becomes increasingly Hispanic.

ST. MICHAEL AND ALL ANGELS' CHURCH, SONORA

The thought of reviving St. Michaels' in Tuolumne County was raised by the Vestry of St. James' Church, Sonora, in January, 1979. On June 20, action was taken. The mission was begun with a service held at the Circus Land Nursery School on Sunday evening. The Rev. Ronald Swanson, then Rector of St. James', was celebrant. Later services were conducted by Canon William Craig, retired in Sonora, and Fr. Robert Olmsted.

In 1901, Archdeacon Emery had opened a mission under the same title in Tuolumne City. He got donations of six lots for the Church, and other help from the lumber company operating there. Deaconness Dorsey did fine work there, and the Sunday School flourished. The mission was organized officially on Candlemas Day, February 2, 1902, and the church building was opened for services on May 25. George Maxwell served as Missioner in 1903, and the building was consecrated on June 3, 1906. W. H. Wheeler was Missionary in 1906, and saw the building of a "bungalow parsonage" in 1907. Why the early effort collapsed, and when, is not recorded in D. O. Kelley's HISTORY OF THE DIOCESE OF CALIFORNIA, p. 403 (1915).

From September, 1981, to November, 1982, Roger Grist was Lay Vicar; priestly services were provided by Fr. Olmsted, Curate at St. James'. In November, 1982, Mr. Grist was ordained Deacon and transferred to St. Paul's, Bakersfield. At a meeting of St. James' Vestry with members of St. Michael's in November, 1982, it was decided to reassign Fr. Olmsted as Vicar of St. Michael's.

On December 12, 1982, a petition signed by St. Michael's members was presented to the Bishop and Diocesan Council, asking that the congregation be organized as a Mission of the Diocese. At the Convention on February 18, 1983, this was formally accepted.

Services continued at the Nursery School for a time while land was sought. In July, 1983, Al and Barbara Carr, members and realtors, found the right kind of building. A method of paying for it was worked out, and the congregation moved into the new church at 19632 Highway 108, at the growing edge of Sonora, in August. The first eucharist was celebrated there on August 21, and Bishop Rivera dedicated the building on November 20. The congregation was greatly assisted in their purchase of the property by a $25,000 grant from the Venture in Mission fund for Mission Advancement in this diocese.

Following Fr. Olmsted's death by cancer, Mr. Joel Hassell was appointed Lay Vicar while he was studying at Church Divinity School of the Pacific. Broadcasts of services from St. Michaels' have been made in an effort to reach a wider community. With the current growth in the Sonora area there is every reason to believe that St. Michaels' will grow as well.

HOLY CROSS MISSION, STOCKTON

The Filipino community in the San Joaquin is quite large. One of its major centers is in Stockton. Since the days of Bishop Charles Henry Brent of the Philippines, the Episcopal Church has had close ties with the Philippine Independent Church; in 1961 this was formalized in full inter-communion. Thus a number of Filipinos were already in full communion with the Episcopal Church, but often separated by language or culture from our established congregations.

Bishop Rivera, in coordination with Fr. Winston Ching, head of "Asiamerica," at National Church headquarters, invited the Rev. Justo Andres and his wife, Raquel Nancy Andres, from the Diocese of Hawaii, to visit Stockton, to ascertain the possibilities of a Filipino ministry there. Fr. Andres accepted and was provided with the use of the facilities of St. John's, Stockton. The first service in the Filipino language was held there on July 3, 1983, with nine people in the congregation.

Previously, Bishop Rivera had attempted to secure the services of Filipino priests directly from the Philippine Island, but these efforts had been frustrated by immigration problems.

At the Diocesan Convention of 1984, the new Mission was formally admitted into union under the title, Holy Cross. The nine original members continued to grow and by December 31, 1986, there were 50 communicants in "good standing" listed. These included not only Filipino, but Hispanic, Southeast Asians, and Anglos. Fr. Justo meets Filipino ships coming into the Port of Stockton, and the Filipino crews of other ships as well.

Holy Cross Mission continues to use the facilities of St. John's Church. It has been designated a "Jubilee Center" by the National Church. As such, it is a branch of the Social Services of the Episcopal Church, under Canon Peter Golden. The Mission's program includes Seamen's Ministry, an hour-long radio ministry every Sunday morning, and a Migrant Ministry. The Mission's two vans provide free transportation seven days a week for church-related trips, and other legitimate needs of members and non-members.

Few in the congregation had previous experience with the pledge system of church support, but almost all have learned and now practice this system. Cultural heritage is encouraged; so folk dancing, music, and bamboo instrument playing typical of the Philippines are a vital part of the Mission's Youth Program, beside Christian Education.

The Mission is deeply grateful to the Rector and people of St. John's for so graciously permitting them the use of the church facility, but the time is rapidly approaching when they will require a place of their own and they are currently making plans to move in that direction as soon as possible.

ST. LAURENCE'S MISSION, STOCKTON

In August, 1981, the Episcopal Mission of North Stockton began holding services in the home of its founders, Richard and Beth Kellogg. Together with Charles Spurlock and Father Eric Yeoman III, the Kelloggs surveyed 1600 homes in the new part of town, north of Hammer Lane. Sunday services soon moved to Camlu Retirement Apartments (where Sunday evening services are still held).

Two years later the Kelloggs resigned to answer a call to the mission field. Their place was taken by Deacon Sylvia Singer (assisted first by Father Yeoman and later by Father Paul Snider and Father Justo Andres). A Sunday morning service began in September, 1983, held first at Parklane School and later in a chapel in the vicarage.

In 1984 Diocesan Convention accepted North Stockton Mission as an Organized Mission, with the dedication of St. Laurence. The work at St. Laurence's Mission has continued to grow — classes for children and adults, good fellowship, and service to our community and the world. St. Laurence's takes pride in having resettled three homeless families in the mission. They look forward to purchasing land for a building site in the near future.

GRACE CHURCH MISSION, GROVELAND

Walt and Eileen DuBridge owned a home at Pine Mountain Lake for several years and planned to retire there permanently. The real estate market in the Bay area where they lived was depressed and their home was not selling. Knowing that there was no Episcopal Church in Groveland, they promised the Lord that if He would approve the sale of their home in Sunnyvale, they would attempt to start a church in Groveland. Their home sold in two weeks.

True to their promise, when they arrived in Pine Mountain Lake in June, 1981, they contacted Fr. Ronald Swanson of St. James', Sonora, and he agreed to come and hold services in their home once a month. Fr. Swanson also arranged for Lay Readers, Bob Woodford and Ron Prescott to hold Morning Prayer on the other Sundays of the month.

Later the facilities of Lake Lodge at Pine Mountain were made available and for six months in 1982 services were held there. Then, in 1983, arrangements were made to rent Mt. Carmel Catholic Church in Big Oak Flat on Sunday mornings at 10 A.M. The Catholic services were conducted on Saturday nights at 5 P.M.

On November 30, 1983, Bishop Rivera met with an enthusiastic group of members to discuss organization procedures and strategy for future growth. The congregation had grown from two to twenty five families in the preceding year, with an average of fifteen persons in attendance every Sunday.

In June, 1984, the Bishop assigned Sister Jeanette Kastorff of the Church Army to the Groveland area to conduct a survey to determine the possibilities of growth for the Episcopal Church in the area. Don Kroeger, who had just graduated from the Church Divinity School of the Pacific and was awaiting ordination to the Diaconate was also assigned to the Mission for the 1984 summer.

In September, 1984, Fr. Martin Risard was assigned to the mission as its first Vicar. In February, 1985, Grace Episcopal Mission (formerly called Groveland Mission, a parochial mission of St. James; Sonora), was received into union with the Convention of the Diocese.

In 1987 the Mission was able to acquire property in Pine Mountain Lake through a $25,000 grant from the Venture in Mission fund for Mission Advancement in this diocese. The congregation has been challenged by the Bishop to raise funds towards a church building which he will match in part.

ST. BENEDICT'S EPISCOPAL MISSION, CERES

St. Benedict's is a parochial mission of St. Paul's Church, Modesto. Preceding its establishment there had been several years of discussion, and when it was finally decided to proceed the decision was to locate in Ceres, eight miles south of St. Paul's in Modesto.

Services began September 9, 1973, in a rented room in the American Legion Hall at Ninth and Lawrence Streets, under the name "St. Timothy's". Clergy from St. Paul's conducted services until the arrival of the Rev. Albert Collins, and resumed conducting services after he left in June, 1975.

The small group of parishioners, with encouragement from Fr. Thomas Foster, Rector of St. Paul's, and the Vestry of St. Paul's began thinking of a more permanent meeting place. In November, 1975, property was purchased at 1941 Butcher Avenue, an unincorporated area. With the move to the new location the name of the mission was changed to St. Benedict's at Bishop Rivera's request and with congregational approval.

The move was not an easy one. On the property was a small house, a double garage and a long shed. A building had been promised to be moved in, but when the moving permit was applied for, the neighbors protested, fearing too much traffic on their narrow country lane. With a great deal of hard, volunteer labor the double garage was turned into a lovely, little chapel. In June, 1976, the Rev. Charles Threewit joined the staff of St. Paul's with responsibility for St. Benedict's. Bruce and Joie Fultz did a great deal of the work.

Father Threewit left in 1977 for a Navy chaplaincy, and the Rev. Will Harvey served for about a year, and, in turn, was followed by the Rev. Robert Slocum. In early 1978, Tom Sutter, of St. Paul's, built a vestibule on the small chapel. At the same time he had the three small rooms which he had previously donated put on foundations. These served as office, Sunday School classroom and nursery. A beautiful hand-made cross by Dr. Chauncey Behrens of St. Paul's and dedicated to the memory of Joseph B. Stanford, was mounted on the roof. On November 12, 1978, Bishop Robert Mize, Assistant Bishop, visited the congregation for the purpose of blessing these additions.

Early in 1981, Fr. Slocum was forced to retire for health reasons. At a joint meeting on August 31, 1981, of St. Paul's Vestry and St. Benedict's committee it was decided that a full time Vicar was needed. On October 1, the Rev. William R. Eastman became the Vicar. This full time ministry was made possible by the commitment of St. Paul's Church to make St. Benedict's the major focus of their concern for outreach and church growth.

In 1982, Marjorie Moon volunteered her talent as an organist to serve the congregation of St. Benedict's. A new Altar Cross was dedicated as a memorial to Ed Soderlund. Again the intricate wood carving was done by Dr. Chauncey Behrens and the mariposite insets were cut and polished by June Barnes, Warden of St. Benedict's. Members of the congregation engaged in outreach by doing hospital auxiliary work, volunteering at the Inter-Faith Food Bank, in the Ralston Tower Auxiliary, as visitors and care persons for the sick and the widows, in their work as nurses, lab technicians and other health fields.

An Altar Guild was formed in 1983 with four teams of two women each. Many new activities have developed, such as study programs in Advent and all during Lent, and E. C. W. was formed and meets monthly, money-raising activities such as a rummage sale and a taco booth at the Diocesan Faire at E.C.C.O., and planning for a "Mardi Gras" Crab Feed in February, 1984.

Recognizing the inadequacies of the location with its limitations on growth the mission began to look for more suitable property. A former Congregational Church building built in 1908 became available and in April, 1986, the Butcher Avenue property was sold and the new facility was purchased located in the center of Ceres. On July 13, the congregation held their first worship service in the newly acquired building. August 6, 1986, being the Feast of the Transfiguration, the new facility was dedicated by Bishop Rivera and Fr. Bill was duly installed as Vicar. The congregation was helped with the finances by a grant of $25,000 from the Venture in Mission fund for Mission Advancement in this dioceses . . . one of seven that have been similarly aided by the VIM fund.

SAINT BARNABAS' MISSION, VISALIA

Saint Barnabas' is a parochial mission of St. Paul's, Visalia. The first gathering of the congregation that was to become the nucleus of the mission was January 30, 1981, at the home of the Rev. and Mrs. John William Burbery, Jr. in Visalia. This home gathering was to typify the life of this mission congregation for their first five years under the leadership of Fr. Bill, Visalia's Parish Missioner.

The first gathering had grown out of the impetus provided by St. Paul's Vestry Mission Committee, under the leadership of the Rector, Fr. Donald D. Cole. They first met on November 2, 1980, and the meeting was chaired by then Deacon Burbery. Plans were made for a potluck and visions shared as to what the ministry of St. Barnabas' was to be. Father Cole laid special emphasis on the need to see this new congregation as focusing on service to the community.

Epiphany 4, February 1, 1981, saw the first meeting for Holy Communion as a congregation. This was conducted in the Burbery's home with Fr. Cole celebrating and Fr. Bill preaching. The Rev. Frank O'Donnell served as priest to the congregation for the first six months until Fr. Burbery was ordained priest in July.

Their first place of meeting after leaving the Burbery's home was the Creative Center, a refurbished ice-house at the corner of Santa Fe and Race Streets in Visalia. Part of the overall facility was used as an educational facility for handicapped adults and it was here that the congregation met Sundays. The artwork produced by these handicapped provided a colorful setting for their worship. It helped, as well, to remind the congregation that this was a special place that ministered to special people during the week and their own need to be of service.

A unique feature of St. Barnabas' was the Adult Class that met each Sunday immediately after worship service. The format was group discussion, usually focusing on the Lessons for the day with Fr. Bill serving as discussion leader and resource person. He often directed their attention to the Old Testament lesson in that his sermons usually related to the Gospel for the day. The class flourished over the five years, with Father Bill insisting that all the adults at worship make every effort to stay, attend and participate in their Adult Class.

Father Burbery resigned from the position at the end of 1985 and the Rev. William Richmond, retired, took over the responsibility for the mission. He was also assisted by the newly ordained Deacon Jeff Smith for a time. The Rev. H. Lee Wilson, retired, is providing Sunday services at the present time.

ST. CLARE'S EPISCOPAL CHURCH AT THE EBBETT'S PASS

A small group of five Episcopalians met infrequently for about a year in the mid-1970s, with Fr. Ronald Swanson, Rector of St. James', Sonora, celebrating the Eucharist at the Pinebrook Picnic Ground near Arnold. Due to various problems, this group dissolved.

On March 8, 1981, the Rev. Robert Downs, Vicar of St. Matthew's, San Andreas, reorganized the group and began celebrating the Eucharist in the home of Bob and Margie Harris in Arnold. There were seventeen communicants at that first celebration. Reg and Mable St. George built a portable altar, and a chalice and paten set was given as a memorial to Bob Harris' mother. Barbara Watson made colorful Eucharistic vestments, and these were dedicated in memory of Peter Harris. Services were continued in homes, once a month at 5 P.M., plus Christmas, Easter, and special occasions, for the next four years. Attendance grew from a yearly total of 225 in 1981, to 465 in 1984. At the beginning of 1984, services were held in the Pinebrook Community Center. Fr. Downs last service was held on February 6, 1985, before leaving for a position in Carmel.

The Bishop appointed the Rev. Martin Risard as Missioner, and he celebrated the Eucharist for the first time at St. Clare's on February 17, 1985. The number of services was increased to twice a month at Pinebrook Community Hall. The Bishop's Committee was officially organized with Marge Harris appointed Bishop's Warden, Rosemary Atkins, Junior Warden, Neil O'Brian, Clerk, Robin Garcia, Treasurer, and Don Feathers member and Lay Reader. Services continued to be held at 5 P.M. In 1986 a Celtic Cross for the altar, carved out of red cedar, was given to St. Clare's by Bob and Marge Harris in memory of their son Peter.

The Diocesan Convention of 1986 received St. Clare's as an organized Mission of the Diocese. Fr. Risard was appointed Vicar. The Mission has continued to grow slowly. The Bishop's Committee decided upon a plan to look for a more visible and accessible location look for a permanent location, and conduct a strong program of evangelism in the communities it serves. In 1986, the Mission, in accordance with its plan, held its first regular Every Member Canvass and Building Fund Campaign, formed a Growth Committee, and set to work implementing the plan.

Jean Feathers was appointed Stewardship Chairman. 1987 saw the formations of a very active E. C. W. group, with Alice Risard as its first President. The group held its first bazaar, for benefit of the Building Fund, raising over $1,800.

With assistance from the Diocese, two acres of land were acquired in Avery, near the Center of the Ebbett's Pass area. The property is located on Highway 4, a main arterial for the south part of Calavaras County. A multi-purpose building providing space for worship, offices, and activities was begun in Dec. '87.

CHAPTER FOUR

HISTORY OF AN EPISCOPATE

Victor Manuel Rivera was born October 30, 1916, in Penuelas, Puerto Rico. The son of the Rev. Victor Rivera and Philomena Toro, he has always known the significance of being raised in a Christian family and environment. He speaks of his mother as being "the greatest missionary he has ever known." "Missionary" not in the sense of going from one's native country to foreign lands, but as one who is on mission for Christ in their daily life wherever they may be. There can be little doubt that her example has played a profound part in influencing his own zeal for mission and evangelism throughout his entire ministry.

Victor Rivera attended the Church Divinity School of the Pacific, and was awarded the Bachelor of Divinity degree in 1944. He subsequently served as Vicar of Grace Church, Martinez, 1943-44, and as Curate at St. John's Cathedral Church, Santurce, Puerto Rico, in 1944. He was called from there to serve as Rector of St. Paul's, Visalia, a position he held until 1968, when he was consecrated third Bishop of the Diocese of San Joaquin.

Married on December 23, 1944, to the former Barbara Ross Lamb, they have spent their entire married life in service to the Church in this diocese. Barbara has been an able helpmeet in that not only has she concurred with Victor's strong commitment to evangelism and mission, she has augmented that interest by taking a Master's degree in Church Growth, and written prolificly on the subject in the diocesan newspaper THE STAR. They have three daughters, all of whom have professional careers.

St. Paul's, Visalia, stands as a testimony to their joint commitment to evangelism. During his tenure the congregation grew not only numerically but spiritually — it is possible to have not only quantity but quality, a much argued point these days of declining church growth among mainline churches. There are those who, viewing the decline, aver that the remainder represent quality and that we should not be unduly concerned about the quantity as long as we have the quality. To that line of argument Dr. Donald McGavran observes that "if one sets out to make a gallon of ice cream, he would be well-advised to have a sufficient quantity of good cream to begin with." In short, it takes both quantity and quality to make a vital Church. This is something Victor Rivera has never doubted.

At the Annual Diocesan Convention, meeting in Church of the Saviour, Hanford, January 26-28, 1968, Bishop Sumner Walters announced his resignation, to take effect on the date of his successors consecration. In his remarks, Bishop Walters expressed his opinion as to the qualities a bishop should possess, although he cautioned that "Few men have them all." He continued, "I put first: a man of God, who loves people. His personal religion is real. His greatest gift should be as a spiritual leader. *If he loves people he will try to bring them to Christ* (emphasis added)." This last has been Bishop Rivera's constant endeavor.

At the special Convention for the purpose of electing a new bishop, held April 26-27, 1968, at St. James' Cathedral, Fresno, there were twelve nominations, including seven from the floor. In the subsequent balloting Victor M. Rivera was elected on the fourth ballot, having been the leading candidate on the three preceding ballots.

In his first Annual Diocesan Convention address, Bishop Rivera, noted the opportunities he saw for establishing Episcopal congregations in this diocese, noting, "We have several places with over 12,000 inhabitants but no Episcopal Church. We have large metropolitan areas where we have only two or three churches but where there should be eight or ten . . . We have been remiss in working among the poor. We have done little missionary work among the Mexicans and Filipinos . . . Work of this nature is almost in its totality missionary work; it will be a long time before it can be self-supporting . . . Our first task as clergy and Christians is to lead people directly to Christ."

In the same address Bishop Rivera dwelt at length upon the importance of Christian Education and noted with concern the decline in Church School enrollment, and the decrease in baptisms and confirmations in recent years. At the same time he pointed out the growth taking place among the so-called Fundamentalist churches; a phenomenon that Dean M. Kelley would write about in his book, WHY CONSERVATIVE CHURCHES ARE GROWING, 1972. It ought to be cause for some deep soul-searching reflection by Episcopalians that for a very long time we have not been converting the unchurched. Our forte, such as it is, has been in attracting the upwardly mobile from other denominations.

Concerning Stewardship, Bishop Rivera challenged the diocese to increased support for mission and missions, "Five thousand dollars for new work does not go very far . . . Let us look carefully at the item in our budget called 'Mission Support.' Of every dollar you gave in 1968 to the Church, only three and one half cents (3.5¢) was used for the support of missionary work in this diocese. What are we going to do about this?", he asked.

In his 1970 Convention address the Bishop said, "I have many concerns, but my chief concern is evangelization. How do we share Christ and His Church with others? . . . I have been reading in THE STAR the accounts of D. O. Kelley and how he started missions in San Joaquin . . . it reads like a modern "Acts of the Apostles." The Bishop was pleased to note that St. Andrew's, Mariposa, was petitioning for admission as an organized Mission at the Convention (and this was approved in the proper place and time).

The budget approved for the diocese reflected a reduction in the amount allocated to the Department of Christian Education. A matter the Bishop deplored, even as he observed that "very few churches have availed themselves of the services of Fr. Wilcox, Christian Education Coordinator . . ." This is a situation that is virtually endemic in the Episcopal Church, and shows little, if any, sign of improvement over the intervening years.

The 1971 Diocesan Convention found the Bishop pleading for a greater commitment to Stewardship and tying it in with Evangelism when he said, "I plead with the clergy, vestries, bishop's committees for a concerted effort to have a well tested, well planned, and well executed evangelistic and stewardship program starting as soon as possible."

The 1972 Convention was marked with the opening of North Fresno Mission (Church of the Holy Family) and the revival of the work in Kernville by Fr. Warren. It was also the year in which the deaneries were expanded from four to the present six " . . . to promote missionary efficiency and inter-parochial cooperation and duties the Bishop may assign."

There was also great satisfaction noted in the Outreach Project begun for missionary expansion and an Outreach Fund begun on the basis of voluntary contributions over and above giving to the local church.

Stewardship was emphasized in observing that fourteen churches had participated in the Dimensions in Stewardship Commitment (DISC) with notable success. The contributions of Elwyn Peterson in the stewardship program of the diocese were noted with appreciation. The average increase by the participating churches was 21% over their giving for the previous year. This year also marked the beginning of the Diocese of San Joaquin's participation in Coalition 14. "Increased stewardship and mutual evaluation of needs and resources, clergy stipends, work with minority groups, continuing education for clergy are some matters of special concern and under consideration."

In the realm of hoped for future ministry development was a desire by the Bishop to start a work among the Spanish-speaking population. A dream that required another ten years to see its realization in the establishment of Santa Margarita de Escocia Mission in Fresno.

The first beginnings of a Diocesan Conference Center were foreshadowed by Sierra Sky Ranch, an independent non-profit corporation owned by individuals in the diocese. Out of this was eventually to come the acquisition and development of what is now known as the Episcopal Camps and Conferences-Oakhurst (ECCO). As such, it represents one of the finest such centers in the Episcopal Church nationwide. Its eventual realization did not come about without considerable trauma on the part of the independent members who owned it. The full measure of their generosity and their selfless service that this diocese might have a conference center is a story that needs telling, but must be done elsewhere.

The Twelfth Annual Convention of the Diocese of San Joaquin also took place in 1972, coming October 6-7; the Eleventh having taken place January 28-30. The Bishop's theme was "Invest in Hope." In his comments the Bishop spoke about a joint lay/clergy meeting held earlier in the year with representatives of the General Convention. There was discussion about the Diocese's feelings with regard to the National Church Program, budget, and priorities. The result was in accord with the findings of a special committee that had been set up by the National Church to ascertain peoples' feelings about its programs, etc. Interestingly enough, although no question was asked about Evangelism, it was a write in by virtually every diocese across the country as being a high priority concern, if not number one. This, the Bishop observed, was true for this diocese as well. On the matter of the budget and its support the Bishop expressed strong objection to any notion of making either diocesan or National Church budgets a matter of voluntary offering, saying, "The Church is not ready at this juncture for a voluntary quota any more than we clergy are ready for voluntary contribution in lieu of salary."

The 1973 Convention saw the admission of St. Raphael's, Oakhurst as a diocesan mission. The General Convention of 1972 was past history, Bishop John M. Allin had been elected the new Presiding Bishop. Liturgical revision and the matter of the ordination of women to the priesthood and episcopate were becoming matters of growing concern throughout the Church.

Again, the Bishop dealt with the topics of Stewardship, Education, and Evangelism. He did this within the context of what had taken place at the General Convention the preceding year. He observed that General Convention had had to take cognizance of the fact that the dioceses had said "... that what people were asking for was for a better program of Christian Education, and a better program of Evangelism. Therefore stewardship, education and evangelism are long term goals and also short term goals for the Church."

As he continued with his address the Bishop strongly emphasized that this is what leading laity and clergy were saying in this diocese, and he then dwelt at some length on each of these. His comments thereon are worthy of repetition, but they are too lengthy to include in this account. Nevertheless, the reader is encouraged to resort to the Journal for Convention 1973 and read pages B-5 to B-15 therein.

At this point it is apropos to note that Bishop Rivera took subsequent steps to provide training and support for evangelism in this diocese. He did so by taking courses at the Fuller Theological Seminary Church Growth program under Dr. Peter Wagner and Dr. Donald McGavran, and with Dr. Win Arn's Institute for American Church Growth, also located in Pasadena. Barbara Rivera was also deeply involved in these programs. Peter Wagner and Win Arn were both brought in as principal speakers for Clergy Conferences in the late 70s, and the latter provided fourteen basic 10-hour seminars on Church Growth principles. A Church Growth Committee was established, and today the Diocese of San Joaquin has one of the largest Church Growth and Evangelism budgets of any diocese in this Church.

In more recent years the diocese inaugurated the L.E.A.D. lab programs developed by Dr. John Savage. Here the Bishop's wife has played a major role. After the initial presentation she and several others in the diocese went through the extensive and intensive L.E.A.D. lab in this diocese certified to conduct the seminars, Barbara Rivera being one of them.

In his 1974 Convention remarks the Bishop wryly commented that he had little that was new to say, "I guess you can say I have a certain obsession about evangelism, and Christian Education." "We need to proclaim Christ, that is our job, the rest of our job is important, but it is ancillary to this. So let us do evangelism, let us be evangelists. Let us not argue the merits of this system or that system, let us not quibble about the connotation of the word." These latter comments are a reflection of the Episcopal predeliction for stressing the need for evangel-ism while all the while assiduously refraining from doing anything much about it other than talk about defining the word.

By this time in his episcopate the Bishop was becoming quite aware that many of the clergy and the laity were "tired of hearing" about evangelism, christian education, and stewardship. In response to the criticism that evangelism as an activity first of all requires that "No person who is not significantly educated in the Christian Faith can be an effective evangelist," the Bishop agreed, in part, "... but we cannot wait," he said, "until we are theologians and then become evangelists. If I had to choose between this egg and this chicken I say let us become first evangelists by the grace of God and then theologians by the same grace. Of course the thing to do is, to learn to talk and learn to think as we grow in grace." The good Bishop might also have noted that among the first evangelists, the Apostles, not a one possessed a theological degree, save Paul. The one thing they all possessed in common was that they knew Jesus Christ as Lord and Savior and knew that it was the most important thing in the world "to proclaim the good news of Jesus." (Acts 5:42).

By the time of the 1975 Convention, issues in the Church had come to a head with the so-called ordination of the Philadelphia Eleven, in which four bishops illegally "ordained" eleven women, averring that they were acting out of conscience. Bishop Rivera's remarks on the whole issue, not only of the action of the bishops, but the matter of ordination of women deserve an attentive reading and consideration. To be sure, Bishop Rivera speaks from a traditionalist conservative viewpoint. Although it is much derided by the liberals now in the ascendancy in the Church, it is nonetheless the position held by the overwhelming majority of those who would call themselves catholic Christians. Something that tiny minority of Christians known as Episcopalians need to bear in mind.

His remarks taken as a whole are notably irenic and sensitive to the fact that "(t)he Church in our times has not given women the opportunity to exercise ministries that have been validated by biblical record or by the Apostolic Church." He further comments in connection with grave issues confronting the Church that "It is too bad that our democratic system of church polity does not have provision for a plebiscite in issues that have been made the concern of every member and thought by many to be of such great importance to the Church at large." The fact is, that our polity is all too capable of manipulation and capture by ideologically motivated minorities purporting to represent the majority.

It is good to remind ourselves that the Thirty-nine Articles of the Book of Common Prayer observes that, in the case of the Authority of General Councils: "And when they be gathered together, (forasmuch as they be an assembly of men, whereof all be not governed with the Spirit and the Word of God,) they may err, and sometimes have erred, even in things pertaining unto God." (p. 872). In any case, at the time of this writing, the matter awaits further consideration by the Lambeth Conference of 1988.

The sad fact is that this and other issues have pretty well polarized the American Church, not to mention the rest of the Anglican Communion. What the end result will be remains to be seen, but one thing becomes clearer with each passing day, it is becoming increasingly difficult to maintain unity in this Church between the opposing groups. "Can two parties walk together except they be agreed?" asks Amos, and the answer is obviously, "no." (Amos 3:3)

In his address for 1976, the year of the General Convention, Bishop Rivera addressed some of the thorny issues facing that Convention and its bishops and deputies. He did so in the presence of the former Bishop Sumner Walters and also of the Presiding Bishop John Allin. In doing so he spoke with wisdom and trenchancy.

On more congenial matters he noted the progress being made by various of the missions and parishes, and rejoiced in the new mission of St. Jude's-in-the-Mountains at Tehachapi, which was received as a diocesan mission. He commented on the fact that St. Paul's, Modesto, was developing two parochial missions; one at Ceres and the other at Patterson. The former is now thriving and has hopes of being admitted as a diocesan mission at the 1988 Convention. The latter has, unfortunately, had to be abandoned.

In his comments about growth in the diocese the Bishop told a fable about a cattleman who started with a herd of 10,000 cattle. Each year for eleven years he lost a number. Some just disappeared, but whatever the reason at the end of the period he found that he had fewer cattle than when he began. "What would be the state of that ranch?" The point of the fable is: "In the Diocese of San Joaquin, at present we have 7,717 communicants in good standing. Since 1964 we have lost, unaccountably removed, from the list 9,991 communicants." The same general trend in the statistics was true throughout the national Church as well.

In the 1977 Convention on February 18-20, Bishop Rivera was obviously speaking out of his own personal travail resulting from the actions taken by the General Convention of 1976 . . . "I have a burden in my heart that I must share with you, not that I want to impose my burden on you, but I must share what I am and what I have, what has been entrusted to me, as your Bishop."

His convictions concerning the ordination of women were expressed as follows, having stated his theological and creedal reasons for not finding such ordination acceptable, " . . . I cannot believe in the ordination of women to the priesthood and the episcopate. But I will never cease to proclaim and acclaim the ministry of women. Ministry is multifaceted, and women have as great a place in ministry — indeed — as Mary the mother of God has such a high place in a magnificent ministry, so can all women, if they are called.

"I was asked, 'What will I do if some lady in the Diocese wants to seek ordination to the priesthood.' My answer is: 'I will tell her where I stand theologically, then I will say, 'Let me show you how you can proceed with the canonical process and let me help you to find a Bishop that will support you in this matter." Those who know Bishop Rivera know that he has remained faithful to those words in every respect, at no little cost to himself emotionally, since one of his daughters presented herself for ordination in another diocese and now serves in the Diocese of El Camino Real. He and his daughter maintain a good personal relationship as father and daughter, but he refuses to recognize her as a priest and will not allow her or any women so ordained to officiate in this diocese for so long as he is bishop. To say the least, this has earned him no little opprobrium from the liberal element in the diocese and the Church at large.

Of necessity, the matters of evangelism and stewardship received less attention from the Bishop than was normally the case. For which, there were no doubt those who heaved a sigh of relief, being tired of hearing about such things year after year. This does not mean they were entirely neglected. He did make comment on these matters but confined himself to short comments for the time being.

Something of a shift in emphasis took place in 1980 at the Convention where the Bishop developed the theme "Committed We Build" and used the tree as an emblem. The emphasis was upon growth, growth that had taken place gradually but encouragingly since 1976. He cited a 5% increase in baptized members. A 1% increase in communicants, not outstanding but at least a halt for the time being in the downward slide of the past.

He dwelt upon the incidents of the Fig Tree in Matthew 21 and in Mark 11, as well as Luke 13. Trees that bore no fruit and did not fulfill their purpose were worthless. He then related these parables to stewardship (he never really gets very far away from the triad upon which his episcopate was based — Evangelism, Stewardship, Christian Education).

Then, he came to what I believe was the *piece de resistance* for the occasion the launching of the program for the new camps and conference center at Oakhurst, the building of the Sumner Walters' Conference Center and associated facilities. Sierra Sky Ranch had been sold at long last and with the proceeds from that sale as nest egg a plan was formulated to seek pledges from every member of the diocese to help build their conference center. In due course it all came about, but not without great travail on the part of many and the Bishop's untiring (some would say relentless) prosecution of the project. Never for very long did he remain silent about the project and was involved in its every detail as it developed and came to fruition.

The same Convention took action in the form of a Resolution for the development of a program for the Hispanic community in the diocese. This was referred to the Bishop and Diocesan Council for study and implementation. There was also the satisfaction of receiving three Missions into union with the Diocese. They were St. Nicholas' Mission, Atwater; Church of the Resurrection Mission, Clovis; and St. Thomas of Canterbury Mission, Mammoth Lakes.

The theme of the 1981 Convention was The River of Life. In 1978 the Bishop had used Rainbow as his theme and deftly woven these varied themes each successive year into colorful and motivating addresses as he pressed forward with the project of building ECCO. In the "Bishop's Charge" he stated: " . . . I want to point to three main areas of concern: outreach, Christian Education, and our new camp and conference center."

The Bishop was able to reflect positively upon the year 1980 for showing significant gains in almost every area of diocesan church life. But he had to qualify his remarks by noting that baptisms were down again, as were confirmations. He urged all church leaders to take cognizance of these facts and to ask, "How can we better integrate new members into the Body so that they do not soon leave by the back door?" He also commented strongly on the need for ever more and better Christian Education, not only for the children but for the adults as well.

But it was on the camp and conference center that he really waxed eloquent. There could be no doubt as to where the Bishop's heart and interests were at the moment. ECCO was paramount in his thinking for the time being. The progress being made was a matter for pride, and the Bishop expressed his deep appreciation for the labors of those who had done so much to make the funding campaign a success. He observed that Sierra Sky Ranch associates had given the diocese $300,000 towards the project and how they were able to acquire 162 acres of prime camp and conference land. Announcement was made of a festive ground-breaking ceremony to take place on April 26 in the afternoon, Low Sunday in the Church calendar, but a high day for the diocese of San Joaquin as they celebrated this important step in the development of the long hoped for center.

1982 was not notably different from preceding years as to the main themes addressed by the Bishop. He dwelt on the Parable of the Talents and its implication for us, clergy and laity alike as we considered our calling in this place at this time. He again stressed the importance of the clergy emphasizing the Confirmation and Inquirers' classes: "New Christians, like new babies, need special attention and special food to nourish them and make them grow."

True to form, he did not neglect to dwell upon Christian Education, Evangelism, and, of course, "Our new camp and conference Center." It would be remiss, however, to leave the impression that the Bishop had no other concerns than those of the Church family. Without exception, from the beginning of his episcopate he spoke of the pressing concerns of the greater world with its grave problems; social, economic, and political. Always in this reviewer's opinion he did so with great sensitivity and insight, but with none of the partisan or ideological spirit that so often characterizes *eminente* pontificating on such themes.

The Hispanic work, so long delayed, was at last undertaken. The Hispanic Commission reported that the Rev. Jeffrey Gonzalez had arrived in the diocese at the end of summer to begin Santa Margarita de Escocia in the Butler Avenue area barrio. Thus, in an unauspicious manner began a work that has grown slowly but surely since and is now worshipping in the Sierra Vista Methodist Church. A fuller account of which can be found in the preceding chapter.

The 1983 Convention had the theme of "One Family In Christ". At the Convention the Bishop expressed his appreciation for the work of the Diocesan staff and welcomed the author of this chapter and editor of the work, as Assistant to the Bishop, having come out of retirement from parish ministry to work with Bishop Rivera whom I admired and respected for his firm and principled stand for "the faith once for all delivered to the saints."

The Bishop observed the State of The Church in the Diocese as being good. Church membership was growing, very slowly, but enough to give encouragement. The most impressive aspect, however, was that increase in giving in what was a time of high inflation and recession in the economy. Giving over the preceding five years had grown by 55%. Accolades were given Elwyn Peterson for his work in stewardship and his persistence in promoting the Tithe as the goal and standard in this diocese.

ECCO and Bliss Grove were proposed for incorporation as separate entities in the diocese with their own board of directors. A step that yet remains to be consummated for various reasons.

The overall thrust of the Bishop's message was one of cautious optimism, and he spoke warmly of the accomplishments of the various para-church activities: e.g., Cursillo, Faith Alive, Marriage Encounter, etc., and their contribution to revitalizing the faith of many. Hopefully these activities would enhance the goal of "One Family In Christ".

Human concerns, Children and Young People, were topics the Bishop addressed. But, then, came the concern that became a major factor in the diocese over the next several years — Venture in Mission. VIM was first propounded as a challenge by Presiding Bishop John Allin, at a time when the Church was in the throes of controversy and turmoil over many issues. Nonetheless, the Presiding Bishop presented the challenge of the national Church seeking the sum of 100 million dollars from its constituency to meet various needs in the world, in the nation, and in the local church and community.

San Joaquin was a late entry into the program because of the effort to fund and develop ECCO. Now, said the Bishop, it is time for us to turn our attention from our own needs to address the larger issues.

It befell me, as the Bishop's assistant, to seek to implement that program in this diocese. In due course plans were laid for a committee to consider the program and to seek input from the diocese at large as to what we ought to be doing, and then to present this in a coherent package for consideration at a special Convention which was finally held on January 28, 1984, in St. James' Cathedral, Fresno.

The committee's recommended goal of $1,111,000 was presented and each program and project considered and approved. In all, fifteen programs and projects were approved, and the recommended monetary goal was approved. The campaign to raise the funds was undertaken by Ward, Dreshman & Reinhardt, who gave invaluable help in developing the campaign. The sum was to be raised over a three-year period. For the most part individual parishes and missions accepted their assigned portion of the total sum. At the time of this writing the diocese has received and disbursed almost 80% of the goal. It was a stipulation of the Special Convention that 51% of the monies raised must go outside the diocese and the remainder could go for programs and projects within the diocese. This stipulation has been strictly adhered to. As the Bishop remarked at the beginning of the campaign: "Venture in Mission is one of the most unselfish things the Episcopal Church has ever undertaken." Certainly, it stands as a testimonial to the concern of Episcopalians about the needs of the world, and the fact that not just 100 million dollars was raised from the inception of the program, but nearly 200 million dollars.

The regular Diocesan Convention of 1984 took place March 30 to April 1 at the Camp and Conference Center-Oakhurst. An opportunity to display the accomplishments of the previous two years in developing the camp. It is no exaggeration to say that everyone who attended that conference was astonished at what had been accomplished and at the quality of the facilities. There is no doubt that ECCO will stand as a monument to Bishop Rivera's and his associates' dream of a truly outstanding camp and conference facility.

The Bishop's theme was "The Field Is The World", which will give you some idea of where he was coming from and where he was going! He was still on the same "old Hobby Horse" some would say, but it was and is a "hobby horse" that has carried the Church a long ways down through the centuries, and the Bishop is not one to abandon tried and proven means for accomplishing the Church's goal of bringing the Gospel to all the world.

"When I was consecrated fifteen years ago, they asked me, "What do you think are the greatest needs of the Episcopal Church in San Joaquin?" I said then, "Three things: Evangelism, Stewardship, and Christian Education". Indeed, he had! The Bishop continued: "I have not changed my mind yet, and I think that this is not just what we need in San Joaquin now, but this is what we need in our Church and all Christian Churches. Evangelism, Stewardship, and Christian Education are the ways of implementing the Divine Commission. We do these things in obedience to Christ. How dare we forget what He said — what He commanded: 'Full authority in heaven and on earth has been committed to me. Go forth, therefore, and make all nations my disciples.'

"Our Church, and many other churches, pass resolutions on subjects about which they know little, and can do less about them. We try to run the house of Caesar, forgetting that we have a Christian home and a Christian family to raise, and that that family cannot be any smaller than the whole world.

"Venture in Mission is our 'aggiornamento'. It is a breath of fresh air; it is the open window from which we can see and relate to Zimbabwe and Namibia and Colombia and Honduras, and closer to home the Filipino and Hispanic brothers and sisters in our Valley and the Asian groups in our cities. Venture in Mission can save our churches and our Church, and, indeed, it is a good step in saving our own souls."

Under the rubric of "Evangelism" the Bishop noted with satisfaction, but not complacency, the accomplishments of various of our parishes in planting parochial missions — and expressed his gratification that with the support of the congregations through their giving for Mission work in the Diocese and the help of Coalition 14 monies that the goal he had set of one new mission every year had been accomplished over the past decade. At the same time congratulations were in order for two new missions being admitted at this Convention: St. Laurence in North Stockton, under the care of Deacon Sylvia Singer; and Holy Cross, Stockton, under the care of Fr. Andre Justo, who has made such significant progress in the development of work among the Filipino community in that city. At the same time work among the Asian refugees in our midst was moving forward under the supervision of Fr. Robert Williams and Mrs. Eleanor Osborn. Once again, what had been only a dream a decade or so before was at last coming to fruition.

The Twenty-fifth Annual Convention of the Diocese of San Joaquin was also its 75th Anniversary. Fittingly enough, the Bishop used the occasion as an opportunity to rehearse the accomplishments of the past, to honor those Saints who had gone before and bequeathed to us such a goodly heritage, and to point to some things we needed to be about in the immediate present and the future. True to his predilections, the Bishop developed the theme of "You Shall Be My Witnesses". "We either obey or disobey. In other words, to quote Bishop Heber Gooden, 'Christ did not tell us to bite the bullet; but to get the lead out!'"

He commented on the founding of this Missionary District in 1910 under Bishop Louis Sanford's leadership, who, at the time, observed that it was beginning with but a dozen clergy, with its people in some twenty-five scattered communities. The Church in what is now designated a Diocese has some fifty-six missions, parishes, and preaching stations, served by fifty clergy (the seeming discrepancy is due to the fact that some clergy are serving in more than one place, and several of the missions are served on a part-time basis). There are, moreover, 39 clergy who are canonically resident but non-parochial. Some are retired, several are in military chaplaincies, and a good number are non-stipendiary.

The Bishop took the opportunity to highlight some of the accomplishments since 1968. He noted one new mission per year had been established: Atwater; Clovis; Holy Family, Fresno; Santa Margarita's, Fresno; Kernville; Mammoth Lakes; Mariposa; Ceres; Oakhurst: St. Michael's, Sonora; Holy Cross, Stockton; and, this year, Groveland. "In 1969," he said, "you set a faith goal of one new mission a year. You did it!" It is doubtful that these would have come to realization had it not been for his constant prodding, although he was gracious and diplomatic to say, "You did it!"

As could be expected, he reminisced about the past and its accomplishments, but not in the manner of one who is satisfied and content to let matters rest there. Rather, as a stimulus for the task that still lies before this diocese. His concluding remarks typify his attitude.

"There are still dreams to dream; purposes to set; goals to establish. There are still many persons of yesteryear that we should pay tribute to on this anniversary; many persons living today that we have not mentioned, but to whom we owe a great deal . . . . I cannot close this address without pleading with you to reach out and bring souls into the Body of Christ."

In 1986 the Bishop chose as his theme "Christ Our Peace". A year in which there was much emphasis upon the concept of "peace" being promoted by many groups. The Bishop began by asking "What is Peace?" "Next to 'love', peace may be the most abused word in the English language . . ." He went on to develop the theme in its great variety of meanings, and without belittling the prevailing idea of freedom from armed conflict, the Bishop pointed out that from the scriptural point of view we are not promised that kind of peace in this world. Rather, Christ said: "I have not come to bring peace, but a sword" (Mt. 10:34). He does offer us a transcendental peace, a "peace that passes all understanding" but it does not mean the absence of conflict. In fact, it promises us conflict in this world if we are faithful to our mission as Christians to bear witness to Him, but at the same time a peace that comes through obedience to His command.

The Bishop went on to detail his plan for a course for Catechists that would be taught by qualified clergy in the diocese, and would have some real substance. "Cathechists," he noted are, "historically disciples who will study, learn and become 'mouth-pieces' of the church, vocal witnesses for Christ and his body." This program inaugurated a long felt desire on his part to bring really solid and sound teaching to the laity, who too often are fed pablum when they ought to be nourished on the strong meat of the Gospel, to paraphrase St. Paul. The program has caught on with a significant number of lay people attending and the first commissioning class for Catechists was held in November, 1987, two years after they began.

The Convention of 1987 saw Bishop Rivera dwelling on the theme of "Lord, Revive Thy Church". Something of deep concern to the Bishop as pastoral leader of this diocese is his awareness of the decline in membership of this Church over the past decade or so, even though the Diocese of San Joaquin does seem to be holding its own. He noted the admission of Arnold as a Mission congregation in union with Convention, and the preaching station organized at Edwards Air Force Base and services instituted at the Chapel of St. Martin of Tours at the Asian Center in Fresno. A total of eighteen mission in seventeen years. Few dioceses can make that claim, but it is not said boastfully — "This is the Lord's doing" and we rejoice in it. At the same time it can be said that it has required faithfulness to the biblical mandate and obedience to "seek and to save the lost" on the part of the Bishop and those who serve these missions.

There was much expectation that the Bishop would announce his intention to retire at the 1987 Convention, and rumors were rife that he would do so. He had sought the counsel of his Standing Committee, the Rural Deans, and the Diocesan Council, earlier in the year as to how best to proceed. Should he call for the election of a Coadjutor or simply serve out the remaining time until he reached the canonical age for retirement at age 72 and leave it to the Standing Committee to call for the election of a Bishop? After lengthy deliberation the advice offered was conflicting and the Bishop was left to exercise his own best judgment in the matter. He did not mention his retirement in the Convention proceedings.

In any case, he did come to the conclusion that he would call for the election of a Coadjutor, and to that end a committee was elected consisting of a clergy representative and lay representative from each Deanery, and six appointed by the Bishop, with Dean George Ruof as Chairman of the committee. They were consituted as the Search, Review and Nominating Committee for selecting candidates for nomination for the position of Coadjutor Bishop of the Diocese of San Joaquin. This committee began meeting in the fall to carry out its important task.

This brief and altogether inadequate record is but a summary of Bishop Victor Rivera's accomplishments and contributions to the history of this Diocese. The selections of noteworthy items and the account is the choice of the author of this chapter. Omissions are many, but choices had to be made; errors of fact there may be, although every effort has been made to not make such errors. In any case, the responsibility is mine alone, and I accept any criticisms with some humility; but would welcome any accolades preferred with greater alacrity. The account is presented with full recognition of its inadequacies, and the biases expressed are mine alone insofar as this account is concerned, although others may share them in some measure. It is altogether fitting, I believe to end on the note of expressing thanks to Almighty God for Bishop Rivera's leadership, and his steadfastness in the Faith, in a most trying time of the history of this Church. "Well done, thou good and faithful servant!"

Elsewhere in this account of the history of the Diocese of San Joaquin you have read about or seen the picture of the clergy with parochial responsibilities at the time of this writing. Here we want to take the opportunity to recognize the retired clergy and the non-parochial clergy.

We begin with Bishop Robert Mize who is not only our senior clergyman, but our beloved assisting Bishop. He is canonically resident in this diocese, and is a collegial member of the House of Bishops, having been consecrated Bishop in the Province of South Africa. He is notably a man of prayer. He visits parishes and missions and confirms on behalf of the Diocesan. His interest in missionary work, especially in Africa, is contagious. But, of course, he will always be remembered as the founder of the St. Francis' Home for Boys, and he will forever be "Fr. Bob" to many.

The Rev. George F. Turney was ordained deacon the same year as Bishop Mize and they were also born in the same year, 1907. Fr. Turney continues assisting at St. Paul's, Visalia, and at other churches in the diocese as need arises. His interest in the Celtic Church in the field of Church History is well known. He also has artistic talent, having made several stained glass windows in past years.

The Rev. John T. Raymond is our senior priest in residence. Fr. Raymond came as Rector of Sonora in 1947. He still assists in Visalia, Lemoore, and, indeed, wherever he is needed.

The Rev. William Richmond is noted for his preaching ability and for his learning. He continues to maintain his skills in both Hebrew and Greek. Fr. Bill was ordained in 1955, and although he is retired he currently is serving the church in Lemoore.

The Rev. Canon Ronald Swanson served in this diocese for many years. He resigned as Rector of St. James', Sonora, in 1987, having served in the diocese since 1959.

The Rev. Norman Van Walterop has been a "tent-maker" priest for a long time. He still helps out wherever he is needed.

The Rev. Raymond Knapp came to the diocese in 1966. Fr. Knapp retired in 1987 having served for twenty years as a priest, first in Delano and then in Lodi.

The Rev. Kenneth Schildt was a worker priest, his field being Insurance, from which he is now retired. He has been associated with this diocese since 1968.

The Rev. Lee Wilson, although retired, is still assisting at St. Barnabas', a parochial mission of St. Paul's, Visalia. His great interest in and knowledge of ornithology (birds) and entomology (insects) is indeed notable.

The Rev. James Trotter was received into the diocese in 1969. He continues to help in Turlock and surrounding areas.

The Rev. James McDonald came to St. Columba's in 1972. After two years he resigned to accept a position as a social worker in Fresno. He continues to assist at Holy Family and other churches as needed.

The Rev. Peter Barker has been in the diocese since 1958; although he left for a short time, he returned in 1973. He is now retired and now supplies in many churches in the diocese as need arises.

Fr. Richard Williams came to St. Stephen's in 1974. He is now retired on disability.

The Rev. Alexander Patience was received into this diocese in 1975. He resigned as Rector of the Church of the Saviour, Hanford, in late 1987 to accept a church position in Dallas, Texas.

The Rev. Leon Plante was received into the diocese in 1979. Although he is retired, he continues to assist at St. Paul's, Modesto, and other churches as needed.

The Rev. James Short served as founding Vicar and Dean of St. Aidan's Mission congregation and school in Fresno. He resigned in 1981 to pursue a career in insurance and financial planning. He continues to assist at St. Mary's, Fresno, and elsewhere as needed.

The Rev. Jeffrey Smith, ordained in this diocese in 1986, served as Deacon Assistant at St. Paul's, Visalia, and Chaplain at King's View Hospital, Reedley. He is now serving a parish in England.

The Rev. Robert Williams was received into the diocese in 1980. Fr. Bob serves as Christian Education consultant and as Director of the Episcopal Asian Ministries in Fresno.

The Rev. Edgar Parrott, after serving as Christian Education consultant, resigned and has been working as a counselor at Kern View Hospital, Bakersfield. He is a great help as a supply priest, especially in the Kern County area. He is noted for his liturgical acumen and his musical talents.

The Rev. Watson Bartholome came to San Joaquin in 1977. Fr. Bart served as Vicar of the church in Tulare until his retirement in 1987. He continues to supply at Hanford and other places as needed.

The Rev. Paul Snider, who came to Tracy in 1977, is now retired but remains active. Most recently he has been serving as *locum tenems* at Hobrook, Arizona.

The Rev. John W. Burberry was ordained in 1979. Fr. Bill served the parochial mission for several years. He continues to assist in Visalia and elsewhere as needed. Fr. Bill's talents as a musician are frequently called upon at various diocesan functions.

The Rev. Brian Endicott was received into the diocese in 1980. He has been Vicar of Avenal and assisted and supplied at a number of churches in the diocese.

The Rev. Robert Richard was ordained in this diocese in 1980. After serving in Selma, the diocesan office, and Merced, he resigned from the latter to pursue a doctorate at the Graduate Theological Union in Berkeley, California.

The Rev. Charles Karoly was ordained in 1981 as a non-stipendiary priest. He served as Vicar of St. Thomas of Canterbury, Mammoth Lakes, until 1986 when he resigned due to the time demands of his position with the town of Mammoth Lakes. He resides in Mammoth Lakes and supplies in the Sierra Deanery when needed.

The Ven. Wayne B. Williamson came to the diocese in 1982 to serve as assistant to the Bishop. He was made Archdeacon in 1985 and served in that capacity until his retirement in 1987. Fr. Wayne continues to assist the diocesan in a variety of ways, and was elected by the Diocesan Search, Receiving, and Nominating Committee for a Coadjutor Bishop to serve as their Secretary.

We would be remiss if we failed to mention a special group of clergymen, to wit, three who are active as Chaplains in the Armed Forces of the United States. We are proud of them: Chaplain John Whitsell, Chaplain Terry Hamilton, and Chaplain Bill Tumbleson. A former Chaplain (Col.) in the U. S. Air Force, the Rev. E. James Kingsley, was received into this diocese in 1983 and served for a short period in Tracy. Subsequently, he served in Lemoore, and is presently serving as part-time assistant at St. James' Cathedral and as a part-time Chaplain for the local Veterans' Administration Hospital.

Canonically resident in San Joaquin, but not domiciled in the diocese are: The Rev. Dr. Connor Lynn, ordained in 1956 at Caicos Island; the Rev. Victor Hatfield, received in 1958, and now living in Cambria, California. The Rev. Harold Thelin, received in 1960, now living in Arizona. The Rev. Howard L. Mather, received in 1961, now living in the Diocese of Olympia; the Rev. David K. Wilson, received in 1966, now serving a congregation in Denver, Colorado; the Rev. Richard Warren, received in 1969, now residing in Cambria, California; the Rev. Percy Jerkins, ordained in this diocese in 1970, living in Ontario, California; the Rev. Francis O'Donnell, ordained in 1977, now residing in Florida; the Rev. Glynn Harper, ordained in 1978, now in Texas; the Rev. Jack Koonce, ordained in 1982, living in Chico, California; the Rev. Albert Walton, received in 1984, residing in New Jersey; and the Rev. James Denson, received in 1984, now residing in the Diocese of California.

As of this writing, we have seven deacons: the Reverends Hugh and Millie Cook, working in Stockton; Scott Murray, serving at Corcoran; Elmer Gould serving in Hanford; and Sylvia Singer, Vicar of St. Laurence's Mission, Stockton; the Rev. Robert Woods, serving in St. Luke's, Bakersfield and assisting in Taft; and the Rev. David Foster serving at All Saints', Bakersfield.

APPENDIX A

HOW THE SAN JOAQUIN ECW "SAVED" THE NATIONAL ECW

Even before women were seated in the House of Deputies at General Convention (1970), there were attempts at the National level to dissolve the Women's Triennial, which had met in parallel to the General Convention since 1874. It was thought by some that the Episcopal Church Women's Triennial had fulfilled its usefulness. San Joaquin's ECW thought otherwise, however, as did many of the Diocesan ECWs in Province VIII.

Province VIII had a long-standing and strong organization, going back to the days of Bishop Sanford of San Joaquin. The ECW or Province VIII adopted by-laws to maintain an annual meeting, at least of officers, even in years when the Provincial Synod did not meet. When the discussion on the national level echoed in talk of dissolving the Province VIII ECW (and in the Diocese of San Joaquin there was talk of withdrawal even from the Provincial meetings for budgetary reasons), many argued strongly that the Provincial meetings provided a forum for people who could not attend the General Convention; furthermore, the Provincial meetings were a learning experience that would otherwise be lost, if discontinued.

San Joaquin's Episcopal Church Women therefore decided, under the leadership of Mrs. Nell Onstad, to present the case for the continuance of the national Triennial. A strong statement to this effect was drafted and sent to every Diocesan ECW President, to the Presiding Bishop, to the Editors of THE EPISCOPALIAN and THE LIVING CHURCH, and to a number of others influential in the Church. Gradually, other diocesan groups took up the cry and circulated letters.

At the Trinennial Meeting in Houston, October, 1970, Nell Onstad was appointed Chairman of the committee to draft a resolution on the matter. The majority of the dioceses were in favor of continuing the Triennial, but the three eastern members of the committee, and the Nation ECW Board "resource person" assigned to the committee, were determined to follow the National Board's suggestion that "women's organizations, as such, were no longer, valid; that all organizations should be open to all people, and that Triennial should be discontinued." Nell argued that women would meet in any case, and that without national ties, the groups would be in danger of becoming ingrown and parochial; and that the women of the Church worked hardest and studied and gave for the missionary outreach of the Church. She managed to get her committee to soften its resolution. After lively discussion the Triennial decided that there would indeed be another Meeting in Louisville, Kentucky, in 1973.

The work was not over. The San Joaquin Resolution was sent to the Presidents of all existing diocesan ECWs in the U.S., with copies for all their delegates to the next Triennial in Louisville. Copies were also sent to the Chairman of the Resolutions Committee, the ECW Presiding Officer, THE LIVING CHURCH and THE EPISCOPALIAN, with covering letters.

When the Triennial convened at Louisville, in the fall of 1973, Ruth Cooper, an attorney (now one of the Chancellors of San Joaquin), was a delegate from San Joaquin's ECW and was involved in the consideration of all resolutions presented concerning the future of the Triennial. The women voted overwhelmingly to continue their meeting simultaneous with the Church's General Convention.

At the Anaheim Convention of 1985, the national organization of Episcopal Church Women was formally re-established, and officers elected. Evelyn Keddie of San Joaquin was elected the National Vice President, and Charlotte Green was named as VIIIth Province Representative to the Trinennial Planning Committee for the Detroit Convention in 1988. Both are past Presidents of the San Joaquin ECW.

From Elizabeth Lyles' Re-write of *DRAFT. January 20, 1987
(with information from Mrs. Ellen Onstad)

THE SAN JOAQUIN DAUGHERS OF THE KING

The Daughters of the King is an international religious order for Anglican women, living "in the world", who take their baptismal vows seriously by committing themselves to a life-long vocation of prayer, service, and evangelism, under the direction of their priest or bishop.

Mrs. Evelyn Walters, wife of the late Bishop Sumner Walters, 2nd Bishop of the Diocese of San Joaquin, was instrumental in forming the first chapter of DOK in the District of San Joaquin, when a group of women at St. John's, Stockton, met with her to make their vows in the mid-1950s. In succeeding years chapters were added at St. Stephen's, Stockton; St. James', Sonora; St. Mary's, Fresno; St. Luke's, Merced; and St. John's, Porterville.

In 1970, Mrs. Joe (Avis) Vieira gathered women at St. Mary's in Manteca, and with the help of St. Stephen's, Stockton, formed a chapter at St. Mary's. Soon after this she called together the first Diocesan Assembly of Daughters of the King, and served as Assembly President for two three-year terms. Under her energetic leadership, new chapters were formed at St. Paul's, Visalia; St. Raphael's, Oakhurst; St. Mark's, Tracy; St. Anne's, Stockton; and several chapters were revived from inactivity. (The chapters at St. Mary's, Fresno; and St. Mark's, Tracy, are now inactive).

Today there are active chapters in the other churches listed above, as well as St. Michael's, Sonora; Grace Church, Groveland; St. Columba's, Fresno; and St. Mattias', Oakdale. There is also a Bishop's Chapter in Fresno, drawing from St. James' Cathedral; Holy Family, Fresno; and the Church of the Resurrection, Clovis.

As chapters serve under the priest, their work varies; yet the consistent emphasis is the life of prayer, service, and evangelism. Chapters are not allowed to pursue money-making activities. Most groups meet monthly. Many have on-going study programs; many visit the sick and minister to the shut-ins. Some provide literature for institutions or tracts for the local church; many sponsor Quiet Days or Retreats. Every chapter has a prayer chain where members pray for whatever is requested of them, as well as for each other, and for "the spread of Christ's Kingdom among women and girls." Every woman in the DOK is expected to keep a Rule of Life.

(by Moina Lucent)

EPISCOPAL CONFERENCE CENTER OAKHURST

ECCO - DREAM and REALITY

> I have spread my dreams under your feet,
> Tread softly because you tread on my dreams.
> (William Butler Yeats)

Twenty years ago a large group of laity, men and women, met to discuss the future needs of the diocese. Emerging high on the list of priorities was the deeply felt need for a conference center where people whom all the parishes and missions of the diocese, and outside the diocese could come together for edification, inspiration, training for ministry, cross-pollination and mutual support.

SIERRA SKY RANCH

The following spring, at a follow-up dinner meeting at the home of the bishop, this group of interested lay people made the decision to seek out a suitable site for the future conference center. Criteria were set and the search began. Important was a central location, ease of accessibility, usable in all seasons, away from urban distraction, etc.

After many months the search narrowed down to the Oakhurst area when — serendipitously — the Holy Spirit put it into the mind of Mr. William Eli to sell the Sierra Sky Ranch. And, he wanted to sell it to us. Since the Sky Ranch was a resort which had long been used by the diocese for special conferences it, and Mr. Eli, were old friends.

However, the asking price for three hundred acres of land, including the lodge, with a 9-hole golf course, swimming pool, barn, corral, horses and parrot was $750,000.

SKY RANCH ASSOCIATES

Since the diocese was not in a position to pay out that large a sum for a conference center — or — anything else, for that matter, a group of twelve laymen decided to form an independent corporation, "Sky Ranch Associates", in order to purchase the property themselves. They did ask the bishop to assist them in obtaining a $100,000 loan for the down payment.

This the bishop was able to do as he applied for and was blessed with an interest-free loan from the Executive Council of the Episcopal Church. With this money as down payment, the property was acquired by SRA for $550,000.

Seeing that the project was underway and in good hands, God heaved a sigh of pleasure and relief and turned His attention elsewhere.

TIMBER TRAILS

"How do you eat an elephant?" someone once asked. The answer? "One bite at a time."

Since the entire Sky Ranch acreage was too big to consume in one bite, the Sky Ranch Associates decided to sell 202 acres to Timber Trails, a company who wanted to develop a sophisticated camping and vacation resort.

Timber Trails bought 40 acres outright. They immediately began the development of water, power, roads and campsites on that property which is situated between Highway 41 and the western edge of the golf course (now known as Bliss Grove).

They also took a purchase option on the 162 acres which were (and, incidentally, still are) located across the entire north edge of the site, above the golf course.

PAYING OFF THE MORTAGE

The Associates then settled down to make a commercial success of the Ranch. The plan was to keep the Ranch and the dining room open to the public in order to pay off the remainder of the mortage. Diocesan, deanery, parish and mission conferences were to be accommodated on a "first Come, first served" basis at the regular commercial rates.

In the Articles of Incorporation of Sky Ranch Associates it was stated that when the property was paid for it would be turned over to the Diocese of San Joaquin, free and clear, for use as a conference center.

NEED FOR EXPANSION

As more and more conferences, retreats, marriage encounter weekends, vestry weekends, etc., were scheduled at Sky Ranch, the need for larger and more comfortable meeting rooms became evident.

Also, during this period, a new mission was being planned by Canon Enrico Molinar. O.A.R., who lived in a mobile home located on the Sky Ranch property. Every Sunday the tiny new congregation crowded into his living room for worship. This mission was subsequently named Saint Raphael's.

SUMNER WALTERS' CONFERENCE CENTER

So in 1975-76, a mini-campaign was held to establish the "Sumner Walters' Conference Center" and $100,000 was raised. This was accomplished throughout the diocese mainly by the hard work and dedication of Bob and Edna Olmsted, but also through the generosity of the Walters family and friends.

Five acres of land were leased by the diocese from Sky Ranch Associates and another beneficence in the form of a grant of $20,000 was bestowed on the project by the United Thank Offering of the women of the Church.

Another godsend appeared at this very moment in the form an ad spotted by the bright eyes of Fr. Tom Foster, offering a second-hand, 60 x 30 foot, modular building for sale. The building was purchased with money from the UTO grant and installed on the five acres.

Members of the congregation of St. Raphael's worked very hard clearing the area, and putting in the foundation for the new facility which they would share.

This modular unit was considered temporary because the bishop had no intention of establishing a permanent building on property which was not free from debt and totally owned by the diocese. The $100,000 raised in the earlier campaign was invested under the able direction of Mr. Tom Doyle to be held and multiplied for future use.

The Sumner Walters' Conference Center on the Sierra Sky Ranch property was dedicated on the first Sunday in June, 1976, with Bishop Walters and his family in attendance. This happy occasion was further glamorized by the first "Faire Day", which has since become an annual event.

... and God looked down and saw we had done it all wrong!

In the fall of 1976 God decided to check back and see how things were going. He waxed wroth and cried out: "You idiots! You sold the half I wanted!!!!"

Timber Trails suddenly went into bankruptcy. The Pioneer Bank of Chicago became the owner of the first 40 acres, and the 162 acres (and the monies due thereon) reverted back to the Sky Ranch Associates.

The bishop immediately sought the advice of the Hon. Charles Hamlin, former judge of the bankruptcy court, who suggested that in order to protect everyone's interests the diocese buy the 162 acres and resell it to another party. For such a desirable piece of land this would not be difficult.

THE 162 ACRES PURCHASED

The bishop, acting on Judge Hamlin's advice and also the recommendation of the Diocesan Council, purchased the 162 acres and several offers were considered. The plan for the sale of the property was announced in Fresno at the Annual Convention held in February of 1977.

That night three laymen, Mark Vasco, Mike ..., and Jim Bishop, with tears in their eyes, called the bishop to their motel room and pleaded with him not to sell the property, but to keep it for the relocation of Camp San Joaquin away from its inconvenient high mountain site.

THE SPECIAL CONVENTION

The bishop explained that the only way this could be done was to have it voted on by Convention; it was too much responsibility for the bishop and Council alone to make such an important decision. The men agreed and a special convention was called in May 1977.

After a day-long debate the special convention of 1977 voted overwhelmingly to purchase the 162 acres for the relocation of Camp San Joaquin and for the development of a permanent Sumner Walters' Conference Center. A development fund campaign was held that very day and $100,000 was pledged on the spot.

CAMPAIGN FOR FUNDS

In the fall of 1978, a feasibility study was carried out by Resource Services, Inc., to determine the potential for a capital funds drive to raise money to build a camp and conference center on the new site.

The results showed that a potential existed if Sierra Sky Ranch were to be sold. The people of the diocese had expressed great confusion about the purpose and financing of Sierra Sky Ranch.

Diocesan Council voted to undertake the campaign under the direction of RSI. Goals were set and the campaign was carried out.

SALE OF THE SKY RANCH

Meanwhile, in response to the request of the people of the diocese Sierra Sky Ranch was put on the market and readily sold. The price was $550,000 for the buildings and 94 acres (including the golf course), with $250,000 down, and the balance to be paid off in three years.

After outstanding debts were paid off, Sky Ranch Associates turned all assets over to the diocese, and the money — approximately $250,000 — was added to the Camp-Conference Center funds that had been raised by the campaign.

THE "40 ACRES"

While all these other things were going on, God prompted the bishop to ask Judge Hamlin to write a letter to Pioneer Bank suggesting that they donate the 40 acres to the diocese as a tax write-off. Pioneer wasn't willing to go that far, but they countered with a very reasonable offer to sell rather than to give the property. After much telephoning and correspondence $85,000 was agreed upon as a price for the site.

Where would the money for the 40 acres come from? Well, it just so happened that Mr. and Mrs. Guy Bliss of Corcoran had left in their wills a legacy for the Diocese of San Joaquin with the proviso that it be used for some project for the elderly. The bishop and Council agreed that this money, which now represented about $40,000, could be used to purchase the land. They further designated that the land would be used for the development of affordable housing for senior citizens.

At about the same time, moved by the Spirit, Mr. and Mrs. David Chambers offered to give $85,000 to the diocese for the purchase of the land if the diocese would let them use five acres for their own use.

The bishop and the council accepted this gift and the purchase of the 40 acres was accomplished. The Chambers later on proposed an alternative to the five acres use.

BLISS GROVE

This property remains separate from the 162 acres. It is governed by a special committee which has, with Council's approval, given it the name "Bliss Grove", in memory of the couple who left the original legacy. This fund was subsequently augmented by a small legacy from the estate of the Rev. Charles Pitkin, late Rector of the Church of Our Saviour, Hanford.

The furtherance of this project into a retirement village has continued separately from, but parallel to, the advancement of the conference center facility. Other than the original legacies no diocesan funds have been raised for, nor allocated to Bliss Grove, but some gifts were received from the Fr. Pitkins and the Effie Davis estates. It is presently planned as a self-sufficient, self-propelled project using only the legacy monies for start-up expenses. As of this writing, the end of 1987, several problems have developed and little has been done at Bliss Grove for the last year.

A FIVE YEAR LEASE

At the time of the sale of Sierra Sky Ranch a provision was included in the deed of sale reserving the five acres leased by the diocese from SRA to be used by St. Raphael's Church and for the conferences which would continue to be held at Sierra Sky Ranch until the new facility was built. This lease of the property and building was to be at no cost to the church or the diocese.

Looking back it is easy to see how God's hand was guiding us and propelling us toward our goals. ECCO has now been in operation for six years. Lewis (Scoop) and Rhoda Beardsley were appointed Director and Cook. The ECCO Board acts very much like a Bishop's Committee. We were authorized by Convention to form a separate corporation. This has not been done for several reasons. If ECCO has to go as a separate entity the liability insurance would be a very great expense and at this juncture difficult to acquire. Making separate corporations of ECCO and Bliss Grove will bring related problems, e.g., providing water and sewer from one source to another. Separate corporations, like those of parochial schools create serious problems dealing with ownership, administration and the like.

-by Barbara Rivera

Advent 1987

ECCO ACTIVITIES

On June 18, 1982, the first group to meet at ECCO, the Aspirants, Postulants, and Candidates Conference, used a 4' x 8' piece of plywood across two saw horses as a table. Their meals were cooked on a borrowed stove and prepared on a card table. That day was just another little step in the fulfillment of a vision Fr. Vic and others had over 40 years before. With Camp San Joaquin and Sky Ranch Associates, those 18 people who met by the pond that summer day in 1982, became the first of many groups who continually come back to our Diocesan Conference Center for retreats, conferences and camps, and the ministry established by Camp San Joaquin and Sky Ranch started a new and exciting phase.

In the five and one-half years since that humble beginning, over 460 groupings have found our facilities conducive to their program goals. In our diocesan family, many parishes and/or missions have had planning sessions. All the E.C.W. functions are held at ECCO. Wardens, Treasurers, Clergy, Lay Readers, Chalice Bearers, Catechists, Clergy Wives, Diocesan Council and many committees come to the Conference Center.

Here, too, other denominations find a welcome for their plans and programs. Our friends come from the Roman Catholic Church, Armenian, the Southern Baptists, the Jewish folk-dancers, the Mennonites, Fresno Bible students, Castle Air Force Base single adults, Nazarene-Latin groups as well as various Lutheran Church leaders.

In our own Church, we are reaching out to the Province of the Pacific with our Speak Spanish Conference which welcomes students from *every* western state. We have hosted many Provincal groups and now are being used by national Church programs ... such as National Bible Institute.

ECCO welcomes all non-profit functions from our local community of Eastern Madera County: Yosemite High School, the Madera County Board of Education. A. A. groups from all over California, the Rotary Club, the Kiwanis Club, the Lions Club, and the local Chamber of Commerce.

With our many meeting rooms, we are enjoying our relationship with State and Federal Forest Service training classes. We reach out to these public servants and they find a deep mutual understanding of their concerns and what the Episcopal Church is all about.

National programs, such as Dr. Tim Savage's Lab II and National Hispanic courses, again contribute to our growth when participants find that the facility is as important as the program.

In the true spirit of mission, we reach out to all. The Association of Retarded Citizens, the Muscular Dystrophy kids, the cancer patients, the elderly, and recovering alcoholics all find compassion and support from a staff that cares.

When we want to sing praises for all He has done to assist us in our growth we can sing along with a Cursillo guitar, a Clovis High School Choir, the Choral Director's Association, the Barbershoppers or the family singing of our neighboring Diocese of El Camino Real.

We are most thankful for the vision of our Bishop, the generosity of the people of our diocese, the commitment of our Board along with a staff who fulfills the purpose of ECCO, which is, "To provide an environment which is sensitive to and supportive of the needs of the community served." In 1987 68 different groups used the facilities at ECCO — many of them repeaters.

-by Lewis "Scoop" Beardsley

CAMP SAN JOAQUIN

We all remember our Lord's example of seeking out places away from the city for retreat, rest, and teaching. The scriptures recount this in many places: "And seeing the multitudes, he went up into a mountain: and when he was set, his disciples came unto him; And he opened his mouth, and taught them." "And the apostles gathered themselves together unto Jesus. And he said unto them, Come ye yourselves apart into a desert place, and rest a while." Again, "And Jesus went up into a mountain, and there he sat with his disciples."

The Diocese of San Joaquin is fortunate to have such a place in Camp San Joaquin, located in the beautiful Sierras midway between Yosemite and Sequoia National Parks. It represents the culmination of a goal which began in the early years of this dioceses.

Louis Childs Sanford, San Joaquin's first Bishop, consecrated January 25, 1911, organized the first general Summer Conference for the then Missionary District. It was held at Camp Sierra during the summer of 1930 and followed by other conferences in successive summers.

The second Bishop of San Joaquin. Sumner Francis Dudley Walters, was consecrated January 6, 1944, and that same year an Episcopal Summer Conference for the district was again held at Camp Sierra.

From 1946 to 1950 conferences were held at Asilomar, with the first, from July 7-13, 1946, billed as "An inspirational, educational, recreational conference" for all from 9 to 90. The Rev. Harry B. Lee was the Dean of that conference. He and our present Bishop, Victor Rivera, were the only two clergy now in our diocese who were in attendance then.

When expense grew and scheduling became difficult, interested and dedicated people made it possible for the district to acquire its own camp, and in the summer of 1951 Camp San Joaquin was opened in the Sequoia National Forest. For more than thirty years our camp and conference programs have continued there.

After Bishop Walters retirement, the consecration of Victor M. Rivera, as third Bishop of San Joaquin on October 15, 1968, only strengthened our commitment to the value of programs begun, and eventually led us to the reality of the dedication of the facility.

Since 1951, summer camps for adults and children of all ages have been held at Camp San Joaquin — Sequoia. Estimating an average of 200 campers per summer times 37 years equals a total of 7,400 people who have experienced the beauty of God's creation through our summer camp programs (and this estimate may be a low figure!) How many lives have been strengthened — how many people, young and old, have had their faith increased through these mountain-top experiences at Camp San Joaquin, only God really knows. We, for our part, give thanks to God for the camp, for Bishop Rivera's dedication and commitment to camps and conferences, and for all those faithful staff members (both lay and clergy) who have helped to make all this possible! (with thanks to Elizabeth Lyles, edited by the Rev. William Fay)

HISTORY OF THE EPISCOPAL ASIAN COMMUNITY SERVICES

In the early 1980's, Fresno experienced a new wave of immigrants unlike any other time in its history. These newcomers were Southeast Asians. From 1977 their numbers grew from a few dozen to 32,000 in 1987. These newcomers were Hmong, Lao Cambodian, Vietnamese and Mien. Ninety-five percent of these people could not speak English.

In early 1983 a young Hmong man, who was baptized Episcopalian, moved to Fresno from Minnesota. He noticed very quickly that there were very few services available for his people. Remembering his association with the Episcopal Church in Minnesota, he sought assistance from the Diocesan Office to encourage the Church to provide direct services for the refugees. For the next several days Vu Yang and Fr. Robert Williams, Diocesan Consultant to Christian Education, began visiting dozens of Hmong families in Fresno. After collecting their interviews, they took their results to Bishop Rivera. The needs of the Southeast Asian were overwhelming. A strategy for advocacy and general assistance was developed. On May 1, 1983 with $1500, the Episcopal Asian Community Services were opened at 3323 E. Belmont in Fresno. Within the first month of operation, over 300 clients had registered at the new Center. As the summer progressed, volunteers from local parishes and missions were providing their services. The problems were divided into four categories: (1) acculturation (2) English skills (3) advocacy and (4) job skills.

For the next four years, the Episcopal Asian Center has concentrated on providing direct services in these four areas. The Center faced the gargantuous task of financing such an endeavor. The cost of services were high, but lives were being changed and shaped.

Funding came from Diocesan sources: United Thank Offering, Presiding Bishops Fund for World Relief, and Coalition on Human Needs. Many local fundraising events brought in needed cash. Many churches and individuals gave donations and gifts. By the end of 1987, over 6,000 Southeast Asians had been served in one form or another by the Center.

In 1986 an industrial sewing project was funded by UTO. To date, this training program has enabled 67 women to be employed. Linda Nelson still trains students and finds employment for them.

Today, the staff of the Episcopal Asian Community Services provides English as a second language, industrial sewing, medical officer training and advocacy.

Many refugees rely upon Vu Yang, Vithaya Xayanath, Kao Yang and others for assistance in critical problems such as arrests and court cases.

As the Episcopal Asian Community Services approaches its fifth year of service, some ask "how long will the refugee center be needed?" From all research and the surveying of trends, The Episcopal Asian Center will be serving the peoples needs well into the next century. As long as Southeast Asian refugees experience the frustration of encountering difficult problems, unemployment, lack of English skills, and a cloudy future. The Episcopal Church, through its refugee agencies, will be there to help when needed. From this encounter, some Hmong and Laotians have become baptized and confirmed in the church. Hopefully, one day, the church will see a Hmong or Lao Episcopal priest on staff guiding the spiritual direction of the Southeast Asian people.

CHARTERHOUSE CENTER

In 1983 there was a vision by some parishioners in the Stockton area and Fr. Robert Williams, Diocesan Consultant for Christian Education, to develop an institute for specializing in adult education. For two years a number of specialized topics were offered to the parishioners. Two of the most popular series were: Theology and Society and Faith and Medicine.

By the mid 1980's Stockton was facing a massive increase in the Southeast Asian population. At the same time, there were very few direct services to meet the needs of the population. The Board of Directors began to explore ways in addressing the needs of the people through Charterhouse. For the very name of Charterhouse was taken from the great English Theological Institute that trained the great theological minds of England.

Charterhouse was to develop into a refugee training center and provide English language classes and a basic support system for the Southeast Asians.

A start-up Grant was awarded by The United Thank Offering of New York to enable Charterhouse to open a Center. The Charterhouse Center opened its doors on October 1, 1986 in the school building of St. Anne's Episcopal Church in Stockton.

The day of opening was marred by a lawsuit against Charterhouse and the Diocese on the part of the Lincoln Village Neighborhood Association. The basic contention was that the Charterhouse Center would destabilize the neighborhood and contribute to an increase of crime and the devaluation of home property.

The County Court of San Joaquin ruled in favor of Charterhouse. The Board of Directors had complied with all County prerequisites and perogatives.

In addition to the three English as a second language classes, the staff operates an advocacy program that addresses the needs of the clients.

The Board nominated Mrs. Judith Bling to be the Director of Charterhouse. Mrs. Bling had many years experience in academic and refugee advocacy activities. She has been instrumental in making Charterhouse an effective and efficient Charterhouse agency for Southeast Asian peoples in Stockton. The Center has been featured on several occasions in the Stockton Record, the cities daily newspaper.

Besides Mrs. Bling, the Center is staffed by Hmong and Lao translators, a curriculum coordinator, part time secretary and a child care worker.

APPENDIX B

NATIONAL CHURCH AND DIOCESAN STATISTICS

National Church - Profile of Church Growth
                  - Profile of Confirmed & Received
                  - Graph of Gains and Losses
                  - Congregational Statistics

Diocese of San Joaquin - Congregational Statistics
                        - Financial Statistics
                        - Attendance Statistics
                        - Profile of Church Growth
                        - Profile of Confirmed & Received
                        - Profile of Church School Growth
                        - Profile of Church Growth
                        - Baptized - Communicants
                        - Average Sunday Attendance
                        - Financial Profile
                        - Hispanic Demographic Profile

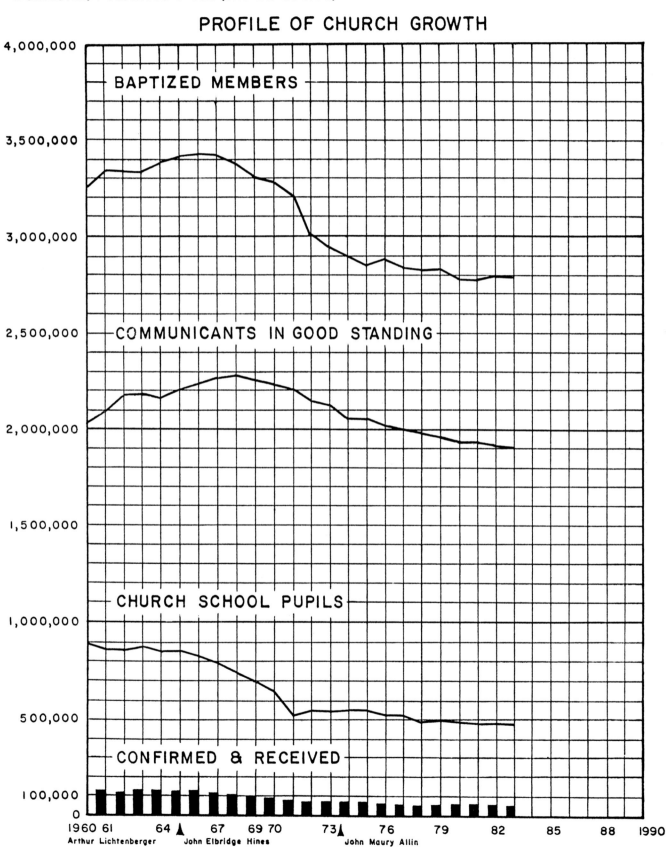

The Episcopal Church in the United States of America
Domestic: Provinces I-VIII (the 50 States)

PROFILE OF CHURCH GROWTH

BAPTIZED MEMBERS

COMMUNICANTS IN GOOD STANDING

CHURCH SCHOOL PUPILS

CONFIRMED & RECEIVED

Arthur Lichtenberger   John Elbridge Hines   John Maury Allin

The Episcopal Church in the United States of America
Domestic: Provinces I-VIII (the 50 States)

PROFILE OF CONFIRMED & RECEIVED

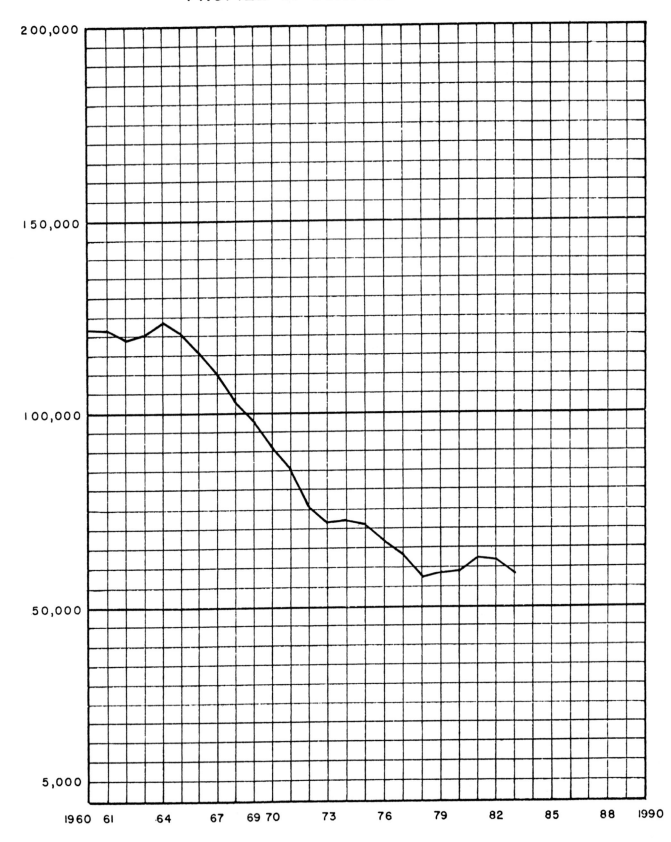

The Episcopal Church in the United States of America

Domestic: Provinces I–VIII (the 50 States)

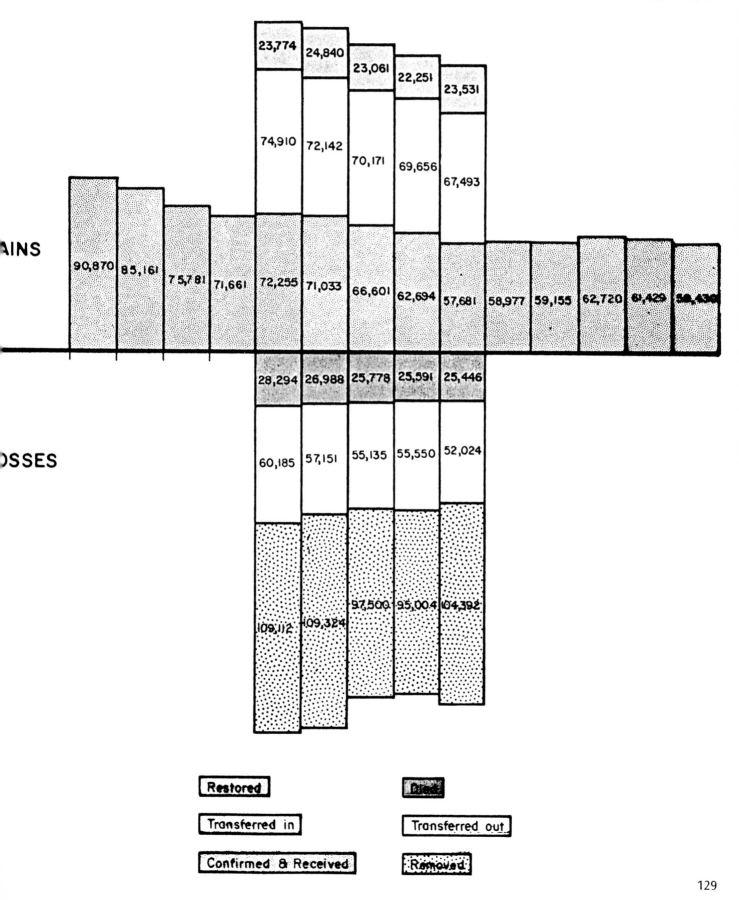

1970	1971	1972	1973	1974	1975	1976	1977	1978	1979	1980	1981	1982	1983

GAINS

Restored (top):
23,774 (1974), 24,840 (1975), 23,061 (1976), 22,251 (1977), 23,531 (1978)

Transferred in:
74,910 (1974), 72,142 (1975), 70,171 (1976), 69,656 (1977), 67,493 (1978)

Confirmed & Received:
90,870 (1970), 85,161 (1971), 75,781 (1972), 71,661 (1973), 72,255 (1974), 71,033 (1975), 66,601 (1976), 62,694 (1977), 57,681 (1978), 58,977 (1979), 59,155 (1980), 62,720 (1981), 61,429 (1982), 59,436 (1983)

LOSSES

Died:
28,294 (1974), 26,988 (1975), 25,778 (1976), 25,591 (1977), 25,446 (1978)

Transferred out:
60,185 (1974), 57,151 (1975), 55,135 (1976), 55,550 (1977), 52,024 (1978)

Removed:
109,112 (1974), 109,324 (1975), 97,500 (1976), 95,004 (1977), 104,392 (1978)

Legend:
- Restored
- Died
- Transferred in
- Transferred out
- Confirmed & Received
- Removed

for The Domestic EPISCOPAL CHURCH IN THE U.S.A. Provinces I–VIII (the 50 States)

FROM PAROCHIAL REPORTS — Compiled by Sr. Jeannette B. Kastorff, C.A.

Admitted as an Organized Mission   Accepted as a Parish

YEAR	Congregation Families	Congregation Individuals	Total Family Units	Total Baptized Members	Baptisms Children	Baptisms Adults	Baptisms Total	Communicants	Add. Confirmed	Add. Received	Add. Transferred	Add. Restored	Add. Total	Loss Died	Loss Transferred	Loss Removed	Loss Total	Present Number in Good Standing
1960				3,444,265					115,233	6,712								2,027,671
1				3,519,685					115,402	5,807								2,095,573
2				3,565,470					112,663	6,158								2,174,202
3				3,587,104					117,682	6,529								2,185,714
4				3,591,164					113,712	6,405								2,168,284
5				3,615,643					109,306	5,974								2,202,607
6				3,647,297					97,217	5,343								2,234,109
7				3,584,613					85,610	5,262								2,267,372
8				3,588,435					79,987	5,174								2,280,077
9				3,536,099					71,606	4,175								2,260,950
1970				3,475,164					67,582	4,079								2,238,538
1				3,445,317														2,208,773
2				3,385,436														2,152,053
3				3,207,702														2,120,482
4	810,379	365,204	1,175,583	2,907,293	54,658	6,080	60,738	2,082,906	67,904	4,351	74,910	23,774	170,939	28,294	60,185	109,112	197,591	2,056,254
5	791,841	380,236	1,172,077	2,857,455	54,888	6,421	61,309	2,077,362	66,008	5,025	72,142	24,840	168,015	26,988	57,151	109,324	193,463	2,051,914
6	734,783	374,278	1,159,071	2,882,064	52,901	6,736	59,637	2,039,637	61,620	4,981	70,171	23,061	159,833	25,778	55,135	97,500	178,413	2,021,057
7	775,064	374,943	1,150,007	2,836,577	53,688	6,935	60,623	2,021,801	57,288	5,406	69,656	22,251	154,601	25,591	55,550	95,004	176,145	2,000,257
8	762,889	380,943	1,143,882	2,825,254	52,519	5,994	58,513	2,015,070	52,490	5,191	67,493	23,531	148,705	25,446	52,024	104,392	181,862	1,981,913
9				2,841,700	53,756	6,520	60,276		53,393	5,584								1,962,060
1980				2,787,444	56,182	7,465	63,647		53,261	5,920								1,933,646
1				2,767,440	58,334	7,231	65,565		55,543	7,177								1,930,690
2				2,795,265	60,601	7,140	67,741		54,315	7,114								1,922,923
3				2,794,690	58,686	7,397	66,083		51,390	7,040								1,906,618
4																		
5																		
6																		
7																		
8																		
9																		
1990																		

Note (Confirmed column, 1967): 1967 Gen. Conv. Journal

CONGREGATION STATISTICS FROM PAROCHIAL REPORTS
for Diocese of San Joaquin (Province VIII)

Admitted as an Organized Mission   Accepted as a Parish   Compiled by Sr. Jeannette B. Kastorff, C.A.

YEAR	CONGREGATION Families	CONGREGATION Individuals	Total Family Units	TOTAL BAPTIZED MEMBERS	BAPTISMS Children	BAPTISMS Adults	BAPTISMS Total	COMMUNICANTS Last Reported	Confirmed	ADDITIONS Received	ADDITIONS Transferred	ADDITIONS Restored	ADDITIONS Total	LOSSES Died	LOSSES Transferred	LOSSES Removed	LOSSES Total	Present Number in Good Standing
1960				15,872	420	285	705	8,879	697	19	528	176	1,420	68	370	400	838	9,461
1				16,624	598	154	752	9,461	802	36			1,449				734	10,176
2				16,875	459	158	617	10,176	603	18			1,310				1,239	10,247
3	4,836	1,376	6,212	17,031	516	150	666	10,247	739	43	491	132	1,405	101	385	710	1,196	10,456
4	4,969	1,411	6,380	16,472	472	145	617	10,456	766	20	357	228	1,371	75	423	949	1,447	10,380
5	4,913	1,339	6,252	16,088	504	161	665	10,380	753	38	359	224	1,374	106	386	711	1,203	10,551
6	4,693	1,548	6,241	16,112	399	125	524	10,551	649	34	441	86	1,210	105	579	1,186	1,870	9,891
7	4,556	1,509	6,065	16,137	383	119	502	9,891	601	17	530	140	1,288	96	457	719	1,272	9,907
8	4,546	1,434	5,980	15,889	373	104	477	9,907	521	25	401	74	1,021	104	444	511	1,059	9,869
9	4,210	1,342	5,552	14,674	302	121	423	9,869	473	22	449	141	1,085	95	438	872	1,405	9,549
1970	4,012	1,395	5,407	14,669	343	95	438	9,545	475	19	346	117	957	92	398	1,189	1,679	8,826
1	3,809	1,525	5,334	14,032	274	95	369	8,821	464	12	325	147	950	103	252	886	1,241	8,474
2	3,635	1,563	5,198	13,306	271	100	371	8,469	394	25	415	77	911	117	289	704	1,110	8,270
3	3,484	1,634	5,118	13,278	308	72	380	8,270	441	20	385	172	1,018	112	349	799	1,260	8,028
4	3,524	1,637	5,161	13,096	336	69	405	8,028	374	26	356	270	1,026	113	288	489	890	8,164
5	3,556	1,741	5,297	12,580	340	69	409	8,164	381	33	340	176	934	108	293	976	1,377	7,717
6	3,578	1,931	5,509	12,706	283	92	375	7,716	326	22	364	180	892	99	319	509	927	7,681
7	3,614	2,022	5,636	13,214	346	90	436	7,681	270	28	521	379	1,198	93	293	421	807	8,072
8	3,580	2,095	5,675	13,005	306	66	372	8,072	303	31	420	219	973	107	274	623	1,004	8,041
9	3,577	2,153	5,730	13,601	380	114	494	8,041	358	30	520	217	1,125	92	320	634	1,046	8,120
1980	3,570	2,270	5,840	14,794	347	116	463	8,120	387	34	433	170	1,024	116	364	471	951	8,193
1	3,532	2,275	5,807	15,305	383	97	480	8,193	300	45	369	157	871	128	349	349	826	8,238
2	3,652	2,201	5,853	16,842	331	96	427	8,238	337	48	422	170	977	129	314	309	752	8,463
3	3,473	2,218	5,691	17,617	373	91	464	8,463	295	46	444	146	931	116	350	472	938	8,456
4	3,509	2,164	5,673	17,349	394	70	464	8,456	243	36	346	133	758	139	266	505	910	8,304
5	3,636	2,140	5,776	17,536	351	61	412	8,304	230	39	338	100	707	123	257	290	670	8,341
6																		
7																		
8																		
9																		

for Diocese of San Joaquin — Compiled by Jeannette B. Kastorff

	RECEIPTS				DISBURSEMENTS					
	For General Purposes					For Work Outside			For Parish Purposes	
YEAR	Plate 51	Pledges 52	Special Offerings 61	Total Receipts G(=E+F) M(=K+L)	Diocesan and General Church Assessments 1864 / 64	Special Offerings 2865 / 65	All Other 1866 / 66	Total for Outside P(64 through 66)	Operating Expenses 1867 / 67	Total for Parish Q(67 through 70)
1960				1,265,604	106,804				357,846	
1				1,261,350	118,452				397,152	
2				1,324,306	135,888				398,074	
3				979,828	154,703				425,722	
4				989,768	162,268				449,650	
5				1,072,827	167,430				480,152	
6				1,057,780	183,432				502,667	
7				1,106,517	201,276				543,447	
8				1,114,408	204,096				556,731	
9				1,155,270	250,275				577,206	
1970				1,122,896	243,595				585,104	
1				1,182,234	263,517				612,025	
2				1,298,790	263,517				627,117	
3				1,347,544	263,517				883,149	
4				1,478,866	263,517				956,038	
5				1,594,220	281,500				1,048,020	
6				1,865,462	307,495				1,211,678	
7				1,982,562	311,627				1,297,479	
8				2,152,007	326,854			408,394	1,395,760	
9				2,269,829	356,976				1,569,555	
1980				2,777,663	404,817	32,885	59,850	497,552	1,765,562	
1				3,098,987	469,945				2,017,923	2,017,923
2				3,329,031	513,412	62,761	79,517	655,690	2,207,067	2,207,067
3				3,797,704	563,998	84,350	94,127	742,475	2,522,111	2,522,111
4				4,011,002	611,781				2,709,993	2,709,993
5				4,242,461	631,656	67,301	196,702	961,057	2,701,282	2,701,282
6				4,620,963						
7										
8										
9										
1990										

ATTENDANCE STATISTICS FROM PAROCHIAL REPORTS

for Diocese of San Joaquin — Compiled by Jeannette B. Kastorff

YEAR	CHURCH SCHOOL Staff & Teachers	Students Pre-school	Grades 1-8	Grades 9-12	Adults	Plotted Total Children Students only	PARISH DAY SCHOOL Students	HOLY COMMUNION Sunday	Weekday	Private	Other	MARRIAGES	BURIALS	SUNDAY ATTENDANCE ALL SERVICES INCLUDING CHURCH SCHOOL — Lent I	Easter	Trinity	Advent I	Sunday Average	TOTAL MON. THRU SAT.
1960	545		4,531	794				2,363		362									
1	514		4,140	550															
2	568		4,251	662															
3	549		3,977	687										6,994	12,762	3,921	6,873	7,638	
4	577		3,956	459										6,966	11,759	5,707	6,179	7,652	
5	545		3,952	520										6,500	12,262	5,902	6,655	7,830	
6	521		3,643	526										6,207	11,646	4,906	6,302	7,265	
7	627		3,672	638										5,531	11,827	4,691	5,427	6,669	
8	574		3,464	480										5,942	11,408	4,689	5,141	6,795	
9	529		3,078	542										4,793	10,809	4,755	4,712	6,267	
1970	489		2,710	509										5,036	9,894	4,361	4,706	5,999	
1	460		2,535	741										4,667	9,383	4,071	4,122	5,561	
2	371		2,076	417		2,056								4,036	8,748	3,734	4,488	5,252	
3	416	467	1,248	341	550	2,056								4,746	9,001	3,429	4,771	5,487	
4	407	492	1,233	351	660	2,076								4,497	9,036	3,984	4,460	5,494	
5	392	474	1,162	383	692	2,019								4,569	9,316	4,319	4,643	5,712	
6	433	425	1,175	288	948	1,888								4,858	9,475	4,216	4,487	5,759	
7	386	411	1,161	366	1,083	1,938	269							4,973	9,462	4,569	4,377	5,845	
8	381	391	1,049	292	1,154	1,732	308							3,861	9,573	4,142	4,777	5,588	
9	350	406	1,009	248	1,065	1,663	346							4,683	9,604	4,017	4,834	5,785	1,346
1980	388	423	1,155	309	1,170	1,887	499					215	276	4,875	9,616	4,578	4,555	5,906	1,593
1	365	463	1,176	280	887	1,919	628	4,371	3,224	2,088	6,949	181	251	4,851	9,741	4,049	4,554	5,799	1,759
2	388	494	1,118	295	942	1,907	544	4,375	3,319	2,164	5,246	157	261	4,864	9,642	4,533	4,629	5,917	1,171
3	364	488	1,007	305	1,085	1,800	662	4,524	3,338	2,331	5,286	194	265	5,286	10,344	4,400	4,670	5,900	1,443
4	341	475	1,039	358	976	1,872	660	4,588	3,259	2,116	5,877	143	276	5,165	10,439	4,178	4,975	6,189	1,366
5	346	523	935	305	869	1,762	688	4,755	3,296	1,844	5,799	132	243	5,062	10,341	4,623	4,394	6,105	1,479
6																			
7																			
8																			
9																			
1990																			

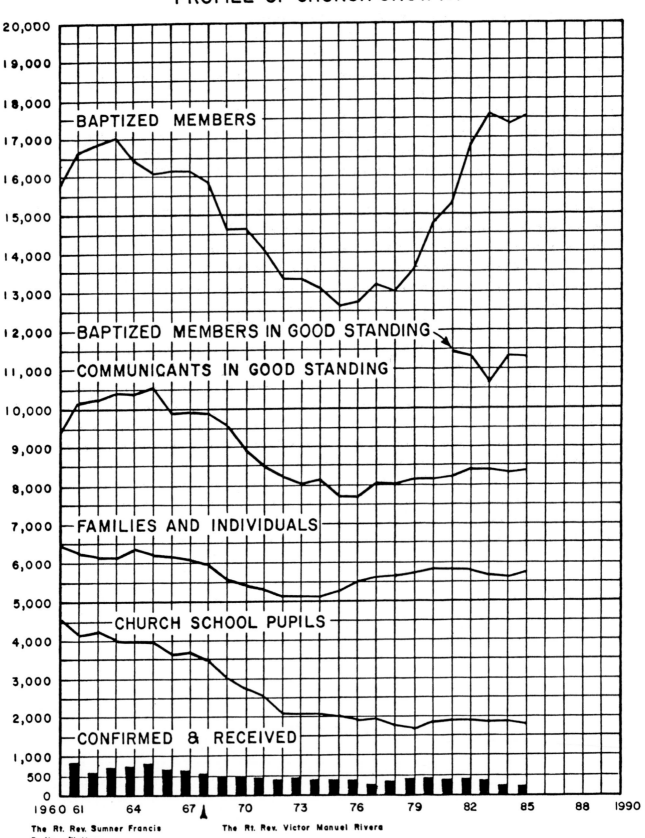

Diocese of San Joaquin
PROFILE OF CHURCH GROWTH

BAPTIZED MEMBERS

BAPTIZED MEMBERS IN GOOD STANDING

COMMUNICANTS IN GOOD STANDING

FAMILIES AND INDIVIDUALS

CHURCH SCHOOL PUPILS

CONFIRMED & RECEIVED

The Rt. Rev. Sumner Francis
Dudley Walters

The Rt. Rev. Victor Manuel Rivera

Diocese of San Joaquin
PROFILE OF CONFIRMED & RECEIVED

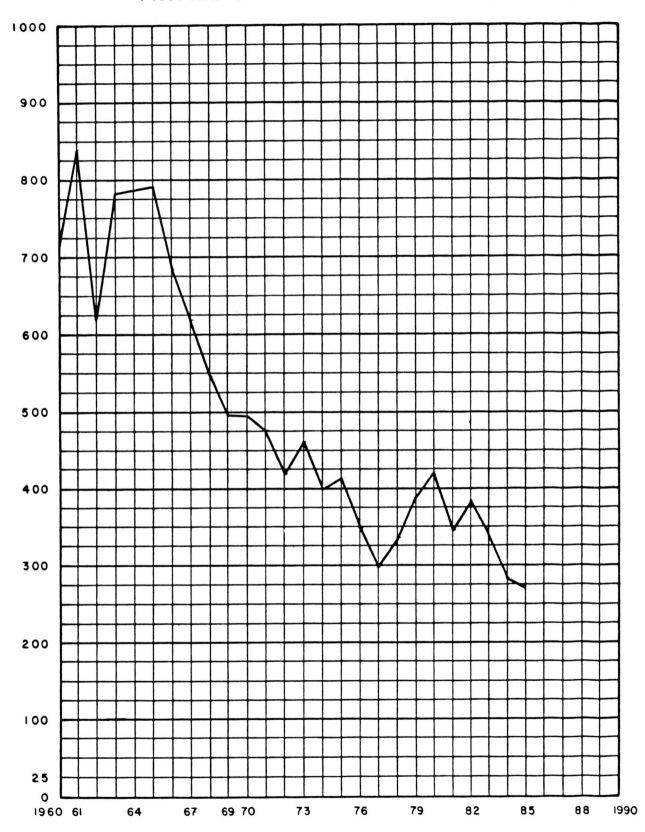

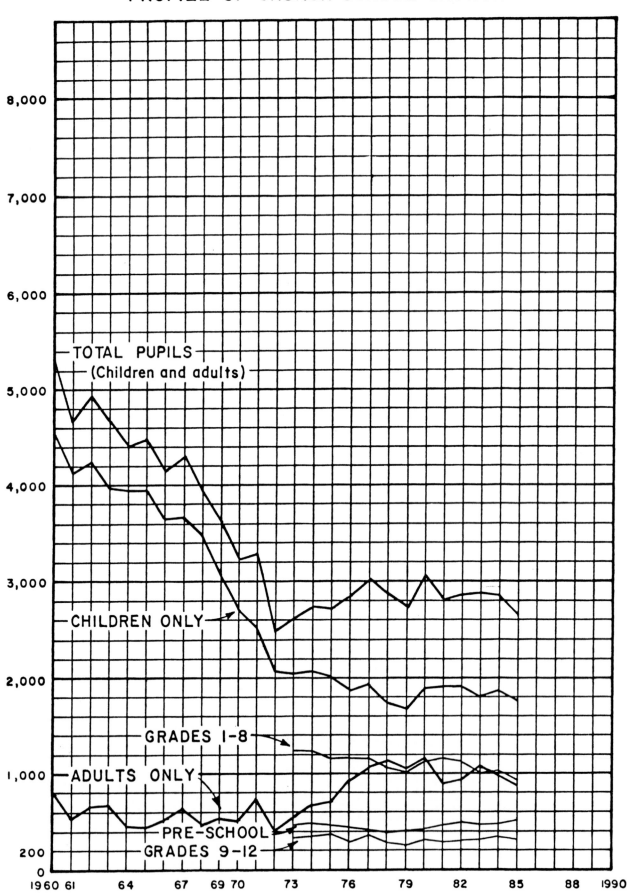

Diocese of San Joaquin
PROFILE OF CHURCH SCHOOL GROWTH

8,000

7,000

6,000

TOTAL PUPILS
(Children and adults)

5,000

4,000

3,000

CHILDREN ONLY →

2,000

GRADES 1-8 →

ADULTS ONLY

1,000

PRE-SCHOOL
GRADES 9-12 →

200

0

1960 61   64   67   69 70   73   76   79   82   85   88   1990

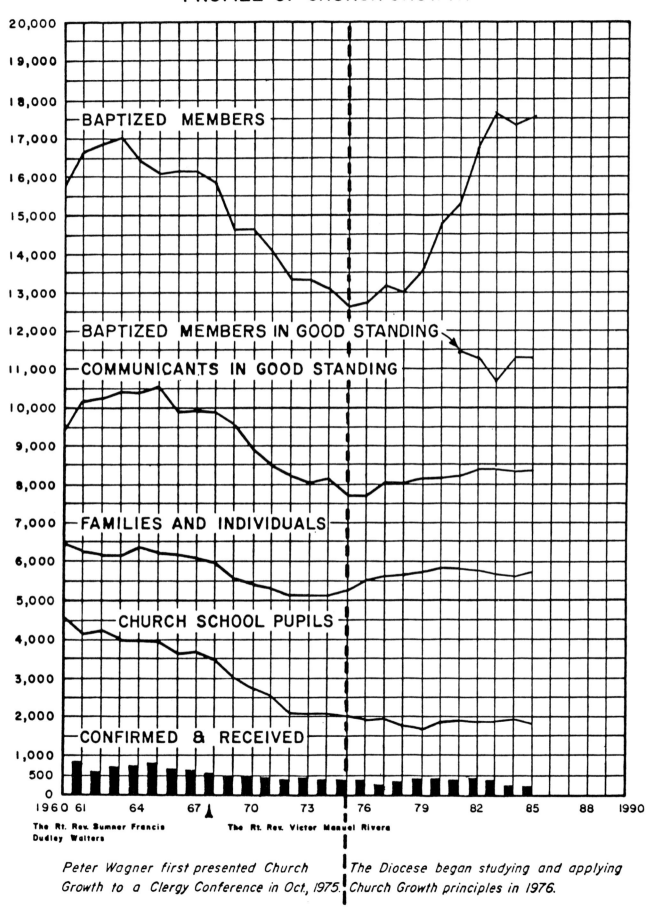

Diocese of San Joaquin
PROFILE OF CHURCH GROWTH

BAPTIZED MEMBERS

BAPTIZED MEMBERS IN GOOD STANDING

COMMUNICANTS IN GOOD STANDING

FAMILIES AND INDIVIDUALS

CHURCH SCHOOL PUPILS

CONFIRMED & RECEIVED

The Rt. Rev. Sumner Francis
Dudley Walters

The Rt. Rev. Victor Manuel Rivera

*Peter Wagner first presented Church
Growth to a Clergy Conference in Oct, 1975.*

*The Diocese began studying and applying
Church Growth principles in 1976.*

Diocese of San Joaquin

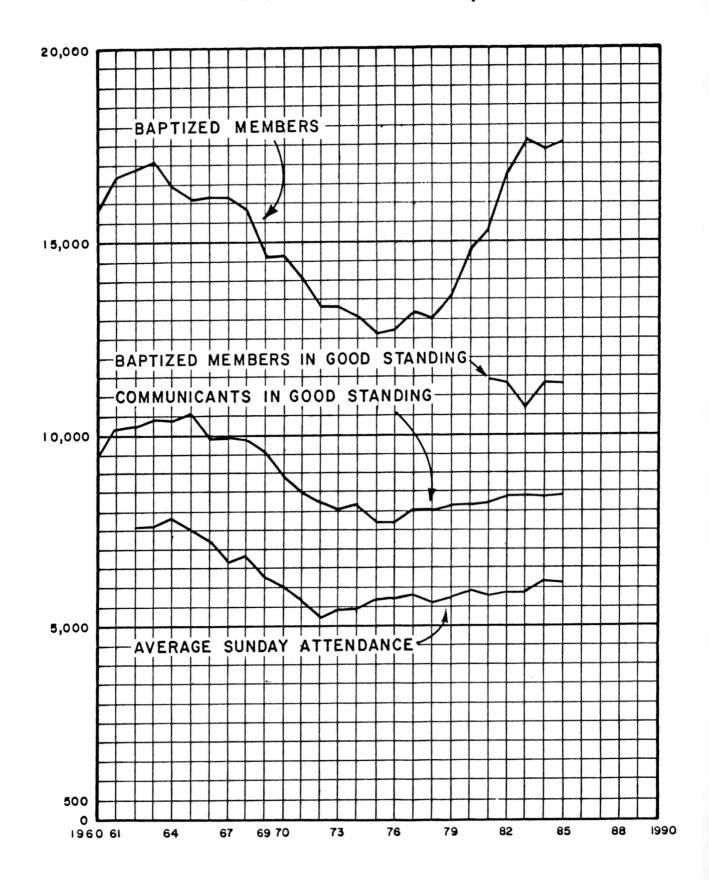

Diocese of San Joaquin

AVERAGE SUNDAY ATTENDANCE

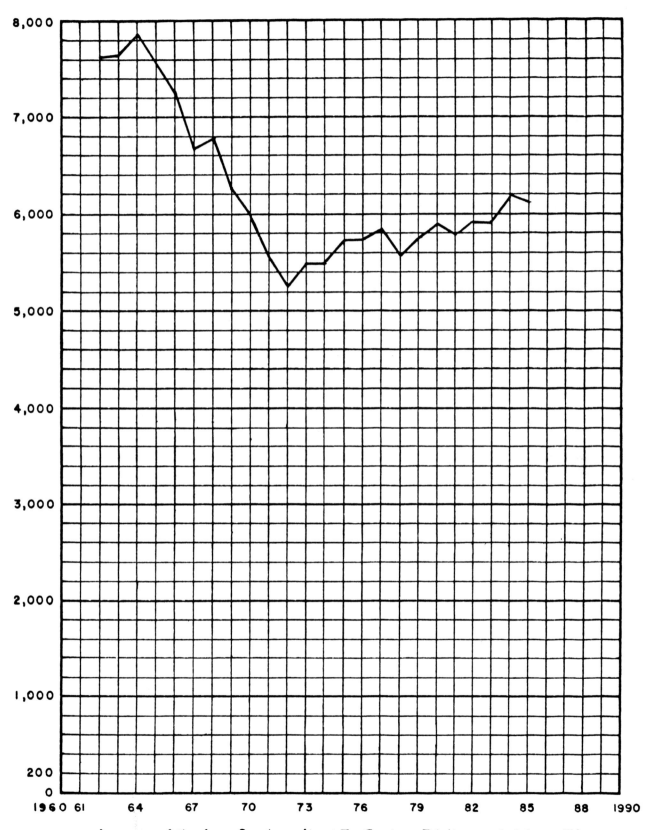

Average of the four Sundays (Lent I, Easter, Trinity, and Advent I)
reported on Parochial Reports.

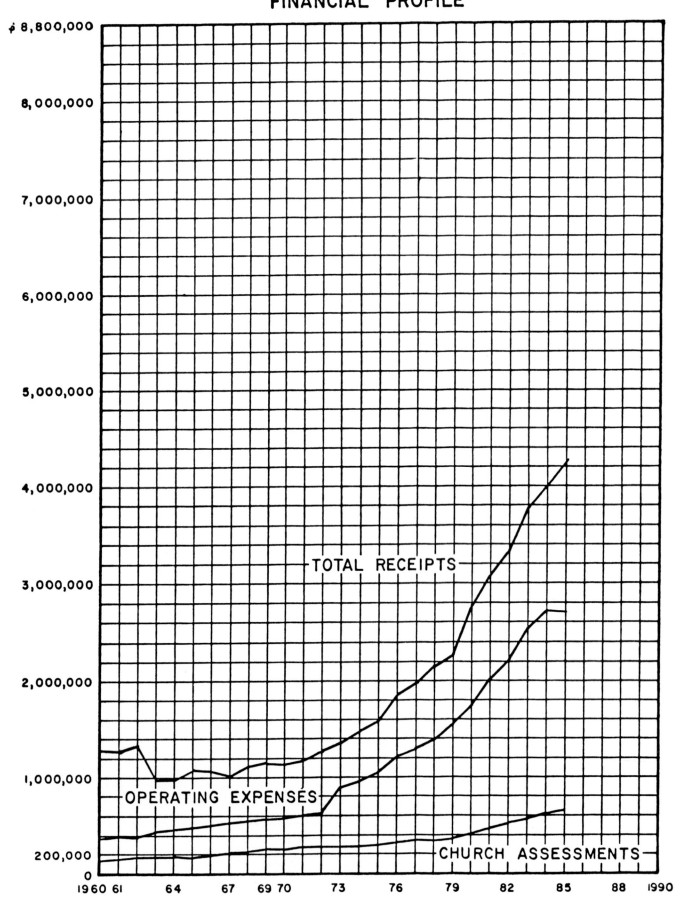

Diocese of San Joaquin
FINANCIAL PROFILE

TOTAL RECEIPTS

OPERATING EXPENSES

CHURCH ASSESSMENTS

$ 8,800,000
8,000,000
7,000,000
6,000,000
5,000,000
4,000,000
3,000,000
2,000,000
1,000,000
200,000
0

1960 61   64   67   69 70   73   76   79   82   85   88   1990

DIOCESE OF SAN JOAQUIN

Hispanic Demographic Profile

Basic Demographics

Estimated Hispanic population in 1986.............559,480
Actual Hispanic population in 1980...................493,050
Percent of all U.S. Hispanics................................3.4%

As a percent of diocese (1986)..............22.5%
Rate of growth, 1980-86......................13.5%

Nationality and Nativity

Mexican origin..448,901
Puerto Rican origin...4,408
Cuban origin...853
Other Spanish origin..38,888
Percent born in state of residence......................56.4%
Percent moved into county in past 5 years............14.0%

As percent of Hispanics in diocese.........91.2%
As percent of Hispanics in diocese...........0.9%
As percent of Hispanics in diocese...........0.2%
As percent of Hispanics in diocese...........7.9%
Percent foreign born...........................26.1%
Percent moved to U.S. in past 5 years.......6.1%

Age Characteristics

Median age--Hispanics........22.1 yrs   White non-Hispanics...........32.9 yrs   Age gap........10.7 yrs
Percent under 5 years ....13.0%   Percent 5 to 17 years............................29.0%
Percent 18 to 65 years......................................53.9%   Percent 65 and over...............................4.0%

Social and Family Characteristics

Average size of households.....................................3.6
Percent of families that are married couples...........77.4%
Percent of men who are separated/divorced...........6.6%
Percent of men who are single.............................35.6%
Percent of men who are veterans.........................16.7%

Average size of families.............................3.9
Percent headed by women....................16.4%
Percent of women separated/divorced....10.4%
Percent of women who are single...........27.3%
Percent of women in the labor force........48.0%

Economic Characteristics

Average family income in 1979.........................$14,555
Per capita income..$4,328
Percent of families below poverty level.................21.7%
Hispanic workers--percent in private sector...........78.8%
Percent self-employed..3.8%
Hispanic-owned firms (1982)...........................7,182

As percent of total per capita income.......61.3%
As percent of all U.S. Hispanics..............94.4%
As percent of all U.S. Hispanics.............101.8%
Percent in public sector........................17.4%
Percent in managerial/professional jobs....8.3%
Annual receipts.........................$446,392,000

Schooling and Language

Median years of schooling.....................................10.3
Percent of men who are college grads...................4.5%
5-17 year olds in Spanish speaking homes..........92,590
18+ year olds in Spanish speaking homes.........243,591

Percent who are high school grads.........34.6%
Percent of women who are college grads..2.7%
Ratio to Hispanics.................................64.9%
Ratio to Hispanics.................................85.4%

Major Concentration of Hispanics in Diocese

The largest concentration of Hispanics is in the southwest portion of the state where more than six out of every 10 Hispanics in the diocese lives. Almost a third (31%) live in Fresno County and 15% in Tulare to the south of Fresno. In the southwest corner of the diocese are 18% of the Hispanics who make Kern County their home. Another major concentration of Hispanics is in the far northwest corner of the diocese in San Joaquin County where 14% of the Hispanics in the diocese reside.

The Rev. Martin Risard

St. Claire's, Arnold

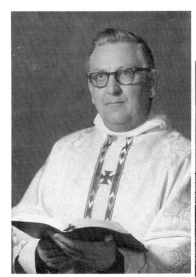

The Rev. Thomas
Corrigan

St. Nicholas', Atwater

St. Thomas', Avenal

The Rev. David Foster,
Assistant

All Saints, Bakersfield

The Rev. Duane H. Thebeau

St. Luke's, Bakersfield

The Rev. John Spear

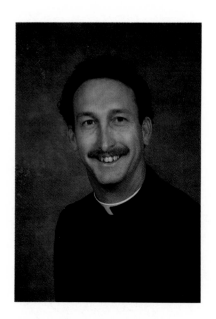

The Rev. Roger Grist

St. Pauls', Bakersfield

The Rev. Philip
Swickard

St. Timothy's, Bishop

St. Benedict's, Ceres

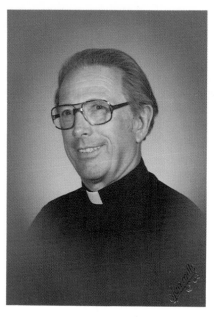

The Rev. William Eastman

Church of the Resurrection
(meeting in United Methodist Church)

The Rev. John Rollinson,
Clovis

St. Philip's, Coalinga

The Rev. Don Kroeger

Epiphany, Corcoran

The Rev. Scott Murray

The Rev. Ed Renner

Church of the Redeemer, Delano

Holy Family, Fresno

The Rev. Robert Lucent

The Rev. Bernard Flynn

St. Columba's
Fresno

The Rev. Fredrick Johnson

St. James Cathedral

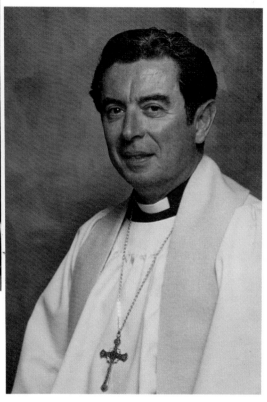

The Very Rev. George C. Ruof

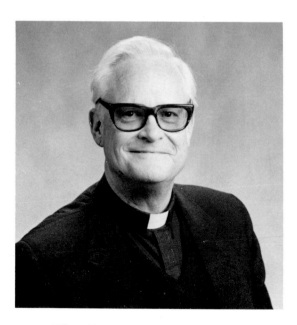

The Rev. James Kingsley

The Rev. Christopher Kelley

The Rev. Dr. Richard Henry

St. Mary's, Fresno

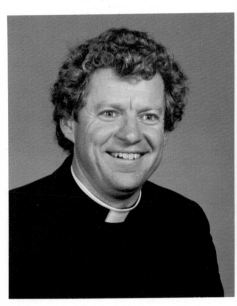

The Rev. Keith Brown

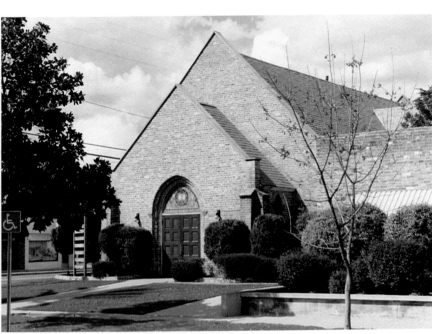

Santa Margarita, Fresno

Grace Church Building Site, Groveland

Church of the Savior, Hanford

The Rev. Alexander
T. Patience

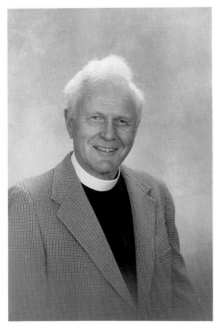

The Rev. David Graham

St. Peter's, Kernville

Christ Church, Lemoore

St. James', Lindsay

The Rev. Greg Waddington

St. John Baptist, Lodi

The Rev. Bruce Bramlett

St. Albans', Los Banos

The Rev. Mark Hall

Trinity, Madera

Trinity, Madera

St. Joseph's R.C. Church, Mammoth Lakes

The Rev. Milt Holmes

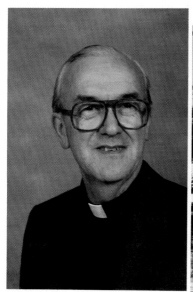

The Rev. Maurice Furlonger

St. Mary's, Manteca

Canon Zealand Hillsdon-Hutton

St. Dunstan's, Modesto

The Rev.
Thomas Foster

St. Paul's, Modesto

The Rev. Lee Peterson

The Rev
Leon MacDougall

St. Mathias, Oakdale

The Rev. David Lueck

St. Raphael's, Oakhurst

St. Andrew's, Mariposa

St. Lukes, Merced

The Rev. Edward Murphy

The Rev. James Thompson

St. John's, Porterville

Good Shepherd, Reedley

The Rev. John Wilcox

St. Michael's, Ridgecrest

St. Matthew's, San Andreas

The Rev. Randy Rainwater

The Rev. Bruce Kirkwood

St. Luke's, Selma

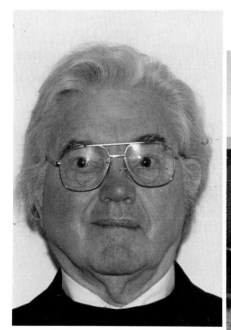

The Rev. Richard Robbins

St. Mark's, Shafter

St. James, Sonora

St. Michael's, Sonora

Joel Hassel, Seminarian

The Rev. Steve Ellis

St. Anne's, Stockton

The
Rev.
James
Booth

St. John's, Stockton

St. John's, Stockton

St. Laurence's Mission, Stockton

Deacon Sylvia Singer

St. Stephen's, Stockton

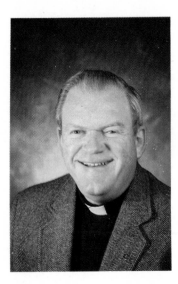

The Rev. Donald Seeks

St. Andrew's, Taft

Cordelia Burt, Bishop's Warden

St. Jude's-In-The-Mountains, Tehachapi

St. Mark's, Tracy

The Rev. John Burk

The Rev. Robert Jordan

St. John's, Tulare

St. Francis, Turlock

St. Francis, Turlock

The Rev. Paul Levine

St. Paul's, Visalia

The Rev. Donald Cole

St. Barnabas Mission, Visalia

The Rev. William Fay

St. Clements', Woodlake

laine Shearer, Star Circulation

Noel Kindred, Secretary

Kay Nelson, Bishop's Secretary

Joyce Cape, Bookkeeper

Gail Powell, Printer

Archdeacon Wayne Williamson

The Rev. Paul Snider

The Rev.
Edgar G. Parrott

The Rev.
Robert Williams

The Rev.
Charles Karoly

The Rev. James Trotter

The Rev.
William Burbery

The Rev. Terrell E.
Hamilton

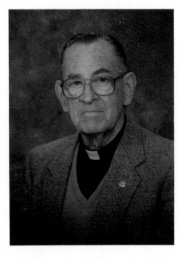

The Rev. William Rich-
mond

Deacon Elmer Gould

The Rev. Kenneth F.
Schildt

The Rev. Leon
Plante

The Rev. Eric Yoeman

The Rev. William Tumbleson

The Rev. Robert Richard

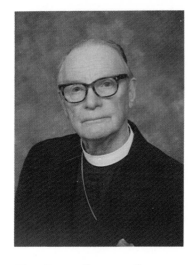

The Rev. Canon George Turney

Bishop Robert Mize

Deacon Claude Cooke

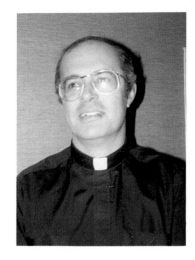

The Rev. Robert Woods

The Rev. Norman Van Walterup

Deacon Millie Cooke

Barbara Rivera

The Rt. Rev. Victor M. Rivera
3rd Bishop of San Joaquin